Ex Libris

Lowell R. Kantzer

WHAT THE BIBLE SAYS

WHAT THE BIBLE SAYS *compiled and edited by* Lewis Drummond

with a foreword by
Dr. Billy Graham

Abingdon Press
Nashville ◆ *New York*

WHAT THE BIBLE SAYS

Copyright © Marshall, Morgan & Scott 1974
First published 1974
U. S. edition by Abingdon Press 1975

Library of Congress Cataloging in Publication Data
Main entry under title:
What the Bible says.
   Includes index.
   1. Bible—Theology.   I. Drummond, Lewis A.
BS543.W48   230   75-17736

ISBN 0-687-44585-X

Manufactured by the Parthenon Press at
Nashville, Tennessee, United States of America

This book is dedicated to

MRS. LEHMAN JOHNSON
our beloved Aunt Sue

One who has faithfully taught
and exemplified in her life
What the Bible Says

CONTENTS

FOREWORD

This book comes at a time of unique opportunity. These are days when Bible distribution is breaking all records. Parallel with this is the flourishing growth of Bible study, both in and out of the church.

Of great need then, is a volume which can serve as a companion to the Scriptures, and which can, with further investigation, amplify its truth. This work of Dr Drummond, *What the Bible Says*, is just that. It is a competent, careful compilation of doctrinal truth, which can be a tool of evangelism, as well as a means to enhance the Christian experience of beginner and saint alike.

Moreover, it is written and edited in a contemporary style that will appeal to every reader. Dr Drummond is a friend of mine whose life has always been an inspiration. He combines the best of several worlds! Coming recently from England to a professorship at the Southern Baptist Seminary in Louisville, Kentucky, he brings into all the work the careful attention to detail of the English, the winsomeness that association with students brings, and the personal experiences of his own committed life. These all provide a practical and effective dimension to his teaching.

What the Bible Says is a worthy successor to Dr R. A. Torrey's book *What the Bible Teaches*. In the Preface of that volume, the author wrote, 'Its most apparent use is as a classbook in Bible Theology . . . The book can also be used in family devotions . . . and . . . it is hoped it may be helpful also in private devotional study.' Just so do I expect that this new volume under Dr Drummond's editorship will have use that is many-faceted.

By his own admission this is not a substitute for a commentary, although every section reveals thorough biblical support. It is a handbook for the sincere student. It is explicit where it can be, and the organization of the material is logical and systematic.

I think the statement at the end of the section on the 'Teaching of Jesus Christ' is a succinct representation of what Christian nurture is all about. The author wrote, 'To study Christ's teaching is our finest education. To understand it is our highest privilege. To obey it is our greatest responsibility. To share it is to bring others to lasting joy.'

The hopeful thrust of the book is exemplified by a phrase in the concluding paragraph—'a day of triumph is sure'. Without hesitation, I commend this volume highly to everyone serious about personal faith.

BILLY GRAHAM

PREFACE

Some years ago, the scholarly evangelist and pastor Dr R. A. Torrey produced a book entitled *What the Bible Teaches*. This volume has remained in print to this day. It has become something of a classic for pastors, teachers and a multitude of laymen who seriously want to know what the Bible teaches.

But many years have elapsed since Torrey first wrote. New insights into biblical truth have emerged. A score of new translations have broken on the scene. With all this advance, there has developed in contemporary man a new interest in the message of the Bible.

It has been the feeling of several that a new work of the nature of Torrey's old classic should be produced. When the publishers Marshall, Morgan and Scott approached me to compile and edit such a work, I seized the challenge and opportunity. This book is the product of that labour.

Of course, the present volume is not intended to replace Torrey's older work. That could not be done. But an effort has been made to update material and present the message of the Scriptures in a contemporary fashion. Moreover, able men of insight who are committed to the biblical message have given the best of their scholarship to produce this volume. They have written in a simple, thorough and readable fashion. Therefore, what is produced is for every person. The pastor, teacher and interested Bible reader will all find help from the pen of these able men.

Further, this volume is intended to be read with Bible in hand. Many hundreds of Scripture references are given. This book is not a mere run-through of evangelical thought. It is a study-reference volume that the reader will want to refer to constantly. A complete table of contents is included that will allow one to study by subject. This should be of extreme value to those who teach the Bible.

I cannot close this brief introduction without paying deep respect and expressing profound gratitude to those who are responsible for this book's production, viz. the contributors. I know these men personally; they are men of God, committed to the faith of the Bible.

So this volume is presented to the reader with the prayer that all who read its pages might be able to grasp more clearly *what the Bible says*.

LEWIS A. DRUMMOND
Spurgeon's College
London 1973

THE CONTRIBUTORS

RAYMOND BROWN, M.A., M.Th., Ph.D.

LEWIS A. DRUMMOND, B.A., B.D., M.Th., Ph.D.

FRANK S. FITZSIMMONDS, B.A., B.D., M.Th.

DONALD MONKCOM, B.A., B.D., M.Th.

PAUL T. MORTIMORE, B.D.

DAVID G. REDDAWAY

STANLEY J. VOKE, B.D.

BOOK I

WHAT THE BIBLE SAYS ABOUT GOD

Throughout the entirety of the Scriptures, the biblical writers never present a rational or philosophical argument for the existence of God. They assume His reality, for they have come to know Him *personally*, and under the inspiration of the Holy Spirit (2 Tim. 3: 16; 2 Pet. 1: 21) they describe both His dealings with man generally and their own personal encounters with Him (e.g. Job 42: 5–6). The Bible says it is only 'the fool' who denies His existence (Psa. 14: 1, cf. 10: 1). God is presented as active in all things and is, therefore, one that can be known. In its description of His multiplied activity, the Bible thus has a good deal to say about the God *who acts*. It is in these descriptive passages that we come to know what He is like.

I. GOD'S DIVINE NATURE

1. GOD IS A PERSONALITY

God is obviously not a 'person' in the sense that we as humans are defined by the term. Still, He has characteristics which are clearly 'personal', e.g. He lives, thinks, feels, speaks, loves, cares, is angry, grieved, pleased, etc. Furthermore, man can enter into the closest possible personal relationship with Him. The Old Testament uses the same word to describe man's experience of personally '*knowing*' God (e.g. Deut. 34: 10) as that used of man's closest possible relationship with his wife; 'he *knew* her' (e.g. Gen. 4: 1). God can be 'known' as a person because, unlike the dead idols of the heathen which cannot speak or help (Jer. 10: 5, 14), He has essential personal attributes.

a. HE LIVES

The Bible constantly describes Him as 'the living God' (Deut. 5: 26; Josh. 3: 10; 1 Sam. 17: 26; Isa. 37: 4; Jer. 10: 10, 23: 36; Dan. 6: 20; Mt. 16: 16; Jn. 6: 69; Rom. 9: 26; 2 Cor. 6: 16; Rev. 7: 2). Because God is alive, man in his deepest personhood cries out for His companionship (Psa. 42: 2, 84: 2), turns to Him in need (Acts 14: 15), trusts Him (1 Tim. 4:10, 6: 17) and serves Him (1 Thess. 1: 9; Heb. 9: 14). But man can also depart from this living God (Heb. 3: 12). This is the essence of sin.

b. HE SPEAKS

God talks with man (Gen. 2: 16, 3: 9 ff, 17: 1–3, 22, 35: 13, 14; Exod. 29: 42, 33: 9–11, 34: 29; Deut, 5: 4, 24, 27; 2 Chron. 6: 15; Psa. 85: 8; Isa. 52: 6; Heb. 12: 25) and man, in response, addresses God (Gen. 18: 27–33; Exod. 8: 12, 15: 25, 17: 4; Num. 12: 13, 20: 16; Deut. 26: 7; Josh. 24: 7; 1 Sam. 15: 11; 2 Sam. 22: 7; 1 Kings 17: 20; 2 Kings 20: 11; 1 Chron. 5: 20; 2 Chron. 13: 14, 14: 11; Psa. 3: 4, 18: 6, 30: 2, 34: 6, 77: 1, 85: 3; Jonah 2: 2).

c. HE PLANS

In biblical thought, history is not a series of disconnected accidents. Rather, it is the unfolding of His divine purposes (e.g. Gen. 50: 20; Job 1: 12, 2: 6; Psa. 40: 17; Prov. 16: 9; Isa. 46: 11; Jer. 26: 3, 29: 11, 36: 3, 51: 29; Rom. 8: 28; 2 Tim. 1: 9; 1 Jn. 3: 8).

d. HE CARES

God watches over men (Mt. 6: 26, 28–30, 10: 29, 30; 1 Pet. 5: 7) and even cares for birds (Deut. 22: 6, 7) and animals (Deut. 35:4). He is particularly concerned about the welfare of widows, orphans, the poor, the homeless and refugees (Exod. 22: 21–27, 23:9; Lev. 25: 35–42; Deut. 15: 7–12) and children (Deut. 22: 8) (see Thomas Cameron, *The Kindly Laws of the Old Testament* for an interesting exposition of the compassionate concern of God as reflected in the Mosaic Law). Naturally, He is concerned about man's physical needs (1 Kings 19: 5–7).

e. HE GRIEVES

God grieves over man's sin (Gen. 6: 6) and disobedience (Psa. 95: 10; 1 Cor. 10:5). Certain things displease Him. e.g. the offering of loveless sacrifices (Isa. 1: 11; Mic. 6: 7, cf. Heb. 13: 16) and the practice of evil deeds (Isa. 65: 12).

f. HE REJOICES

He is pleased with the sincere praises of His children (Psa. 69: 30, 31). A good man's behaviour (Prov. 16: 7; Heb. 11: 5), ambitions (1 Kings 3: 10; 1 Thess. 4: 1) and a consistent Christian life (1 Thess. 4: 1; 2 Tim. 2: 4) please Him. Christ set Himself to please His Father at all times (Jn. 8: 29, 4: 34), and God was pleased with Him (Mt. 3: 17, 12: 18, 17: 5). Those who lack faith cannot possibly please Him (Heb. 11: 6), and He is clearly displeased when men oppose His servants (1 Thess. 2: 15).

g. HE BEFRIENDS US

He meets with man (Exod. 4: 24, 27, 5: 3, 19: 17, 33: 11; Num. 23: 4, 16) and counts Himself as man's friend (e.g. Abraham 2 Chron. 20: 7; Jas. 2: 23).

2. GOD IS A SPIRIT

Although we may describe God with the aid of human personal categories, He obviously does not have a physical form or body as does man (Lk. 24: 39; Deut. 4: 15). God is Spirit (Jn. 4: 24). He cannot be seen by man (Jn. 1: 18, 5: 37; 1 Tim. 6: 15, 16; 1 Jn. 4: 12), though on rare occasions in Old Testament times He did reveal Himself (Exod. 24: 9, 10, 33: 18–23). Of course, God's full revelation comes through His self disclosure in His son (Jn. 14: 7, 9). This we shall see in much detail later. God in His glory is the Invisible One, (Col. 1: 15; 1 Tim. 1: 17; Heb. 11: 27) and He is not confined to geographical locations even though He may choose to reveal Himself in distinct and special places (Gen. 28: 16; Exod. 25: 22, 29: 42, 30: 6, 36; Num. 23: 15, 16; 1 Kings 8: 13, cf. 2 Chron. 6: 18).

Therefore, when the Bible says that man was made 'in the image of God' (Gen. 1: 26, 27, 5: 3, 9: 6) it does not refer to physical likeness but rather to moral affinity. In this respect man is clearly distinct from animal creation. His addressability (God chooses to talk to him) and moral accountability to God make him unique.

3. GOD IS A UNITY

God is described by Jesus Christ as *'the only true God'* (Jn. 17: 3, cf. Jude 1: 25). He is the *One Lord* (Deut. 6: 4) and there is no other god besides Him (Deut. 4: 35, 39). The Hebrew people were given clear proof of this while they were slaves in Egypt (Exod. 8: 10, 9: 14). Centuries later the exiled Hebrews in Babylon, surrounded by pagan altars and images, were reminded of the same truth (Isa. 43: 10, 11, 44: 6, 8, 45: 5, 6, 14, 18, 21, 22, 46: 9). It is precisely because there is no other God that the prophets and others despise the multiplicity of heathen deities who are powerless to save and unable to deliver those who offered precious gifts to gain their favour (Isa. 45: 20). The Israelites mock these idols and pour scorn on those who make them and worship them (Isa. 44: 9–20; Jer. 10: 1–5, 14: 22). Idolatry is always viewed as an offence in the Bible (Isa. 2: 8, 18, 20, 31: 7, 57: 5; Jer. 50: 2, 38; Ezek. 8: 10, 20: 7, 8; Hosea 4: 17; 8: 4; Micah 1: 7;), Hab. 2: 18; Zech. 10: 2, 13: 2, for it is God who forbids it (Exod. 20: 3, 4). Within this unity God is known in three persons: Father, Son and Holy Spirit (Mt. 28: 19; 2 Cor. 13: 14).

4. GOD IS ETERNAL

The idols made by men are worth no more than the precious metal of which they are made. In time of calamity or adversity they are utterly worthless (Isa. 46: 5–7). The prophetic word vividly portrays the distressed Babylonians hurrying from the city as the armies of Cyrus approach. They carry their idols to safety (Isa. 46: 1, 2).

However, when the Hebrew people are in trouble, they have a God
who safely carries them (Isa. 46: 4). Idols are made in time and will
perish as any other manufactured thing, but Israel rejoiced in a God
who was eternal and would never fail them. He is known as the
eternal (Deut. 33: 27; 1 Tim. 1: 17) and everlasting God (Gen.
21: 33; Psa. 41: 13; Isa. 40: 28; Jer. 10: 10; Hab. 1: 12; Rom.
16: 26), the everlasting Father (Isa. 9: 6). There is no beginning
(Psa. 90: 1, 2, 93: 2) or ending with Him (Job 36: 26; Heb. 1: 11,
12). He inhabits eternity (Isa. 57: 15) and is the first and the last
(Isa. 44: 6). He anticipates everything and everybody (Gen. 1: 1).
He is unique and because of this He can be described in terms which
could not possibly be used of any mere man. Men change, but He is
the unchanging God (Mal. 3: 6; Heb. 1: 12; Jas. 1: 17). Men fail
their friends, but He is utterly dependable and trustworthy (Num.
23: 19; Heb. 6: 17, 18). Men sometimes break their promises. But
we can rely upon His unfailing word (Josh. 21: 45, 23: 14; 1 Kings
8: 56). Men change in their affections and loyalties; He never fails
(Deut. 31: 6; Josh. 1: 5; Psa. 89: 28).

II. GOD'S DIVINE CHARACTERISTICS

God is sometimes described by the use of three terms; Omnipotent
(His power is greater than any other), Omniscient (He knows
everything) and Omnipresent (He is present everywhere). These
terms themselves are not found in Scripture (with the sole exception
of Omnipotent in Rev. 19: 6), but the ideas conveyed by them are
frequently illustrated in the Bible.

1. GOD IS OMNIPOTENT

This theme 'the Almighty reigns' is the song of the redeemed in
Heaven (Rev. 19: 6). It expresses a truth continually expounded in
Scripture and the text provides us with two basic aspects of the
concept; the Almighty God and the Sovereign God.

a. THE ALMIGHTY GOD

When God talked with Abraham, He announced Himself as
'God Almighty' (Gen. 17: 1). Abraham's son Isaac used the title in
his blessing of his son Jacob (Gen. 28: 3). When God later revealed
Himself to Jacob it was as 'God Almighty' (Gen. 35: 11), and Jacob
also used the same name when he spoke of God (Gen. 43: 14, 48: 3,
49: 25). The name of God used in these patriarchal narratives is the
Hebrew word, *El-Shaddai*. It indicates a God who is all-powerful and
impregnable. The term is not confined to these familiar and meaningful Genesis stories alone, it is used throughout both the Old and
New Testament (Exod. 6: 3; Num. 24: 4, 16; Ruth 1: 20, 21;
Job 5: 17, 6: 4, 8: 5, 13: 3, 21: 15, 29: 5, 33: 4; Psa. 68: 14, 91: 1;

Ezek. 1: 24, 10: 5; Joel 1: 15; 2 Cor. 6: 18; Rev. 1: 8, 4: 8, 11: 17, 15: 3, 16: 7, 14, 19: 15, 21: 22).

i. Incomparable in quality

The biblical writers frequently note the fact that God's power is unique. It is futile to try to compare it with any kind of human power. In conversation with Job, the young Elihu said that God is 'exalted in His power' (Job 36: 22, cf. 37: 23). King Jehoshaphat knew that God's power and might was so great that 'none is able to withstand it' (2 Chron. 20: 6). The psalmist recognized that power 'belongs to God' (Psa. 62: 11) and that it was so great that enemies cringe before it (Psa. 66: 3) and are scattered by it (Psa. 59: 11). He describes it as abundant power (Psa. 147: 5). It is sovereign power in that He can use it to cast down or to raise up; He uses it exactly as He chooses (2 Chron. 25: 8). This power is unique. Believing people love to sing and talk about it (Psa. 145: 11). Men praise God for it (Psa. 21: 13, 59: 16), knowing how weak and ineffective they would be without it. They long to proclaim it to the generations to come (Psa. 71: 18).

ii. Displayed in creation

The subject of God's creative power is often mentioned in Scripture, even outside the obvious Genesis narratives (e.g. Job 26: 7–15; Psa. 65: 6). Prophets declared that God made the earth by His power. It is a favourite prophetic theme, e.g. in Isaiah (40: 21–28, 42: 5, 44: 24, 45: 12, 18) and Jeremiah (10: 12, 27: 5, 32: 17, 51: 15). The exultant song of praise in Heaven focuses on this same theme, 'Worthy art thou, our Lord and God, to receive glory and honour and power for thou didst create all things, and by thy will they existed and were created' (Rev. 4: 11). Even the unbeliever can discern God's power and deity by observing the created world (Rom. 1: 20).

iii. Manifested in history

The deliverance of Israel in the exodus-event is a superb illustration of God's power. The mighty Pharaoh was but an instrument in God's hands (Rom. 9: 17). But Pharaoh rebelled against God's will even though he was told of God's invincible might (Exod. 9: 16). And once God delivered His people, the Hebrews sang about their deliverance and acknowledged it was due to God's power (Exod. 15: 6). It was recognized that it was by God's great power and mighty hand that they had been saved (Exod. 32: 11; Deut. 4: 37, 9: 29; 2 Kings 17: 36; Neh. 1: 10; Psa. 66: 5, 6).

The Hebrews rejoiced in this event. He even used the winds for His purposes (Exod. 14: 21, 15: 10). No obstacle was allowed to stand in their way (Psa. 106: 9), and all this was done that subsequent generations might know of His delivering power (Psa 106: 8).

The later prosperity of the Hebrew people was also due to God's power (Deut. 8: 17, 18; Psa. 111: 6). Even though the Lord God manifested Himself in supernatural events, so great is His power that even on these occasions His power was veiled (Hab. 3: 4).

iv. Revealed in Christ

The unique circumstances attending the conception of Jesus were due to the 'power of the Most High' (Lk. 1: 35). Christ Himself is described as 'the power of God' (1 Cor. 1: 24). His healing miracles were due to God's power (Lk. 9: 43). Men were allowed to use their limited power to crucify Him (John 19: 10, 11), but by God's unique power Christ was raised from the dead (Acts 2: 24; 1 Cor. 6: 14; Eph. 1: 19, 20). By that same power of God we too shall be raised (1 Cor. 6: 14; 2 Cor. 13: 4).

v. Proved in experience

Christians have rejoiced in the truth that the power of God is not reserved for dramatic, spectacular events or confined to certain occasions in history. It is available *now* to believers. They have proved that God's power sustains them in weakness and trouble (Psa. 68: 35; Isa. 40: 29; Rom. 16: 25). David knew this to be true in his afflictions (2 Sam. 22: 2, 33), and Paul realized its truth in physical suffering (2 Cor. 12: 9, 10). The early Christian people soon came to realize that God was pleased to use weak men and women in His service so that man could not take the glory to himself (1 Cor. 1: 26–29; 2 Cor. 4: 7). The Christian message could be communicated effectively only when the messengers were entirely dependent on God's power (2 Cor. 6: 7; Eph. 3: 7; 1 Thess. 1: 5).

This power was not an occasional and dramatic intervention in human life, but a constantly renewed experience of inward strength (Eph. 3: 20, 6: 10; Col. 1: 11). With this assurance men can endure suffering in the cause of the Gospel (2 Tim. 1: 8). It is by this same power that believers are kept, even though they are tested by severe and harassing experiences of affliction (1 Pet. 1: 5; Jude 24, 25). This transforming, saving and keeping power of God is the theme and corollary of the Gospel of redemption (Rom. 1: 16; 1 Cor. 1: 18). His power sustains those who are in danger of death (Psa. 79: 11).

The Bible says that God's voice is powerful (Psa. 29: 4). His word has power to effect what He commands; 'God said . . . And it was so' (cf. Gen. 1: 6, 7, 9, 11, 14, 15). Under various images the word of God is described as a powerful instrument for God's purposes (Jer. 23: 29; Eph. 6: 17; Heb. 4: 12), yet it is tragically possible to be familiar with the letter of Scripture and remain ignorant of the power of God (Mt. 22: 29). God is described as the *Everlasting* King (Exod. 15: 18; Psa. 10: 16, 29: 10, 66: 7, 145: 13; Jer. 10: 10; Dan.

4: 3; 1 Tim. 1: 17). He is in complete control and does whatever He chooses (Psa. 115: 3, 135: 6; Dan. 4: 35). His purposes cannot be thwarted (Job 42: 2).

God's omnipotence also means that God is Sovereign.

b. THE SOVEREIGN GOD

This sovereignty is seen in several ways:

i. In the affairs of His world

This Almighty, Sovereign God is the Lord who reigns over the whole world (Psa. 103: 19). He rules even the nations which do not openly acknowledge Him (2 Chron. 20: 6; Isa. 40: 15, 17). He works in the hearts and minds of heathen leaders and accomplishes His purposes by using them as He wills. For example, even a cruel and ruthless nation like Assyria became the rod of His anger to chastise the wayward and disobedient Israelites (Isa. 10: 5). And when He had finished with the heathen oppressors they too were judged (Isa. 10: 12). In their arrogance the Assyrians foolishly imagined that they had the freedom to plan their campaigns and plot their military manoeuvres (Isa. 10: 13–19). Similarly, at a later date, Nebuchadnezzar was used as God's servant and was described as such (Jer. 25: 9, 27: 6, 43: 10). Later still God raised up a previously insignificant tribal leader, Cyrus, and made him a great king to effect the deliverance of God's people from Babylon (Isa. 41: 2–4, 25, 45: 1–5, 46: 11). Cyrus is therefore referred to as God's Shepherd (Isa. 44: 28) who fulfils His predetermined purposes (cf. 2 Chron. 36: 23).

The Hebrew people obviously recognized that God had delivered them both from their Egyptian and (later) Babylonian oppression. He was directly responsible for their desert journeys (Amos 2: 10). But Amos discerned that God's sovereignty was such that he plotted the movements of heathen nations as well (Amos 9: 7). God reigns over the heathen (Psa. 47: 8; Jer. 10: 7) and appoints their kings as He chooses (Dan. 2: 21, 5: 21). Earthly kings vainly imagine that they can frustrate His purposes (Psa. 2: 2), but they have to bow down before Him (Psa. 2: 4, 72: 11). Any power they have is derived from God (Job 24: 22–24) and He withdraws it at His will (Isa. 37: 21–29). His Kingdom rules over all (Psa. 47: 2, 7, 103: 19; Dan. 4: 17, 25, 32, 5: 21).

ii. In the destiny of His people

There is a unique sense in which the Sovereign God can be described as the King of Israel (I Sam. 12: 12; Psa. 89: 18, 149: 2; Isa. 43: 15, 44: 6; Ezek. 20: 33). When the Hebrew people appointed kings as other nations, they were in danger of forgetting the kingship of the Lord their God (Hosea 13: 9–11, cf. Jdgs. 8: 23; 1 Sam.

12: 13–18). Because God is Israel's ruler (Psa. 59: 13), He accepted full responsibilty for their welfare. God frequently defeated and frustrated heathen kings when they rose against His people in order to destroy them. This theme is often developed both in psalmody (Psa. 105:'14, 135: 8–12, 136: 17–22) and in the Hebrew prophetic tradition (e.g. Jer. 51: 20–24). The prophets eagerly anticipated a time when God's sovereign control over the whole world would be given practical expression in the establishment of His peaceful kingdom. They saw Jerusalem as the centre of this dominion and as that which would attract worshippers from all nations who would come before God in gratitude and submission (Mic. 4: 1–7, cf. Isa. 2: 2–4).

iii. In the lives of His children
He is not only sovereign in the ordering of national and community life but also in the ways of individual men and women; a truth which is both encouraging and comforting to those who trust Him. The Psalmist refers to God as 'my King' (Psa. 5: 2, 68: 24, 74: 12, 84: 3) and thus realizes that He is to be extolled (Psa. 145: 1). This King reveals Himself to individuals in times of great need, for example when the throne of Judah was without a king (Isa. 6: 1).

The death of a king was always a time of particular danger in any near-eastern country. It was always an open invitation to rebellion, intrigue, or attack from neighbouring enemies. But Israel was made to see that, although Judah's throne was empty, God's eternal throne was not (Isa. 6: 5). The prophet realized that this sovereign God would bring salvation to His people (Isa. 33: 20–22). Similarly, Jeremiah, in time of national apostasy and personal spiritual hardship, rejoiced in the fact that 'a glorious throne set on high from the beginning' was the place of sanctuary (Jer. 17: 12, cf. 14: 21). Perhaps the most superb illustration of God's sovereignty in the life of an individual is in the familiar story of Joseph. He looked back on a life of hardship, affliction, misunderstanding and deep personal sorrow; but in it all he could discern the providential control of a sovereign God (Gen. 50: 20).

iv. In the work of His Son
Christ came to fulfil God's sovereign purpose for lost mankind (Lk. 19: 10; Jn. 3: 17, 4: 34, 5: 30, 6: 38, 17: 4). His death on the Cross was not an accident. He knew it was ahead (Jn. 2: 4, 7: 6, 8: 20, 12: 27, 17: 1, cf. Mk. 8: 31, 9: 31, 32, 10: 33, 34). The early Christian preachers quickly realized that Christ's sacrificial death was part of God's sovereign and saving purposes. Judas, Pilate and the priests played merely subsidiary roles in the events of the Passion. The death of God's Son was allowed in that it was 'according to the definite plan and foreknowledge of God' (Acts 2: 23). The

prophets had predicted it (Acts 3: 18), and it was all part of God's sovereign plan (Acts 4: 27, 28, cf. 1 Pet. 1: 20).

v. In the extension of His dominion

It is surely significant that the Lord Jesus made great use of the term 'Kingdom' to describe God's work among men. The word (*basileia*) obviously does not mean kingdom in the sense of geographical territory. It indicates the kingly rule of God and the sphere where that kingship is openly and freely acknowledged. In Christ's teaching the Gospel was a message of God's kingly rule (Mk. 1: 14, 15; Lk. 8: 1). Men can enter that Kingdom only by repentance and faith (Mk. 1: 15). It is the work of God's Spirit; a new birth (Jn. 3: 3, 5).

The things of the Kingdom are to be of the greatest importance and priority to those who believe (Lk. 12: 31). But note that it is clearly described as *God's Kingdom* (Lk. 12: 32, 17: 20, 19: 11; Acts 8: 12, 14: 22, 19: 8, 20: 25, 28: 23, 31; 1 Cor. 4: 20, 6: 9ff; Gal. 5: 21; Col. 4: 11; 2 Thess. 1: 5; Rev. 12: 10). It is an unshakeable Kingdom (Heb. 12: 28) and one that will continue to grow however fiercely men may work against it (Mt. 13: 31, 32; Lk. 1: 33; Acts 5: 39, 8: 1–8, 9: 1–18).

Note the recurrence of the term 'multiplied' in the Acts of the Apostles. It is a story of inevitable and irresistible growth (Acts 6: 1, 7, 7: 17, 9: 31, 12: 24). Longing for the time when God's will is eagerly sought and gladly pursued by all men, His disciples pray 'Thy Kingdom come' (Lk. 11: 2).

2. GOD IS OMNISCIENT

This All-powerful God is fully aware of everything. He is not limited, as man is, by ignorance and uncertainty. Everything is clearly visible to Him (Heb. 4: 13; Psa. 139: 3). He has perfect knowledge (Job 36: 4; Psa. 73: 11). He keeps watch on the nations (Psa. 66: 7). And He does not confine His interest to the nation of Israel alone. Amos told his hearers that God knew about the sins of one heathen nation against another. Many Israelites were amazed to realize He was grieved about the vindictive cruelty of the Moabites to the King of Edom, or about the transgressions of Gaza and Tyre in taking slaves to Edom, especially if the captives were not Israelites (Amos 2: 1, 1: 6, 9). Before the prophet exposes the sins of Judah (2: 4, 5) and Israel (2: 6–16), he shows the people that God has seen all the atrocities of their vicious neighbours even the sins which did not in any way affect the people of the Northern Kingdom! Nothing can be hidden from His gaze. His eyes are in every place (Psa. 94: 9; Prov. 15: 3; Heb. 4: 13). He is 'a God of knowledge and by Him actions are weighed' (1 Sam. 2: 3). He knows about individuals (2 Sam. 7: 20; Job 34: 21; Jer. 12: 3) as well as empires. The biblical writers develop this theme of God's omniscience in a number of ways:

a. HE DISCERNS OUR SECRETS

It is only ignorant and unbelieving men who suggest that God cannot see what they are doing (Psa. 73: 11; Isa. 29: 15, 16, 47: 10). Men foolishly imagine that they can have their secrets, but God knows of their plans and ambitions even before they have had time to work them out in detail. He knows 'the secrets of the heart' (Psa. 44: 21), and He knows the hearts of all men (1 Kings 8: 39; Acts 1: 24, 15: 8). It is ridiculous to imagine that we can keep anything from Him (Job 34: 22, 25). There will be a Day when God will judge these secrets of men (Rom. 2: 16). Everything will then be made manifest (Jer. 32: 19; 1 Cor. 3: 13, 4: 5).

b. HE READS OUR THOUGHTS

Man is easily deceived. He goes by outward appearances, but God looks into the hearts of men (Jer. 20: 12; 1 Jn. 3: 20) and knows them as they really are (1 Sam. 16: 7). He does not see as man sees (Job 10: 4). Psalm 139 is a detailed and moving exposition of this serious theme (cf. Psa. 139: 2, 4). He knows what man is thinking about (Psa. 94: 11, 139: 23; Isa. 66: 18). Long before man puts his ideas into words, God knows about them (Psa. 139: 4). He also knows what we talk about (Jer. 17: 16). He knows about our private generosity (Mt. 6: 4), prayer life (Mt. 6: 6) and personal discipline (Mt. 6: 18).

c. HE REALIZES OUR LIMITATIONS

Because He made us (Psa. 139: 13), He knows all about us (Psa. 139: 16). He knew us before anyone else knew us (Psa. 139: 15) and He obviously knows us better than anyone else. He understands our physical limitations; 'He knows our frame; He remembers that we are dust' (Psa. 103: 14, cf. Psa. 78: 39).

d. HE SEES OUR TROUBLES

God knew all about the distress of His people in Egyptian bondage (Exod. 2: 24, 25, 3: 7). He knew them in the wilderness (Hosea 13: 5). He knew what they would do even before they came into the Promised Land (Deut. 31: 21). Once they came into the land of Canaan, they proved that God continued to keep His eye on them from the beginning of each year to its end (Deut. 11: 12). When the exilic experience of divine judgment came upon them, some who remained in the land were tempted to believe that God had forsaken them and no longer looked upon them (Ezek. 8: 12, 9: 9). They forgot that He knew of their sins as well as their sorrows (Ezek. 8: 17). Because His eye was upon the exiles (Jer. 24: 6), they would certainly return to their own land. Once they were back in the land, God continued to look upon them in favour in times of trouble (Ezra 5: 5).

Individuals have also been comforted by realizing that the All-seeing God knows about their adversities and difficulties. Jeremiah, for example, knew that God was aware of the hostility of his enemies (Jer. 18: 23). As a matter of fact, God revealed their cruel plans to His servant (Jer. 11: 18). Another sufferer, Job, knew that God was conscious of his grief and that the fires of adversity would both prove and purify him (Job 23: 10). Obviously, He knows all about our needs (Mt. 6: 8, 32) so there is no reason to be anxious. Moreover, He knows how to deliver us (1 Cor. 10: 13; 2 Pet. 29: 9).

e. HE UNCOVERS OUR SINS

Jeremiah's enemies plotted against him, but God knew of their evil designs. Men may try to hide their sins, but God sees them all (Jer. 16: 17, 23: 24). The sinner foolishly imagines that he can sin in secret (Job 24: 14, 15). Further, He knows all about our past sins (Psa. 69: 5). Achan imagined that nobody was aware of his theft, but God knew about it (Josh. 7: 10–26, cf. 22: 20–22). David thought his sin against Bathsheba was a matter solely between themselves. He did it in secret (2 Sam. 12: 12), but he was publicly condemned (2 Sam. 12: 7). It was evil *in God's sight* (2 Sam. 12: 9; Psa. 51: 4); He sees iniquity (Job 11: 11) however men may try to cloak it. He knows our secret faults (Psa. 19: 12). They are set in the light of His countenance (Psa. 90: 8). The believing man asks that these sins will be revealed to himself so he may forsake them (Psa. 139: 23, 24). God tries and tests the hearts and minds of sinful men (Psa. 7: 9, 26: 2) and, knowing their sins, longs to forgive them if only they will confess their iniquity (1 Jn. 1: 8, 9). It is ridiculous to say we have not sinned. God knows the facts (1 Jn. 1: 10). It is man's pride which keeps Him from God. And He knows full well about our arrogance. This is one of the worst sins. It leads to self-satisfaction and self-display. Christ knew that this was the basic trouble with the Pharisees and made it clear God knew their sinful hearts (Lk. 16: 15).

f. HE KNOWS OUR FAITH

By far the greatest illustration of God's omniscience is that He knows those who will believe on Him in the future (Rom. 8: 29). Because He knew those who would put their trust in Christ's saving work, He set them apart as His own believing people (Eph. 1: 5, 11, 12; 2 Tim. 1: 9; 1 Pet. 1: 2). Although there is more in the biblical idea of predestination, at least this much is quite clear in the Scriptures.

g. HE DETERMINES OUR DESTINY

There is a special sense in which 'the eye of the Lord' is upon those who love and obey Him (Psa. 33: 18, 34: 15). He knows them intimately and treasures that relationship (Nah. 1: 7; 2 Tim. 2: 19). Jeremiah, for example, was assured that God knew him even before birth and planned that he should be a prophet. This was God's purpose for young Jeremiah (Jer. 1: 5). The Apostle Paul could say the same (Gal. 1: 15). The Psalmist is amazed that God takes such a personal interest in insignificant man (Psa. 144: 3, 4). He knows all about the path we will take (Psa. 142: 3). The movements of every day are His concern (Job 3: 4; Psa. 139: 2), and with His infinite knowledge He promises to guide us through life (Psa. 32: 8). He shows us His way and purpose for our lives (Psa. 25: 8). The God who knows us by name (Exod. 33: 12, 17) and numbers the hairs of our heads (Lk. 12: 7) is obviously concerned about every single detail in our lives.

3. GOD IS OMNIPRESENT

God is not a 'localized' God. The Hebrews, like other near-eastern people, were always in danger of thinking of God as a 'God of the land'. Their neighbours believed that their gods ruled over their own territories, but they could hardly conceive of a God who ruled over all and who could therefore manifest Himself anywhere and everywhere. Naaman, the Syrian Commander, who was cured of his leprosy, may have had these ideas in his mind when he took home a bag of Israelite soil so that he could stand on it as he worshipped Israel's God (2 Kings 5: 17).

In marked contrast to this 'tribal-god' thinking, the Old Testament asserts that God is everywhere. He fills both heaven and earth. He is 'a God at hand and not a God afar off' (Jer. 23: 23). Just as man cannot hide anything from God, neither can he escape from His presence. He is always near to us (Psa. 139: 7–10; Amos 9: 2–4; Acts 17: 27). It is in Him that 'we live and move and have our being' (Acts 17: 28). God is described as 'the High and Lofty One who inhabits eternity'. Yet, *at the same time,* He dwells with the man of a humble and contrite spirit (Isa. 57: 15). The Eternal God is known as the One who dwells in the high and holy place, yet 'earth is His footstool' (Isa. 66: 1).

How was God made manifest on earth? His presence among men can be traced in three areas of experience.

a. TO INDIVIDUALS

Certain men in Old Testament times were uniquely aware of God's presence with them, even though He dwelt in the heavens (Psa. 2: 4, 115: 3, 123: 1). Six examples among many to be found in the Bible illustrate this truth;

(1) *Jacob* (Gen. 28: 16, 17)
(2) *Joseph* (Gen. 39: 2, 3, 6–20, 21, 23)
(3) *Moses* (Exod. 33: 14, 34: 5, 6)
(4) *Joshua* (Josh. 1: 9, 17)
(5) *David* (Psa. 23: 2, 4)
(6) *Jeremiah* (Jer. 1: 8, 19, 15: 20, 20: 11)

b. TO ISRAEL

It can be argued that God's presence with *specific* individuals in no way indicates that He is everywhere at the same time. But the Hebrew people rejoiced in the certainty of the presence of God amongst all of them and at all times and in all places. God went before them (Deut. 1: 30, 9: 3). Moses told the Israelites that the Lord was with them (Deut. 31: 6, 8). Isaiah told his contemporaries, 'God is with us' (Isa. 8: 10). The exiled Israelites in Babylon were told that God was with them in their tribulations (Isa. 43: 2, 5). Ezekiel was given this truth in visionary form. He saw the chariot-throne of God not where he would expect it in Jerusalem, but in Babylonia. He is there because He is everywhere (Ezek. 1: 26–28). He is able to do this because He is not confined to one place. His presence is said to fill heaven and earth (Jer. 23: 24), yet He also walked with the Israelites as they journeyed (Deut. 23: 14).

c. TO BELIEVERS

Christians are assured that God is with them. The promise made to Joshua, that the Lord will not forsake him (Josh. 1: 5), is repeated to the early Christian people (Heb. 13: 5). Other New Testament epistles close with the confident assertion that 'the God of Peace' is with every believer (Rom. 15: 33; Phil. 4: 9). It is a New Testament way of expressing the truth that the God who dwells 'in the high and holy place' also lives 'with him who is of a contrite and humble spirit' (Isa. 57: 15).

III. GOD'S DIVINE ATTITUDES OR ATTRIBUTES

The Bible is very explicit about the attitudes or attributes of God (the two terms are virtually synonymous when applied to God). Five of these are of supreme importance.

1. GOD IS LOVE

Love is an expression of God's very nature. He is love and He loves us (1 John 4: 16). He sets His love upon us to care for us as we cleave to Him in love (Psa. 91; 14). In biblical thought, this love of God is expounded in many marvellous ways.

a. SUPERLATIVE LOVE

There is no love on earth like it. Parental love makes astonishing sacrifices, but God's love is far greater than even this (Jn. 3: 16). The Lord abounds in love and is said to keep 'steadfast love for thousands' (Exod. 34: 6, 7; Jer. 32: 18). Isaiah tells of 'the abundance of His steadfast love' (Isa 63: 7). It is said to extend to the heavens (Psa. 36: 5).

b. UNMERITED LOVE

God's love is all the more wonderful in that it is so totally undeserved. He sets His love upon men even though they are utterly unworthy of it. There are two clear biblical illustrations of this principle;

i. God's love for the Hebrews

God did not choose the Hebrews because they were great or mighty, but solely because He loved them (Deut. 7: 7, 8, 10: 15). God continued to love them even though they were not worthy of such love. He loved them when they were disobedient and rebellious (Jer. 31: 3; Hosea 11: 1–4). He was known to be the God who loved His people Israel (Deut. 33: 3; 2 Chron. 2: 11, 9: 8; Psa. 47: 4; Isa. 43: 4, 48: 14).

ii. God's love for the sinner

God loves us even though we may not love Him. He loves us 'even when we were dead through our trespasses ' (Eph. 2: 1, 4, 5). God shows His love for us supremely by the fact that 'while we were yet sinners Christ died for us' (Rom. 5: 8).

c. PARDONING LOVE

Overwhelmed by a sense of guilt, David prayed that God would have mercy on him according to His steadfast love (Psa. 51: 1). Even though we may wander away from Him, He loves us and longs for us to return that He may forgive and heal us (Hosea 14: 4). He is a God who pardons iniquity; this is because He delights in steadfast love (Mic. 7: 18). Jonah knew that God would forgive the Ninevites because He abounded in steadfast love (Jonah 4: 2 cf. Joel 2: 13).

d. GENEROUS LOVE

God's love is clearly expressed in His many gifts to us. The Hebrew people recognized that the benefits of everyday life were an indication of God's love for them, e.g. the gift of children or a good harvest (Deut. 7: 13). It is the same Father who loved us who also gave us eternal comfort and good hope through grace (2 Thess. 2: 16). Our sonship is yet another expression of God's love for us (1 John 3: 1).

e. PATIENT LOVE

Even in our stubbornness and sinful disloyalty, God goes on loving us; 'How can I give you up . . . my compassion grows warm and tender' (Hosea 11: 8). Hosea knew this, for it was mirrored in his own tragic domestic experience. Although his wife had gone after other lovers, he could not give her up. The prophet knew also that the Lord continued to love His people even though they had gone after other gods (Hosea 3: 1, 2).

f. EVERLASTING LOVE

It was not the kind of love that changed or vacillated. God's love was utterly dependable. Man can rely on that love without any fear that it will let him down. Even though He is grieved by our sinning, He does not cease to love us; 'If they . . . do not keep my commandments then I will punish their transgression with the rod . . . but I will not remove from him my steadfast love' (Psa. 89: 31–33). Just as our sins cannot separate us from that love, neither can any other experience in life—or even in death (Rom. 8: 38, 39). His love is everlasting (Isa. 54: 7, 8).

g. CORRECTIVE LOVE

Yet God's love is never mere sentimentality. It is reliable and strong—the kind of love which points out our mistakes and corrects us when we go wrong. The very act of correction is an unmistakable expression of His love for us. He disciplines those He loves (Prov. 3: 12; Heb. 12: 6; cf. Rev. 3: 19).

h. PROTECTIVE LOVE

God's love is not merely negative in pointing out our sins. It is positive and practical in that, because He loves us, God protects us and surrounds us in the everyday experiences of life. An Old Testament example of this can be found in the Balaam story where it says that God did not listen to Balaam 'but the Lord your God turned the curse into a blessing for you, because the Lord your God loved you' (Deut. 23: 5). The Holy One of Israel is described as Israel's 'Saviour', the One who said, 'Because you are precious in my eyes, and honoured, and I love you, I give men in return for you, peoples in exchange for your life' (Isa. 43: 3, 4). Even though the Hebrew people were to pass through the waters of distress and fires of affliction, the Lord would protect them (Isa. 43: 2) because He loved them infinitely.

i. INCARNATE LOVE

The coming of God's Son is, without doubt, the supreme manifestation of God's love; 'In this the love of God was made manifest among us, that God sent His only Son into the world' (1 Jn. 4: 9, cf. Jn. 3: 16; Tit. 3: 4–7).

j. SACRIFICIAL LOVE

God's love is further displayed in His redeeming love; 'He loved us and sent His Son to be the expiation for our sins' (1 Jn. 4: 10; cf. Rom. 5: 8).

k. ACTIVE LOVE

It can clearly be seen from the above references that God's love is an alert, practical love. It is revealed through historical events and in pragmatic ways. It is not a theoretical attribute of a distant God. God's love is such that it must express itself in action. The biblical writers expound the theme of the God who takes the initiative; 'In His love and in His pity He redeemed them; He lifted them up and carried them all the days of old' (Isa. 63: 9). He loved us long before we had any love for Him (1 Jn. 4: 10). We love Him because He first loved us (1 Jn. 4: 19).

l. DEMANDING LOVE

But this costly and active love of God makes demands upon us. Both Old and New Testament passages emphasize the importance of making a response to God's love by loving others. 'He . . . loves the sojourner, giving him food and clothing. Love the sojourner therefore . . .' (Deut. 10: 18, 19). If God loves, we must love also (1 Jn. 4: 11, 21). Christians are taught by God to love one another (1 Thess. 4: 9). Almost every epistle in the New Testament makes some reference to the necessity of Christian love.

m. IMPARTIAL LOVE

We are often selective in our loving, but God loves all men and longs for them to come to Him. God loved *the world* so much that He gave His only Son (Jn. 3: 16). The love of God is with us *all* (2 Cor. 13: 14).

n. PERSONAL LOVE

And yet, although God loves all, His love for us is deeply personal. An Old Testament example illustrates a universal truth; '. . . and he called his name Solomon. And the Lord loved *him*.' David gave the name 'Jedidiah' to his newborn child; it meant 'beloved of the Lord' (2 Sam. 12: 24, 25). The name was an expression of a profound biblical truth. Even though David had grieved God and brought sadness to others, yet the Lord loved him and gave him a son. God also loved the child. He loves us all and yet He loves us individually and personally; we matter to Him (cf. Gal. 2: 20).

2. GOD IS RIGHTEOUS

The Hebrew terms *tsedeg* and *tsedagah* are variously translated in the R.S.V. as 'justice', 'righteousness', 'deliverance', 'victory', 'salvation', and 'vindication'. This is an indication of the wealth of meaning which is meant to be conveyed by these words and their cognates. It is far more than 'doing right' or 'being upright' in a moral sense, though that too is obviously intended. It has been suggested that their root meaning is something like 'that which is as it should be' (R. T. France, *The Living God*, 1970, p. 92). It is God acting in a way we would expect, or manifesting Himself in a manner which is entirely consistent with everything else we know about Him.

This righteous God is clearly concerned about those who are oppressed by unrighteousness. God puts wrong things right, and so we move into the realm of ideas indicated by terms like 'salvation', 'deliverance', 'vindication', etc. The Bible does not discuss these various aspects of God's nature and attributes in a cold, theoretical, detached fashion. It has been said that God is known for what He is by what He does. It may help us to understand what is meant by God's righteousness if we trace five ways in which His righteousness is revealed. God is righteous in:

a. HIS UNCHANGING INTEGRITY

The prophet Jeremiah, surrounded by unrighteous men intent on killing him (Jer. 11: 18–21), came before God in prayer. He began, 'Righteous art thou, O Lord' (Jer. 12: 1; cf. Ezra 9: 15; Psa. 119: 137). He knew that it was not merely that God judged righteously (Jer. 11: 20); God was Himself utterly righteous. The word gave rich expression to the divine integrity. The Psalmist says, 'Gracious is the Lord and righteous' (Psa. 116: 5). Elihu says he will 'ascribe righteousness to his Maker' (Job 36: 3). In one of the 'Songs of Ascent' which the Hebrew pilgrims sang as they made their way up to the Holy City, they recalled the fact that as a nation they had often suffered but went on to remind one another of this great truth: 'The Lord is righteous' (Psa. 129: 1–4; cf. 2 Chron. 12: 6). The Lord God is said to be One who practises righteousness in the earth and delights in it (Jer. 9: 24). In prayer Daniel said righteousness 'belonged' to God (Dan. 9: 7). Jesus described God as a righteous Father (John 17: 25).

In the Bible God's righteousness is seen to be:

i. Unique

God is obviously not righteous in the sense that any good man may be described as 'righteous'. The prophet said, 'Only in the Lord, it shall be said of me, are righteousness and strength' (Isa. 45: 24). No man living is righteous before God because of his own deeds (Psa. 143: 2).

ii. Consistent

The Psalmist rejoices that 'The Lord is just in *all* His ways' (Psa. 145: 17).

iii. Dependable

God's righteousness is 'like the mountains of God' (Psa. 36: 6). It is an everlasting righteousness (Psa. 111: 3; Isa. 51: 6, 8). Moreover, God is righteous in:

b. HIS SAVING ACTIVITY

The biblical writers are hardly interested in detailed and remote theological abstractions. For them God is alive and active in nature and in history. If it thunders, it is because God is at work. If a huge tribe migrates from one place to another, it is because God has plotted the course of their movement. We have observed that *tsedeg* and its cognates can be accurately translated by words from the vocabulary of salvation like 'victory', 'deliverance', 'vindication', etc. These terms express truths about a God who is determined to see that right is done. God's righteousness is an active, saving righteousness. Micah reminds the people that God has acted for them in history. He tells them of specific occasions when they have seen 'the saving (righteous) acts of the Lord' (Micah 6: 5).

This concept is often found in Isaiah. The second half of the book, especially chapters 40–55, depicts a situation at the close of the Babylonian exile. God has pardoned their iniquity (Isa. 40: 1, 2) and now proves Himself to be their righteous Deliverer. The exiled people are naturally afraid as they contemplate the long journey home through hundreds of miles of barren desert, but they are told that their righteous God will uphold them (Isa. 41: 10). To effect the deliverance from Babylon, God has raised up King Cyrus. 'I have aroused him in righteousness . . . he shall build my city and set my exiles free' (Isa. 45: 13). His deliverance (A. V. 'righteousness') is said to be near (Isa. 46: 13). The moment of Israel's release is at hand 'Righteousness', as used here, is a synonym for 'salvation'.

A good example of this principle can be found in Isa. 51: 15:

'My deliverance (A. V. righteousness) draws near speedily,
My salvation has gone forth.'

This is an illustration of Hebrew parallelism, a poetic form whereby the same kind of truth is set forth in different ways. His righteousness is expressed in the act of deliverance. It is obviously right that God's people should now be free to return to their own land. The period of divine chastisement is over. He manifested His righteousness as He judged them. He displays it yet again in the manner He effects their deliverance.

'Soon my salvation will come
and my deliverance (A. V. righteousness) be revealed' (Isa. 56: 1)

Obviously, the New Testament doctrine of salvation has to be seen against this rich Old Testament background (cf. Rom. 3: 25, 26; 10: 3, 1 Cor. 1: 30; 2 Cor. 5: 21).

And God is righteous in:

c. HIS TRUSTWORTHY REVELATION

God's word is a further expression of His righteousness. It is the upright and reliable message of a God who cannot lie and will not deceive us (Num. 23: 19; Heb. 6: 18). The word of God is often described as a righteous word. It will not mislead. God's message in the Bible assumes different forms. Sometimes there is a promise, on other occasions a word of instruction or rebuke. But whatever God says to us, we may be assured that it will be entirely in keeping with His righteousness. For example;

i. Promises

Ezra addressed God in a prayer of confession and said, 'Thou hast fulfilled Thy promise, for Thou art righteous' (Neh. 9: 8). Ezra was referring to the Covenant promises of God. He knew that God had promised to give the land of Canaan to the Hebrew people, and they had proved the reliability of His word. His promises are righteous promises. They will certainly be fulfilled (Psa. 119: 123).

ii. Ordinances

The Psalmist took up the theme of God's ordinances and said, 'The' ordinances of the Lord are true and righteous altogether' (Psa. 19: 9).

iii. Testimonies

The famous 'Psalm of God's Word' (Psa. 119) says that God has appointed His testimonies 'in righteousness' (Psa. 119: 138). The 'testimonies' of God's word might well refer to those passages which bear witness to what He is, to what He has done and what He will yet do for those who trust Him.

iv. Laws

The Bible says of God: 'Thy righteousness is righteous for ever and thy law true' (Psa 119: 142). God's people are reminded of their unique privilege in having such a law: 'And what great nation is there, that has statutes and ordinances so righteous as all this law which I set before you this day?' (Deut. 4: 8).

v. Commandments

If God instructs us to do something or to refrain from some particular action we may be assured that this is another expression of His righteousness. He knows what is best for us and for others. 'All thy commandments are right' (Psa. 119: 172).

God says, 'I the Lord speak the truth. I declare what is right' (Isa. 45: 19). His word is both true and unchanging; 'by myself I have sworn, from my mouth has gone forth in righteousness a word that shall not return' (Isa. 45: 23).

Righteousness is further revealed in:

d. GOD'S PROVIDENTIAL DIRECTION

Obviously, God guides us through His written word. The Bible further assures us that He reveals His sovereign will and purpose for us as we commune with Him. And God's plan for our lives is always the best for us. It is the right one, for it is chosen by a righteous God. He leads us in 'paths of righteousness' or 'right paths' (Psa. 23: 3). Our part is to seek His will and pray 'Lead me O Lord in Thy righteousness . . . make Thy way straight before me' (Psa. 5: 8).

Finally, God's righteousness is seen in:

e. HIS ABSOLUTE JUSTICE

The Bible often expounds the theme of God's righteousness in the setting of judgment, not only in the future at the great Day when we must all give an account of our lives (2 Cor. 5: 10) but also in the present. The judgment-theme in Scripture is not confined to the Last Judgment. Men are compelled to see that in this life we all have dealings with Him whether we like it or not. If we disregard His laws and refuse His mercy, we may well meet Him in wrath. 'The wrath of God is the contrary wind of the divine will. He soon discovers who runs against it.' (Emil Brunner.) The Bible illustrates this truth in a threefold manner.

i. National judgment

The Hebrew people knew all about this. Daniel gave expression to the truth when he said, 'We have not entreated the favour of the Lord our God turning from our iniquities and giving heed to Thy truth. Therefore the Lord has kept ready the calamity and has brought it upon us; for the Lord our God is righteous in all the works which He has done' (Dan. 9: 13, 14). Daniel could see that God's judgment upon His people was yet another expression of His righteousness.

A similar truth is found in the Book of Lamentations. Jerusalem is broken and forsaken, but it was the Lord who 'summoned an assembly' against her (Lam. 1: 15). Yet it is no act of injustice on God's part: 'The Lord is in the right,' says the sufferer, 'for I have rebelled against His Word' (Lam. 1: 18). The Israelites also knew times when, because of His righteousness, God had judged those nations who had acted unrighteously towards them (Psa. 9: 5–8). He always judges the world with righteousness (Psa. 9: 8, 72: 2, 96: 13, 98: 9).

ii. Personal judgment

There are many occasions in the Bible when individuals cast themselves upon God in that they have suffered personally because of the sins of others. They wisely call upon their righteous God to put things right. In the moral world which He has made, vindication belongs to Him (Psa. 35: 24). They recognize that they could easily be mistaken or unjust in their judgments, but God judges with absolute righteousness. Jeremiah is a good example of an Old Testament character who suffered at the hands of his contemporaries. He realized that God knew the thoughts and evil intentions of his persecutors (Jer. 11: 20). Similarly, when David was oppressed by an enemy, he put the case into the hands of a righteous God (Psa. 7: 9, 11). He realized that the same Lord who 'judges the peoples' was his judge too (Psa. 7: 8). Perhaps the most striking biblical reference to personal trust in God's righteous judgment is that of Christ Himself. He was reviled by sinful men, but 'when He suffered He did not threaten; but He trusted to Him who judges justly' (1 Pet. 2: 23).

iii. Future judgment

Although God acts in justice in the present, there is no doubt also that there will be a Day of Judgment at which His righteousness will be further manifested. This is a familiar New Testament theme in the Book of the Revelation. One of the angels is heard to say, 'Just art Thou in these Thy judgments' (Rev. 16: 5), and a voice came from the altar; 'Yea, Lord God the Almighty, true and just are Thy judgments' (Rev. 16: 7). The heavenly multitude also cry, 'Salvation and glory and power belong to our God, for His judgments are true and just' (Rev. 19: 1, 2). The apostle Paul rejoices in 'the Lord, the righteous Judge' who will award him 'the crown of righteousness' and that there will obviously be millions of others who will receive it (2 Tim. 4: 8).

3. GOD IS MERCIFUL

Throughout the centuries Christian people have acknowledged the undeserved goodness (Isa. 63: 7) of 'a gracious and merciful God' (Exod. 34: 6; 2 Chron. 30: 9; Neh. 9: 31) and have reminded one another that 'our God is merciful' (Psa. 116: 5; Deut. 4: 31). He is 'the Father of mercies' (2 Cor. 1: 3). David, for example, realizes that God's mercy is 'very great'. He would far rather fall into the merciful 'hand of the Lord' than 'the hand of man' (2 Sam. 24: 14; 1 Chron. 21: 13).

God does not manifest His mercy on the basis of merit. It is often shown to those who least deserve it. Ezra said of the idolatrous Israelites, 'Even when they had made for themselves a molten calf . . . and had committed great blasphemies, Thou in Thy great mercies didst not forsake them in the wilderness' (Neh. 9: 18, 19). When God's people cried to Him in trouble He answered them in mercy (Neh. 9: 27).

Sometimes the Lord withholds His mercies, but it is only that we might see our need of Him and so turn to Him in sincerity (Psa. 77: 9; Isa. 45: 7, 8, 54: 8, 60: 10, 63: 15; Jer. 16: 5). Even when His mercies are not evident, His mercy is still the same. In the experience of the Hebrew people these periods of chastisement were an essential part of their spiritual training. Without them, they were in danger of becoming careless and selfish. When the time of discipline is over, the God of mercy returned with His mercies (Zech. 1: 16; Psa. 103: 8, 9; Isa. 14: 1, 2). There are times when He waits to be merciful to us (Isa. 30: 18).

We can ask two important questions: *What* is God's mercy like and *why* is God merciful? The Bible describes the mercy of God as:

a. UNDESERVED

Men cannot demand it (Exod. 33: 19), and they cannot earn it. It is not given in return for good works. Daniel once prayed and said, 'We do not present our supplications before Thee on the ground of our righteousness, but on the ground of Thy great mercy' (Dan. 9: 18). We are not worthy of God's mercy; Jacob knew that (Gen. 32: 10). It comes to us not only when we least deserve it, but even when we seem to reject it. Bunyan wrote about a God who followed the wayward 'with pardon in His hand'. That was the experience of Lot. It was a merciful God who sent the delivering angels to Sodom, the doomed city. Yet it says of Lot 'but he lingered' so the angels seized him by the hand and led him away, 'the Lord being merciful to him' (Gen. 19: 16).

b. RELIABLE

Men can be merciful in one moment but ruthless in another. The false gods of the ancient world were seen as capricious and unsure. One day they might favour you, but in the next they could harass you. The Hebrews took delight in a God whose mercy was trustworthy and sure. He had promised to be merciful and would not change His mind (Psa. 119: 58, 132). God declared Himself on the issue; 'I am merciful, says the Lord' (Jer. 3: 12), and He does not change and vacillate as we do (Mal. 3: 6; Jas. 1: 17). The mountains may depart, but God's mercy will not (Isa. 54: 10). Even though there are times when He has to speak against us, yet God says to us as to Israel; 'I will surely have mercy' (Jer. 31: 20).

c. UNIVERSAL

The Lord Jesus described His Father as One who was kind to the ungrateful and the selfish (Lk. 6: 35). David confessed that 'the

Lord is good to all and His compassion is over all that He has made' (Psa. 145: 8, 9).

The New Testament abounds in references to 'the tender mercy of our God' (Lk. 1: 78). The Magnificat (Lk. 1: 46–55) and the Benedictus (Lk. 1: 68–79) are two of Luke's superb songs; both contain references to God's mercy. Paul reminds his readers that we have received mercy (2 Cor. 4: 1); that God is rich in mercy (Eph. 2: 4); that the mercy of God is often manifest in times of sickness (Phil. 2: 27); that it is by God's mercy that we are saved (Tit. 3: 5). The apostle rejoiced in this immense truth because for him it was something more than a theological issue. God met him in mercy and transformed the persecutor into a preacher. He 'received mercy' (1 Tim. 1: 13, 16).

We are also reminded in the New Testament epistles that the path of prayer is the way to mercy (Heb. 4: 16), and in our personal experience the new birth is the outcome of God's great mercy (1 Pet. 1: 3). The blessing of our corporate life in the Church is equally dependent on God's mercy (1 Pet. 2: 10). We 'glorify God for His mercy' (Rom. 15: 9) and have many an occasion when we rejoice that 'the Lord is compassionate and merciful' (Jas. 5: 11).

But when we have said all this about God's mercy we have hardly begun to understand it. We have seen *what* His mercy is like, but we now ask the question as to *why He is merciful*? For our answer we must look carefully at an important Hebrew word. It is a word packed with rich meaning which defies accurate translation by any single English noun. This term *chesed* and its cognates appears in the Old Testament about 200 times. In our English versions it is variously translated; 'mercy,' 'kindness,' 'loving kindness,' 'steadfast love' (R.S.V.). The word really indicates the kind of compassion one would expect from someone to whom you were bound in covenant or agreement.

It has sometimes been translated 'covenant-love'. It is a word which cannot be separated from the covenant idea. It means faithful-love or loyal-love. The covenant idea was a familiar one in the ancient near-east. Kings and countries, traders and merchants all made covenants or agreements with their neighbours and associates. An agreement was drawn up and promises were made. Both parties were obviously expected to be loyal to the covenant. Many covenants indicated the benefits which would accrue if the agreement was kept and the curses which would follow if the promises were broken. It is against this background that we must understand God's covenant with His people. Loyalty was expected, blessings were promised and warnings were given. Both parties were expected to have *chesed*. Both must be faithful and loyal to the covenant. The covenant-keeping God of the Hebrew people showed steadfast love (*chesed*) to those who loved Him and kept His commandments, i.e. the agreement (Exod. 20: 6, 34: 7; Deut. 5: 10). He is 'the faithful God who keeps covenant and steadfast love (*chesed*) with those who love Him' (Deut. 7: 9, 12). He will not fail in His part of the covenant, for His steadfast love (*chesed*) endures for ever (1 Chron. 16: 34, 41; 2 Chron. 5: 13, 7: 3; Psa. 106: 1, 107: 1).

But Israel certainly failed in their part of the agreement. They pledged their loyalty to God but then went after other gods. Their *chesed* did not endure; it was like morning dew which quickly disappeared once the sun came out (Hosea 6: 4). True, they went on with their sacrificing, but God did not want it unless it was a genuine expression of their love. When His people came out of Egypt He did not talk to them initially about sacrifices. Rather, He was concerned about their *obedience* (Jer. 7: 22–26). God wanted *chesed*, not sacrifice (Hosea 6: 6).

This theme of God's *chesed* forms a natural link with the next of God's 'attitudes' that we are to consider, viz. His faithfulness. The scores of references to *chesed* in the Old Testament all support the concept of God's faithfulness. He will not fail. His *chesed* 'meets' us to meet our need (Psa. 59: 10) and then follows us wherever we go (Psa. 23: 6). It surrounds us (Psa. 32: 10) and saves us (Psa. 109: 26); it satisfies us (Psa. 90: 14) and sustains us (Psa. 33: 18).

4. GOD IS FAITHFUL

Perhaps we may ask a further important question; how can we be sure that God will be true to His covenant-love? The answer rests in the fact that He has declared Himself to be a righteous God. His whole nature and name is at stake, and that divine nature is one of steadfastness and fidelity. It is in the setting of the covenant that He is described as 'the faithful God' (Deut. 7: 9).

The Psalmist often reminds us that God is faithful; His word to us is faithful and sure (Psa. 119: 86, 138). His chastisement of us is faithful (Psa. 119: 75). God's faithfulness is immense (Psa. 36: 5), lasting (Psa. 119: 90) and attentive (Psa. 143: 1). Psalm 89 is 'the Psalm of our Faithful God'. His faithfulness is firm (Psa. 89: 2), incomparable (Psa. 89: 8), active (Psa. 89: 23, 24), reliable (Psa. 89: 33). Such faithfulness is surely worth talking about (Psa. 40: 10, 89: 1, 5, 92: 1, 2).

God has a plan for our lives and this is a further indication of His faithfulness (Isa. 25: 1). It is a faithful God who calls us into fellowship with Christ (1 Cor. 1: 9). He sets us apart (sanctifies) for Himself and keeps us (1 Thess. 5: 23–24). He will not allow us to be tested beyond our breaking point (1 Cor. 10: 13); He will strengthen us and guard us (2 Thess. 3: 3). Yet he pardons us when we fail Him (1 Jn. 1: 9). In times of suffering and persecution we must only do what is right and commit ourselves to our 'faithful Creator' (1 Pet. 4: 19). Each new day reminds us of the faithfulness of God (Lam. 3: 23). He is faithful to us not only because it is His nature to be so, but also because He loves us so much; 'I will betroth you to me in faithfulness' (Hosea 2: 20). It is the faithful Lord who has chosen us (Isa. 49: 7).

5. GOD IS HOLY

Our holy God has been described as 'wholly Other'. When we come to consider God's holiness we are thinking about His transcendent glory. He is so utterly different from us. 'I am God and not man, the Holy One in your midst' (Hosea 11: 9). Hannah knew that 'there is none holy like the Lord' (1 Sam. 2: 2). We might briefly summarize the biblical teaching about God's holiness, His majestic separateness from us, in this way:

a. GOD DECLARES HIMSELF AS HOLY
'I am the Lord your God . . . I am holy' (Lev. 11: 44, 45, 19: 2, 20: 26, 21: 8).

b. THE TITLES OF GOD DESCRIBE HIM AS HOLY
His name is 'a holy name' (Lev. 20: 3, 22: 2, 32; 1 Chron. 16: 10, 35; Isa. 57: 15). The term is often found in the Psalms (e.g. 103: 1, 105: 3, 106: 47) and Ezekiel (e.g. 20: 39, 36: 20, 39: 7). It is a Hebraic way of saying that God is holy. He is constantly described in Isaiah as the Holy One of Israel (e.g. Isa. 1: 4, 5: 19, 24, 12: 6, 30: 11, 45: 11, 47: 4). Further, the title is used elsewhere in the Old Testament (e.g. 2 Kings 19: 22; Psa. 71: 22, 78: 41, 89: 18).

c. HIS SERVANTS ACKNOWLEDGE GOD TO BE HOLY
Joshua reminded the people that the God they professed to serve was 'a holy God' (Josh. 24: 19). In a moment of dark despair, David recalled the fact of God's holiness (Psa. 22: 1–5). The Psalmist calls upon men to extol God because 'Holy is He' (Psa. 99: 5).

d. GOD'S HOLINESS DEMANDS OUR HOLINESS IN RESPONSE
We are never allowed to study the biblical doctrine of God in theological and intellectual isolation. Scriptural truth demands a practical response. These are not merely truths to treasure in our minds. *They must be applied to our daily lives.* They will affect our behaviour. If God is love, we must be loving (1 Jn. 4: 11). If God is righteous, we too must do what is right (1 Jn. 2: 29; Psa. 11: 7). The good news of a merciful Father means that we not only believe it but act upon it by being merciful to others (Lk. 6: 36). If God cares, we must care (Deut. 10: 18, 19). Similarly, if God is holy, we must also be holy (Lev. 11: 45; 1 Pet. 1: 15, 16). In biblical thought the doctrine of God must be studied alongside the doctrine of the Christian Life.

IV. GOD'S DIVINE PERSONHOOD: THE TRINITY

The biblical doctrine of God is presented in a trinitarian context. Obviously, the concept of the Triune God cannot be fully comprehended by the human mind. Even though it is an immense challenge to our intellectual powers, few would dare to pretend to have grasped the doctrine in all its magnitude and splendour. But where we cannot fully understand, we are to adore and walk by faith. Thus it is better simply to accept the biblical data by faith, confessing that here we are in the realm of intellectual *mystery* as well as theological and spiritual *certainty*.

The doctrine of the Trinity is expressed in various *Old Testament* contexts. In some passages God speaks of Himself in the plural (Gen. 1: 26, 3: 22, 11: 7; Isa. 6: 8). Furthermore, the ordinary Hebrew word for God, *Elohim*, is plural in form. As Alan Richardson says, 'It represents a deep biblical insight: God is not, and never was, a lonely God. There is personality in God, and a person could not exist alone . . . a (as) 'unitarian' (Torch Bible Commentary *Genesis I-XI*, London 1953, p. 46).

There are also narratives which refer to the Holy Spirit and 'Wisdom' both of which suggest a plurality of activity within the one Godhead. Moreover, many of the passages in which these titles occur suggest aspects of 'personality'. Take for example, the Old Testament doctrine of the Holy Spirit. He comes from God and is known as 'the Spirit of the Lord' (Jdgs. 13: 25). He empowers men (Jdgs. 14: 6, 15: 14), directs (Psa. 143: 10) and teaches (Neh. 9: 20) them. He came down upon men (Jdgs. 14: 19; 1 Sam. 11: 6). There were times when He was grieved (Isa. 63: 10). It is clearly revealed that the Spirit of God will come upon God's Servant (Isa. 42: 1). So if we maintain that our Lord Jesus Christ was the Suffering Servant (Mt. 12: 17–21), then there is a clear Trinitarian reference in Isa. 42: 1. The title 'Wisdom' is also found in the Old Testament in a highly personalized setting as one capable of emotional reactions (Prov. 8: 1, 2) and an active participant in the work of Creation (Prov. 8: 22–31). This title and function were used by New Testament writers to describe the person and work of Christ (e.g. 1 Cor. 1: 24, 30; Col. 1: 15–17, 2: 2; Heb. 1: 1–3).

When we come to the *New Testament*, the concept of the Trinity is no longer in the theological background. In several important contexts the doctrine is made quite explicit. In the Gospel narratives, for example, it becomes necessary to consider the Lord God in trinitarian terms in order for the stories to have real meaning. The angel who visits Joseph brings a word from *God*. He is told that the virgin to whom he is engaged is to give birth to a child (later to be named *Emmanuel,* i.e. 'God with us') and this miracle is possible because that which is conceived in her is of the *Holy Spirit* (Mt. 1: 20–23). All three persons of the Trinity are mentioned in this brief passage.

The same thing can be observed in the words of the angel to Mary. She is told that she has found favour with *God* (Lk. 1: 30). The child is to be 'called the *Son* of the Most High; and the Lord God will give to Him the throne of his father David . . . of his kingdom there will be no end' (Lk. 1: 32–33). When puzzled as to how this can happen to a woman without a husband (Lk. 1: 34) she is clearly told that the *Holy Spirit* will come upon her (Lk. 1: 35). The child born of the Holy Spirit is to be called 'the Son of God' (Lk. 1: 35).

This trinitarian presupposition emerges yet again in the birth stories of the Gospels at the point where the devout man Simeon holds the child *Jesus* in his arms (Lk. 2: 28). It explicitly says that the *Holy Spirit* was upon him (Lk. 2: 25) and he blessed *God* (Lk. 2: 28). There is a further indication of the Triune God in the account of Christ's baptism in the river Jordan. The narrative says that 'when Jesus had been baptised and was praying, the heaven was opened, and the *Holy Spirit* descended upon him in bodily form as a dove, and a voice came from heaven, 'Thou art my *beloved Son;* with thee I am well pleased' (Lk. 3: 21, 22, cf. Mt. 3: 16, 17). A reference to Christ's ministry in Acts 10: 38 is clearly trinitarian.

Throughout the rest of the New Testament there are many trinitarian statements. It finds its most striking appearances in the Great Commission of Jesus (Mt. 28: 19) and the famous benediction used by the apostle Paul (2 Cor. 13: 14). But these are not isolated or solitary references; e.g. Acts 2: 33, 38, 39, 20: 28 ('the blood of his Own'), Rom. 14: 17, 18, 15: 16, 30; 1 Cor. 12: 4–6; 2 Cor. 1: 21, 22, 3: 3; Gal. 3: 11–14, 4: 6; Eph. 2: 18, 2: 20–22, 3: 14–16; Col. 1: 6–8; 2, Thess. 2, 13, 14; Tit. 3: 4–6; 1 Pet. 1: 2; Jude 20, 21; Rev. 1: 4, 5.

The trinitarian idea possibly reaches its climax in the teaching of John's Gospel about the person and work of the Holy Spirit. Jesus refers to Him as the Counsellor 'whom the Father will send in my name' (14: 26). The 'Spirit of Truth' proceeds from the Father and will bear witness of Christ (14: 26). Nothing could be more definite and explicit. Again, the Lord Jesus says the Spirit will assume a convicting ministry among men because Christ is going to His Father (16: 8–10). In the upper room the risen Christ said, 'As the Father has sent me, even so I send you. . . . Receive the Holy Spirit' (20: 21, 22).

More than one New Testament scholar has observed that even the form and outline of the New Testament epistles have been influenced by the doctrine of the Trinity. Arthur W. Wainwright (*The Trinity in the New Testament,* London 1962) observes that the first eight chapters of Romans are dominated by this important biblical idea, e.g. Introduction (1: 1–17), the judgment of *God* (1: 18–3: 20), Justification through faith in *Christ* (3: 21–8: 1), Life in the *Spirit* (8: 2–30); and it is interesting to observe that trinitarian references are found in the concluding section of Romans 8; the *Spirit* helps our weaknesses and intercedes for us (8: 26) and we rejoice in the fact that *God* predestined us to be conformed to the image of His *Son* (Rom. 8: 29).

The same kind of thing can be said of Paul's argument in 1 *Corinthians; Christ* is the power and wisdom of *God* (1: 18–2: 9), and our grasp of these Christian certainties is dependent on the work of the indwelling *Spirit* (2: 10–16, 3: 16, 17). *Galatians* is a further illustration of the trinitarian foundation of the New Testament doctrine of Salvation. Paul rejoices that his apostleship is not of merely human origin, but 'through Jesus Christ and God the Father' (Gal. 1: 1). God is the One who 'sent forth His Son' (Gal. 4: 4) and who 'raised Him from the dead' (Gal. 1: 1). He also sent the Spirit of His Son into our hearts (Gal. 4: 6). Believers walk by the Spirit (Gal. 5: 16, 25), they belong to Christ Jesus (Gal. 5: 24), knowing that by God's grace (Gal. 2: 21) they are part of the Church of God (Gal. 1: 13); they are Sons of God (Gal. 3: 26). Now let us examine each 'person' of the Triune Godhead.

1. GOD IS A FATHER

Most of us find comfort and security in the concept of God's divine Fatherhood. Earlier we surveyed the nature, characteristics and attitudes of God. It is important for us now to draw attention to the Bible's teaching about God as *Father*. It must be recognized at the very start that the concept of 'fatherhood' in biblical thought is dominated by authority and responsibility as well as providential care and compassion. It is possible to sentimentalize the idea of 'fatherhood', especially in the light of the contemporary disregard of parental authority. When we say we are thankful that God is our Father, we are not merely grateful for His undeserved love, but for His sovereign control as well. He is the Head of His people. The biblical narratives emphasize four aspects of God's Fatherhood:

a. THE FATHER'S PERSONALITY

Jesus refers to God in prayer as 'Father' (Mt. 11: 25; Lk. 11: 2, 22: 42, 23: 34, 46; Jn. 11: 41) and encourages His disciples to address God in this way (Mt. 6: 9; Lk. 11: 2). Jesus describes the Father as holy (Jn. 17: 11), righteous (Jn. 17: 25), loving (Jn. 16: 27), living (Jn. 6: 57), omnipotent (Mk. 14: 36), forgiving (Mt. 6: 14; Lk. 15: 21, 22, 23: 34), merciful (Lk. 6: 36), perfect (Mt. 5: 48), omniscient (Mt. 6: 4, 6, 8, 18) and generous (Mt. 5: 45, 7: 11; Lk. 11: 13).

In the teaching of Jesus, the Father reveals truth (Mt. 16: 17; Lk. 10: 21), answers prayer (Mt. 18: 19), exacts justice (Mt. 18: 35) and sustains life (Jn. 6: 32). It is the Father who determines the precise moment of His Son's return (Mt. 24: 36; Mk. 13: 32) and the ultimate destiny of this world (Acts 1: 7).

Jesus clearly said it was the Father who appointed the Kingdom for Him (Lk. 22: 29), who sent Him into the world (Jn. 6: 57, 8: 16, 20: 21), who gave believers to Him (Jn. 6: 65, 10: 29) and has the power to keep them (Jn. 17: 11). Christ spoke out of a unique and intimate relationship with His Father (Jn. 10: 30). He had seen (Jn. 6: 46), knew (Jn. 10: 15), loved (Jn. 14: 31) and honoured (Jn. 8: 49) the Father. He had been taught by Him (Jn 8: 28, 15: 15). He manifested and declared Him to others (Jn. 1: 18, 14: 6–11). The many 'signs' He performed before men were 'good works from the Father' (Jn. 10: 32, 37). God had set His seal on the person and work of His Son (Jn. 6: 27); the seal was the sign of authenticity and consecration (Jn. 10: 36).

b. THE FATHER'S AUTHORITY

In the eastern countries, in their early history, the father had complete and final jurisdiction over his children. There were serious penalties for acts of disrespect and rebellion against a father (Exod. 21: 15, 17; Lev. 20: 9; Deut. 21: 18–21). The Law of Moses insists that parents be honoured (Exod. 21: 12; Deut, 5: 16), and the Book of Proverbs constantly reiterates the responsibilities of children towards father and mother (Prov. 10: 1, 15: 20, 19: 26, 20: 20, 23: 22–25, 28: 24, 29: 3, 30: 11, 17). The idea that 'authority' is an ingredient of the father image when used in the Bible is confirmed by the fact that the term 'father' is frequently used to describe people in positions of special dignity and national or religious importance, e.g. priests (Jdgs. 17: 10, 18: 19), prophets (2 Kings 2: 12, 6: 21), kings (2 Kings 14:3, 18:3, 22:2), military commanders (2 Kings 5: 13) and state officials (Gen. 45: 8). This is particularly evident in Isa. 22: 15–25, where it is said of Eliakim 'I will . . . commit your authority to his hand; and he shall be a father to the inhabitants of Jerusalem' (Isa. 22: 21).

It is to be regretted that we do not always recall this emphasis on 'authority' when we come to expound God's Fatherhood. For before the idea of fatherhood tells us about God's provision, it insists on our *subservience* to Him. The Hebrew people were told to *submit* to His Fatherhood because He is the Father who created them (Deut. 32: 6, Isa. 64: 8; Mal. 2: 10), displayed the fatherly qualities of justice (Deut. 32: 4) and faithfulness (Deut. 32: 4) and demonstrated His unrivalled authority and power by giving the nations their inheritance and geographical boundaries (Deut. 32: 8). Jesus taught that the Father's will must be obeyed (Mt. 7: 21). When we approach Him in prayer as our Heavenly Father, we are to say 'Thy Will be done' (Mt. 6: 9, 10). Jesus is our perfect example in this, for He surrendered His own will; longing to be obedient to His Father (Mt. 26: 39, 42; Mk. 14: 36; Lk. 22: 42; Heb. 10: 7, 9). The Fatherhood of God is not only a sublime truth to ponder, it is a spiritual challenge to obey. To acknowledge God as Father is to say 'Yes' to His perfect will (Mt. 12: 50; Jn. 6: 38).

c. THE FATHER'S RESPONSIBILITY

In eastern thought, the father assumed all necessary responsibility for his children's shelter, clothes, food, moral and religious instruction. Similarly, God undertakes to provide for the entire needs of His children. His responsibility is sixfold.

i. To care

God declares Himself to be 'Father of the fatherless and protector of widows' (Psa. 68: 5, cf. Psa. 27: 10). In Jewish society the committed believer had a moral responsibility to care for those who had no human source of help and comfort (Exod. 22: 22; Deut. 10: 18, 14: 29, 16: 11, 14, 24: 17, 19–21, 26: 12, 13, 27: 19). The reason for this was because God Himself is deeply concerned about the needs of such people. Therefore, His worshippers should be like the God they professed to adore. The Lord Jesus continually emphasized this aspect of God's fatherly provision as He urged His followers not to be anxious for earthly necessities (Mt. 6: 26, 32; Lk. 12: 30).

ii. To love

A Hebrew father cared for his children because he loved them so passionately. Similarly, God the Father 'pities His children' (Psa. 103: 13). It is an expression of His steadfast love for them (Psa. 103: 11). This covenant-love is the basis of His unlimited forgiveness (Psa. 103: 3, 12), healing mercy (Psa. 103: 3) and ungrudging generosity (Psa. 103: 5, 10). He understands our human frailty (Psa. 103: 14) and knows how much we need His fatherly compassion. Jesus insisted that those who profess to serve their Heavenly Father must be equally compassionate (Mt. 5: 43–48); only in this way could they be 'sons of your Father who is in heaven' (Mt. 5: 45). He is merciful and they must be merciful too (Lk. 6: 36).

iii. To teach

The father of a Jewish family was the person responsible for the provision of his children's education. In the Hebrew wisdom literature children are urged to attend to the instruction given by their fathers (Prov. 1: 8, 4: 1, 6: 20, 13: 1). Some of this parental exhortation takes the form of clear and serious warnings about the sad

consequences of irresponsible behaviour (e.g. Prov. 1: 8–19). Similarly, the Lord God teaches and trains His children and imparts
true wisdom to those who look to Him for help (Prov. 2: 1–6;
Jas. 1: 5).

iv. To correct
Children do not always heed parental advice. There are occasions,
therefore, when it is necessary to enforce discipline (Prov. 13: 24,
19: 18, 22: 15, 23: 13, 14, 29: 15). Believers are exhorted to remember the corrective ministry of the Lord God in their lives (Prov.
3: 11). He reproves those He loves (Prov. 3: 12; Heb. 12: 5–11).
There are important illustrations of God's fatherly correction in
Isaiah 63–64. Isaiah 63: 10–19 recalls the rebellious attitude of
God's People. They grieved His Holy Spirit (Isa. 63: 10); and He,
in turn, makes them aware of His anger (Isa. 63: 15). But the
people insisted that God was their Father (Isa. 63: 16) and pleaded
with Him to end this period of admittedly deserved chastisement
and necessary discipline (Isa. 63: 17–64: 7). They repeated their
earlier affirmation that He is Father (Isa. 64: 8) and asked that,
having learned from their sins, they will not be afflicted any more
(Isa. 64: 8–12). God had to explain that He was ready to be sought
by those who, unhappily, did not trouble to ask for Him (Isa. 65: 1).
The word 'Father' might well be on their lips, but its truth had no
place in their hearts. Jeremiah gave eloquent expression to a similar
complaint (Jer. 3: 4, 5, 19, 20). They used the word 'Father' in
addressing God, but He was grieved that they did not mean it
(Jer. 3: 5).

v. To lead
The father does not correct his children from a distance. He sets
them an example and points out the right way for them in life.
Although Jeremiah knows of the people's rebellion, he rejoices that
God's stubborn people will return to the Lord. He will ·'lead them
back . . . in a straight path', because He is 'a father' to Israel
(Jer. 31: 9).

vi. To protect
The Jewish father was responsible for his children's safety, and the
Psalmist rejoices that God has promised to protect His people.
Psalm 89 is of importance here. The Davidic King is obviously in
mind (Psa. 89: 19), and he is told that 'the enemy shall not outwit
him, the wicked shall not humble him' (Psa. 89: 22). When surrounded by foes the King will rely on the steadfast love of God and
cry to Him 'Thou art my Father, my God, and the Rock of my
Salvation' (Psa. 89: 26). All these titles confirm a sense of security,
for God is in the closest relationship with the needy King. He is

known in the intimacy of personal experience (*my* Father, *my* God, *my* salvation), and He is reliable and strong ('The Rock'). In unbroken relationship with our Father God all believers are secure. Christ told an unsympathetic and partially hostile crowd (Jn. 10: 19–26, 31) that those who are in the Father's hand will never perish (Jn. 10: 27–29).

d. THE FATHER'S GENEROSITY

The impartial generosity of the Father finds rich expression in the teaching of Jesus. Even the ungrateful and the selfish (Lk. 6: 35) alike experience His goodness. The evil and the good, the just and the unjust alike are recipients of His bounty, and just as He gives impartially in this life, so He judges impartially in the next (1 Pet. 1: 17). It is in this sense that Paul describes God as 'the Father of all' (Eph. 4: 6, cf. 3: 14, 15). At the same time, the New Testament constantly emphasizes the generosity of the Father towards those who have put their trust in Him. The believer is uniquely aware of the Father's gifts in salvation. He enjoys blessings and benefits from the Father that the unbeliever can hardly imagine (Eph. 1: 3–14). The Christian knows that the Father has manifested His grace (Gal. 1: 3, 4; 1 Jn. 4: 14), displayed His mercy (1 Pet. 1: 3), imparted His comfort (2 Cor. 1: 3, 4), revealed His treasures (Eph. 1: 17–19) and bestowed His love (2 Thess. 2: 16; 1 Jn. 3: 1; Jude 1).

He is the unchanging (Jas. 1: 17) and omniscient (1 Pet. 1: 2) Father who assures our sonship (Rom. 8: 15; Gal. 4: 6), expects our holiness (1 Thess. 3: 13), encourages our fellowship (1 Jn. 1: 3) and deserves our thanks (Eph. 5: 20; Col. 1: 12, 3: 17).

2. GOD IS A SON

a. THE PERSON OF JESUS CHRIST

When John brought his gospel to a close, he observed that if everything about Christ was to be set down in writing 'the world itself could not contain the books that would be written' (Jn. 21: 25). The Old Testament anticipates His coming and the New Testament expounds it.

Any attempt to set forth the biblical doctrine of Christ in a few pages is bound to neglect some important aspects of His person and work. Still, the following guide-lines may encourage a deeper enquiry and serve as a foundation for further study.

i. The promised Christ

It is a mistake to imagine that we can give a satisfactory exposition of the immense theme of Christology by confining ourselves to the New Testament. One must go further back. The story of Christ begins long before 'Bethlehem'. Old Testament prophets are said to have seen His glory (Jn. 12: 41). We begin, therefore, with a brief survey of the Old Testament doctrine of Christ.

i) His coming was anticipated

There was no shortage of outstanding national leaders in Old Testament times. And despite the failings of many, there are vivid accounts of dedicated and gifted kings, priests and prophets. Still, the Hebrew people recognized that this kind of leadership was transitory, uncertain and inadequate. They looked forward to the coming of God's chosen ones, the 'Messiah', the anointed leader of God's people.

The expectation of the Messiah took various forms. At different points in Hebrew history, the people anticipated the coming of One who would teach them as a prophet (Deut. 18: 15–18), lead them as a shepherd (Isa. 40: 11), rule them as a king (Zech. 9: 9), represent them as a priest (Psa. 110: 4), atone for them as a sacrificial lamb and suffering servant (Isa. 52: 13–53: 12). During His ministry Jesus Himself mentioned three outstanding biblical personalities (Abraham, Moses and David) who faced the future with this keen sense of anticipation that God's appointed Deliverer would come: 'Abraham rejoiced that he was to see my day' (Jn. 8: 56); 'Moses . . . wrote of me' (Jn. 5: 46) and 'David thus calls Him Lord' (Mt. 22: 45).

ii) His life was predicted

The predictions of the coming Messiah were not presented in a vague sense, i.e. Old Testament believers with appropriate insights peering into an obscure future as they described some kind of coming Deliverer. It is far more precise than that. There was an astonishing amount of detail in the way that the Old Testament writers predicted the life of the promised Christ. Micah foretold where He would be born (Micah 5: 2); Isaiah described the nature of His ministry (Isa. 61: 1–3); and in the famous 'servant songs' vivid descriptive detail is given of His persistent gentleness (Isa. 42: 1–4, cf. Mt. 12: 18–21), His universal appeal (Isa. 49: 1–6), His submissive attitude (Isa. 50: 4–7) and willingness to go to the extreme limits in suffering love.

The manner of His rejection by men is vividly portrayed and the purpose of His sacrificial death is carefully expounded (Isa. 52: 13–53: 12). This prophet and other Old Testament writers discern further detail about His suffering, e.g. the silence before His arrogant accusers (Isa. 53: 7), the betrayal by a disloyal friend (Psa. 41: 9), that He was suddenly forsaken by those nearest to Him (Zech. 13: 7). Even the form of His death was not missed, e.g. the piercing of hands and feet (Psa. 22: 16) as well as other supplementary details such as the mockery of the crowd (Psa. 22: 6–8), the soldiers' action in casting lots for His garment (Psa. 22: 18) and giving Him vinegar as He hung on the Cross (Psa. 69: 21).

Of course, the Old Testament prophecies do not finish at the Cross. They look on to the vindication of Christ's Sonship and the completion of His saving activity as they anticipate the Resurrection (Psa. 16: 8–11; Isa. 53: 10–12) and the Ascension (Psa. 110: 1). The apostles and evangelists of the early Church were quick to discern the importance of these Old Testament predictions and made effective use of them in their preaching (e.g. Acts 2: 24–36, 3: 21–26, 4: 10–12, 13: 32–41).

iii) His sacrifice was portrayed

In addition to predictions, there are also Old Testament passages which assume a far deeper significance as they are seen in the light of Christ's sacrifice. Jesus Himself obviously viewed His death as the fulfilment of such prophecy. During the Emmaus Road conversation He told His companions that it was 'necessary that the Christ should suffer these things and enter into His glory' (Lk. 24: 26, 27). He proved this by reference to the Old Testament. It is likely that His exposition at this point made reference to well-known Old Testament ceremonies, sacrifices, personalities, promises and events in which His victorious death had been pre-figured and anticipated. These would include the *Passover Lamb* (Exod. 12: 1–20, cf. Jn. 19: 36; 1 Cor. 5: 6–8; 1 Pet. 1: 18, 19), the *Levitical Scapegoat* (Lev. 16: 1–22, with hints in Jn. 1: 29 [bearing away sin], Heb. 13: 12–13; 1 Pet. 2: 24 R.S.V. margin 'carried up our sins in His body') and the *Suffering Servant* (Isa. 50: 4–7, 52: 13–53: 12, cf. Acts 8: 27–35; 1 Pet. 2: 21–25).

To note just these few aspects of such an immense theme is to oversimplify. Bible students have found helpful allusions to Christ's sacrificial work in many other Old Testament passages as well, such as those which describe the Levitical offerings and ceremonial and cultic detail. But these passages pointed out at least introduce this vital theme.

iv) His activity was described

It is important further to note that there are narratives in the Old Testament which clearly suggest that in some 'theophanies' (as the divine appearances are described) we have an account of the activity of the pre-existent Christ. Some have regarded 'the Commander of the Lord's army' who met Joshua by Jericho (Josh. 5: 13–15), or the 'fourth man' who appeared in the flames as the three Hebrew loyalists were cast into the furnace (Dan. 3: 24, 25) as manifestations of the Lord Himself.

In writing to the Corinthians, the apostle Paul refers to a well-known rabbinic tradition about 'the rock' in the wilderness and relates this story to the pre-existent Rock, Jesus Christ (1 Cor. 10: 4). Obviously, there is little room for rigid dogmatism as to the precise identity of these supernatural appearances, but many would find them descriptive of one aspect of Christ's pre-existent activity. It is significant that these manifestations are only given to men in moments of extreme trial and serious adversity.

We have obviously not exhausted the Old Testament teaching on this superb theme, but it is necessary to turn now to the New Testament writings in order to outline their important teaching about Jesus Christ.

ii. The unique Christ

The biblical writers hold together in perfect balance the two immense theological claims that the Lord Jesus Christ is truly God and truly man. He is not merely a devout man honoured by God, nor is He some remote divine or angelic being utterly out of touch with human problems. He is unique in His deity as the Only-begotten Son of God and at the same time complete in His humanity. But, unlike ourselves, He lived in perfect obedience to His Father's will; unstained by sin, selfishness or rebellion (Heb. 10: 7, 9). The New Testament asserts the uniqueness of Christ as it expounds:

i) His equality with God

Jesus said, 'I and the Father are one' (Jn. 10: 30). Some of these truths were outlined in considering the biblical doctrine of the Trinity. At this point it is only necessary to draw attention to two other important ways in which Christ's Deity is expressed in New Testament teaching: viz. His pre-existence and His pre-eminence.

1) *His pre-existence.* Jesus referred to His unique relationship with God in the pre-temporal terms: 'Before Abraham was, I am' (Jn. 8: 58)—a truth which irritated many of His contemporaries. He spoke naturally of God as His 'Father' (Jn. 2: 16, 5: 43, 6: 40, 10: 29, 14: 23). He talked about the glory He had with the Father; it preceded the work of Creation (Jn. 17: 5). He described the love He enjoyed in intimate communion with His Father 'before the foundation of the world' (Jn. 17: 24).

The fourth Gospel opens with a series of important Christological statements which include the assertion that the 'Word' was 'in the beginning' (Jn. 1: 1). He had always been 'with God' (Jn. 1: 1; 1 Jn. 1: 2). In another context Paul describes Him as One who was 'before all things' (Col. 1: 17). We have already referred to Old Testament theophanies, but our evidence for Christ's pre-existence does not rely solely on these narratives.

These may support our claim, but we construct our doctrine of
Christ's pre-existence primarily on the words of Jesus Himself
(Jn. 8: 58, 17: 5, 24).

The New Testament writers often referred to His pre-existence
in the context of Creation. Christ shared in the creation of the
world (Jn. 1: 3; Col. 1: 16; Heb. 1: 2). It was made for Him
(Col. 1: 16) and is sustained by Him (Col. 1: 17; Heb. 1: 3).

2) *His pre-eminence.* Jesus is clearly described as sharing in the
Trinity (Jn. 1: 1). John's Gospel begins and ends with impressive
expositions of the uniqueness and essential deity of Christ (1: 1,
14, 18, 20: 28–31). And these recur throughout the Gospel in a
number of different contexts. Christ was deeply aware of this
unique relationship with His Father. It was for this reason that the
Jews hated Him and determined to kill Him: 'because He . . .
called God His Father making Himself equal with God' (Jn.
5: 18). The vivid account of Christ's compassionate humility as
He washed the disciples' feet opens with a reference (Jn. 13: 3) to
our Lord's knowledge of His *authority* ('knowing that the Father
had given all things into His hands'), His *origin* ('and that He
had come from God') and His *destiny* ('and was going to God'). He
knew Himself to be the chosen and appointed Messiah (Jn. 4: 25,
26), the Son of God consecrated by the Father and sent into the
world (Jn. 10: 36).

It was not only that Christ referred to Himself by these titles of
deity, God addressed Jesus as His 'Son' (Mt. 3: 17, 17: 5; Mk.
1: 11; Lk. 3: 22, 9: 35; Heb. 1: 5). When He came into this
desperately needy world He was called 'Emmanuel' which means
'God with us' (Mt. 1: 23). Throughout His life Christ was aware
that God was not only with Him (Jn. 16: 32) but in Him (Jn.
17: 21). In New Testament teaching, personally to confess the
deity of Christ is to enter into an eternal relationship with the
Father and, conversely, to deny that Christ is the unique Son of
God is to cut ourselves off from the Father (1 Jn. 2: 22, 23, 4: 15,
5: 1). Christ is God's Son 'manifested in the flesh' (1 Tim. 3: 16).

But the marvellous story of Christ's redemptive work is an
account of willing renunciation. Equal with the other persons of
the Godhead, He shared the Father's love for the world and so,
eager to transform sinful, rebellious man, 'He . . . came to live
amongst us at great sacrifice, subjecting Himself to rejection by
men and death on a Cross. God became man, the sovereign became a servant and the Giver of our life was robbed of His own.
The Son who was honoured by the Father was humiliated before
men, but the rejected Christ has become the Exalted Lord.
Those who bowed the knee to Him in scornful mockery will one

day prostrate themselves before Him in submission as the entire universe acknowledges His Lordship' (Phil. 2: 5–11, Paraphrase).

ii) His revelation of God

Many Old Testament prophets and leaders endeavoured faithfully to explain all they knew of the God who addressed them. The revelation was inevitably of a fragmentary nature, however (Heb. 1: 1). Christ came to reveal God to man in a unique and complete way. Paul viewed the Lord Jesus as 'the image of the invisible God' (Col. 1: 15). Christ is described at the beginning of another epistle as One who 'reflects the glory of God and bears the very stamp of His nature' (Heb. 1: 3). All the fullness of the Godhead dwells in Him (Col. 1: 19, 2: 9). Looking at Him we see the Father's glory (Jn. 1: 14) in a way it cannot be seen elsewhere. He is the likeness of God (2 Cor. 4: 4). To see Him is to see the Father (Jn. 12: 45, 14: 8–11), to honour Him is to honour the Father (Jn. 5: 23), to hate Him is to hate the Father (Jn. 15: 23), to know Him is to know the Father (Jn. 8: 19), to trust Him is to trust the Father (Jn. 12: 44, 14: 1) and to receive Him is to receive the Father (Lk. 9: 48; Jn. 13: 20). He reveals God's nature (Jn. 1: 18), speaks God's word (Jn. 3: 33, 34, 17: 8, 14) and manifests God's glory (2 Cor. 4: 6; Heb. 1: 3).

But men on their first encounter with Christ did not always understand this unique revelation. It often took time for the truth to dawn. Two magnificent stories in John's Gospel illustrate this. Look at the narrative in John 4 which relates Christ's encounter with the woman at the well. A gifted early Christian commentator, Ephraem the Syrian, expounded the passage in this way:

> .... first she caught sight of a thirsty man, then a Jew, then a Rabbi, afterwards a prophet, last of all the Messiah. She tried to get the better of the thirsty man, she showed her dislike of the Jew, she heckled the Rabbi, she was swept off her feet by the prophet, and she adored the Christ.

John 9 gives a vivid account of the healing of the blind man. Initially he refers to Christ as 'the man called Jesus' (9: 11), then as 'a prophet' (9: 17), later as 'a man . . . from God' (9: 33) and finally as 'Lord' (9: 38).

The small group of disciples knew that He came from God (Jn. 17: 8, 25), but the majority who met Him were slow to discern who Christ was (Jn. 16: 9). They still are! But God bore witness to His Son (1 Jn. 5: 9), and the Holy Spirit continues to testify to Him (Jn. 15: 26). God not only publicly announced Christ as His Son (Mk. 1: 11) but constantly attested this truth by miraculous signs and compassionate miracles (Jn. 5: 36, 10: 37; Acts 2: 22). One of the remarkable things about the gospel narratives is that, although many people did not recognize Him as God's Son, the demons always did so (Lk. 4: 41). In their unsought and inevitably disturbing encounters with Christ they openly declared Him to be 'the Son of God' (Mk. 3: 11), 'the Holy One of God' (Lk. 4: 34) and 'Son of the Most High God' (Mk. 5: 7).

iii) His work for God

Other men have viewed their life's work with a deep sense of vocation. Yet Christ's sense of mission was unique. He made the unequivocal claim that He had been sent into the world with a distinct and 'once for all' redemptive mission.

As far as the Godhead is concerned, Jesus came forth from God the Father (Jn. 3: 31, 6: 46, 16: 28). God gave Him to us because He loved us so much (Jn. 3: 16). He came to do God's will (Jn. 4: 34; Heb. 10: 7–9), to show God's truthfulness (Rom. 15: 8) and to display God's mercy (Rom. 15: 9).

As far as man is concerned, Christ came to call sinners to repentance (Mt. 9: 12, 13), to serve (Mt. 20: 28), to give men life (Jn. 10: 10; 1 Jn. 4: 9) and to bring blessing into our needy lives by turning us from our iniquities (Acts 3: 26). He came to condemn sin (Rom. 8: 3), to make expiation for our transgressions (1 Jn. 4: 10) and save sinners (1 Tim. 1: 15; 1 Jn. 4: 14). He came to preach peace (Eph. 2: 17), to bear witness to the truth (Jn. 18: 37) and impart it to men (1 Jn. 5: 20), to bring light into a dark world (Jn. 12: 46) and to abolish death (2 Tim. 1: 10) by bringing men hope of eternal life (Jn. 3: 16).

As far as the Devil is concerned, Christ came to judge him (Jn. 16: 11), cast him out (Jn. 12: 31), destroy his works (1 Jn. 3: 8) and ultimately destroy him (Heb. 2: 14, 15).

It is only through Christ that man can have access to God (Jn. 14: 6; Rom. 5: 2), find peace (Rom. 5: 1) and achieve reconciliation with God (2 Cor. 5: 18). The New Testament offers no other way of salvation (Acts 4: 12). These are astonishing statements. Moreover, they are not philosophically debated in the New Testament; they are simply authoritatively declared.

iv) His authority from God

Jesus is clearly described as One who is 'from God' (Jn. 6: 46). He had a clear purpose in life. Unlike unredeemed man, He knew both where He came from and where He was going. Without Christ we know neither our own origin and destiny nor His. He knew these things (Jn. 8: 14). Uniquely aware that God had sent Him (Jn. 13: 20, 16: 27), He made no secret of His unique status. The Father had given Him such authority. And this power was operative in the entire universe (Mt. 28: 18).

All things had been committed into Christ's hands (Jn. 3: 35). The early Christian preachers loved to refer to him as 'Lord of all' (Acts 10: 36). He was 'heir of all things' (Heb. 1: 2); infinitely superior to the angels who incessantly worship Him (Heb. 1: 4, 6). Yet during His earthly ministry He openly acknowledged that His authority was derived from God the Father (Jn. 5: 30). It was not a self-exalting kind of authority, but of a kind that made men deeply aware of the sovereignty of God. This leads us naturally to Christ's dependence on God.

v) His reliance on God

One of the most arresting aspects of the doctrine of Christ in John's Gospel is that, side by side with the uninhibited claims which Christ made for Himself as the Son of God, He also spoke frequently of His utter reliance on the Father. He said He had received the Father's life (Jn. 5: 26), the Father's authority (Jn. 5: 27) and the Father's glory (Jn. 17: 22, 24). He distinctly stated that He did nothing on His own authority (Jn. 4: 34, 5: 19, 30). He did not come into the world simply of His own accord, but because He was sent by God (Jn. 5: 38, 8: 42, 17: 3, 18). He only spoke as the Father had taught Him (Jn. 8: 28, 12: 49, 50, 14: 10, 24). He did not seek to glorify Himself (Jn. 8: 50) but constantly reflected the glory of the Father (Jn. 8: 54). When He performed miracles, they were not for self-exaltation. Rather, they bore witness to the Father (Jn. 10: 25). He even regarded His followers as those who had been given to Him by the Father (Jn. 10: 27–29, 17: 6). He never saw them as enlisted by His own persuasive appeal.

vi) His submission to God

The entire life of Jesus is viewed as one of total surrender to the Father's will (Jn. 5: 30). When writing about the Incarnation, the author of Hebrews states that on coming into the world the Lord Jesus said, 'I have come to do Thy will, O God' (Heb. 10: 5–9). During the temptations in the wilderness Christ testified that man's greatest happiness and satisfaction was to be found in complete obedience to God's word (Mt. 4: 4). During the course of His earthly ministry Jesus assured His disciples that His obedience to the Father was the dominating concern of His life. His great longing was to fulfil God's purposes. He longed to complete His ministry on earth (Jn. 4: 34, 17: 4) and keep His Father's commandments (Jn. 15: 10). He had no ambition to please Himself (Rom. 15: 3). When He came to the hours of trial and death, He prayed earnestly to the Father for help, but nevertheless repeated His conviction that God's will must be courageously pursued (Lk. 22: 41, 42).

Loving submission is constantly characteristic of our Lord's relationship with the Father. Although He enjoys complete equality with God, He insists on perfect obedience to God (Heb. 5: 8, 9), and this submissive attitude continues to the triumphant end (1 Cor. 15: 24–28).

iii. The incarnate Christ

In considering Christ's person we turn now to some further details about His life among men.

i) His birth

The birth narratives in the Gospels of Matthew and Luke make specific reference to Christ's virgin birth. This fact is declared to Joseph (Mt. 1: 18–25) and to Mary, the virgin to whom he was betrothed (Lk. 1: 26–38).

Both are told that this unique birth is due to the direct intervention and miraculous activity of the Holy Spirit (Mt. 1: 18, 20; Lk. 1: 35). In compiling his account of Christ's birth, Matthew referred to a relevant prophecy made by Isaiah centuries before (Mt. 1: 22, 23; Isa. 7: 14).

It must be noted that some early manuscripts give a singular rather than a plural reading to the text of John 1: 13, 'who owe their birth neither to human blood, nor to physical urge, nor to human design, but to God'. Two outstanding early Christian writers (Tertullian and Augustine) both read the text as singular, therefore as a reference to Christ rather than to believers i.e. '*He* was born not of blood, nor of the will of the flesh, nor of the will of man but of God'. In his famous *Confessions*, Augustine quotes the text in this way as a clear reference to Christ's virgin birth.

There are those who question the doctrine of Christ's virgin birth because it does not appear in the New Testament outside the gospels. But we must remember that there are numerous themes which are expounded by Christ and not by Paul. By the same token, there are other subjects which are highly important to Paul and yet are unmentioned in the gospels. We do not thereby doubt their authenticity. It is not always proper interpretation to assess the importance of a doctrine by the number of times it appears in Scripture. The fact that it is there at all demands our reverent attention.

ii) His titles

We have already noted that Christ claimed to be God's Son (Jn. 10: 36, 19: 7). By His parents He was named 'Jesus' which is a translation of a Hebrew name (Joshua) meaning 'God's salvation' (Mt. 1: 21). He was also called Rabbi (Mk. 9: 5, 11: 21), 'Teacher' (Mk. 4: 38, 9: 17), 'Master' (Lk. 5: 5, 8: 24, 9: 33), the 'Prophet' (Mt. 21: 11; Lk. 7: 16, 39), 'Christ' (Mk 8: 29, 14: 61) and 'Son of David' (Mk. 10: 47, 48).

In describing His own person and work, Jesus made use of other highly important titles: 'Son of Man' (Mk. 2: 10), the 'Bread of Life' (Jn. 6: 35, 41, 48, 51), the 'Light of the World' (Jn. 8: 1, 9: 5, 12: 46), the 'Door of the Sheep' (Jn. 10: 7, 9), the 'Bridegroom' (Mk. 2: 19, 20; Jn. 3: 29), the 'Good Shepherd' (Jn. 10: 11, 14), the 'Resurrection and the Life' (Jn. 11: 25), the 'Way, the Truth and the Life (Jn. 14: 6), 'the true Vine' (Jn. 15: 1), 'Alpha and Omega' (Rev. 22: 13), 'Lord' (Lk. 20: 41–44, cf. Psa. 110: 1).

His followers called Him the 'Son of God' (Jn. 1: 49), the 'King of Israel' (Jn. 1: 49, 12: 13). John the Baptist called Him the 'Lamb of God' (Jn. 1: 29, 36). The early Christian preachers added to these arresting and meaningful titles by referring to Christ as God's 'Servant' (Acts 3: 13), the 'Holy and Righteous One' (Acts 3: 14), the 'Author of Life' (Acts 3: 15), the 'Stone' (Acts 4: 11), the 'Prophet' (Acts 3: 22), the 'Just One' (Acts (22: 14), 'Lord of All' (Acts 10: 36), 'the Judge' (Acts 10: 42).

The writers of the New Testament continue to reflect on the nature and achievements of Jesus and describe Him as the 'Head of the Body' (Col. 1: 18), 'Advocate' (1 Jn. 2: 1), 'Mediator' (1 Tim. 2: 5; Heb. 9: 15, 12: 24), 'High Priest' (Heb. 2: 17, 3: 1, 4: 14, 5: 5 and elsewhere in Hebrews), the 'Image of God' (2 Cor. 4: 4; Col. 1: 15), the 'Power and the Wisdom of God' (1 Cor. 1: 24), the 'Last Adam' and the 'Second Man' (Rom. 5: 12–21; 1 Cor. 15: 22, 45–49), the 'Beloved' (Eph. 1: 6), the 'Word' (Jn. 1: 1), the 'Apostle' (Heb. 3: 1) and the 'Amen' (Rev. 3: 14).

Dr Vincent Taylor has observed that these names and titles of Jesus provide us with illuminating insights into the Christo-centric thought of the early Christian people. He has pointed out, 'they are the signs and seals of the earliest Christology, and by their subsequent use throughout the centuries the Church has endorsed their permanent validity. A striking confirmation of this claim is the fact that the Church has never been able to add other names in any significant degree.' The one exception is the name 'the Redeemer', a title of Christ not found in the New Testament although His redemptive activity is often described. Dr Taylor reminds us that the 'classic names are those of the New Testament. . . . and they are the only names with a foreseeable future. This fact is one of the neglected arguments for the plenary inspira-tion of Holy Scripture, and a vindication of the claim that the examination of the names and titles is a necessary prelude to the study of the Person of Christ' (*The Names of Jesus*, London 1953, 173ff).

iii) His life

Obviously, the precise details of Christ's life can best be grasped by careful study of the four Gospels, even though none of the writers presumes to present an exhaustive account of the Lord's ministry. At the beginning of his Gospel, Luke tells us that others had compiled similar narratives to his own (Lk. 1: 1–4). John, as he draws his Gospel to a close, confesses that he has had to be very selective in his use of material. Christ did many things which John was not able to record. He had simply chosen a number of significant miracles and sayings in order to convince his readers of Christ's deity and so enable them to receive eternal life (Jn 20: 30, 31, 21: 25).

Jesus was born in Bethlehem (Mt. 2: 1–12) but was quickly taken to Egypt because of Herod's threat to kill Him (Mt. 2: 13–18). Joseph and Mary later came back to Israel and settled at Nazareth where Joseph worked as a carpenter (Mt. 2: 19–23, 13: 55). We know little of Jesus' childhood. Luke says most about it, but even so the details of this period are confined to two brief comments about Christ's development. We are told about His increase in physical strength, intellectual wisdom and spiritual stature (Lk. 2: 40), and also that the favour of God was upon Him (Lk. 2: 40, 52), as well as the commendation of man (Lk. 2: 52). The only detailed reference to Christ's youth is an account of His visit to Jerusalem as a boy of twelve (Lk. 2: 41–51). By this time He had an astonishing grasp of the Jewish law (Lk. 2: 46, 47) and was aware of a unique relationship with the Eternal Father (Lk. 2: 49).

We know nothing of the next eighteen years. Then at the age of thirty Jesus commenced His public ministry. It was initiated by two highly important events; His baptism, when the Father openly declared Christ's Sonship (Mt. 3: 13–17; Lk. 3: 21, 22) and His temptations when the Devil persistently cast doubt on it (Mt. 4: 1–11). Jesus began His work as a wandering teacher in His home area of Galilee (Lk. 4: 14, 15). When He came to Nazareth, He spoke openly of His unique mission (Lk. 4: 16–27), a fact which so angered His listeners that they tried to kill Him (Lk. 4: 29, 30). After this event His life was in constant danger, for His opponents were intent on His destruction (Mk. 3: 6). Despite this opposition Christ continued His ministry undisturbed, deeply aware that His ultimate death would be by God's design rather than man's intrigue.

Over the next two or three years Jesus' time was spent largely in teaching and healing. He made several journeys throughout

Israelite territory and, in order to train a group of men who would continue His work, He called twelve 'disciples' to share His company and ministry (Mk. 3: 13–19). At times the disciples were ungracious, harsh and cruel (Lk. 9: 51–56), afraid (Mk. 9: 6), ineffective (Mk. 9: 18, 28, 29), embarrassed (Mk. 9: 33, 34), exclusive (Lk. 9: 49, 50), impetuous (Mk. 14: 29–31), thoughtless (Mk. 10: 13), proud (Mk. 10: 35–37; Lk. 9: 46–48) and indignant (Mk. 10: 41). Yet for all this Christ loved them (Jn. 13: 1) and valued them as His close companions (Lk. 22: 28), affectionately referring to them as His 'children' (Jn. 21: 5). These privileged men witnessed His miracles (Mk. 5: 40–42), heard His teaching (Mt. 5: 1), confessed His Sonship (Mt. 14: 33) and received His commission (Mk. 3: 13–15).

Throughout His ministry, Christ grasped every opportunity to teach. He preached in synagogues (Mk. 1: 39, 6: 2) both in the north (Lk. 14: 15) and south (Lk. 4: 44) of His country, in the open air by lakesides (Mk. 2: 13), from boats (Lk. 5: 1–3) and on the slopes of the mountains (Mt. 5: 1). Compelled to preach, it was with a deep sense of urgency (Mk. 1: 38; Lk. 4: 43) He travelled throughout Israel's villages (Mk. 6: 6) and visited the larger cities also (Mk. 10: 46). He was not concerned about numbers. At times He taught in the Jerusalem Temple (Mk. 14: 49) and at others in small houses (Mk. 2: 1, 2; Lk. 10: 38, 39). We shall consider the form and content of His teaching later.

The first miracle He performed was at Cana of Galilee, not many miles from His home town of Nazareth. At Cana He turned water into wine (Jn. 2: 1–11). With some exceptions most of His miracles were not spectacular demonstrations of power over nature but acts of compassionate mercy on those who were in physical, mental and spiritual distress. He healed lepers (Mt. 8: 1–4; Mk. 1: 40–45; Lk. 17: 11–19), paralytics (Mt. 8: 5–13; Lk. 6: 6–10), the blind (Mt. 9: 27–31; Mk. 10: 46–52), dumb (Mt. 9: 32, 33), deaf (Mk. 7: 31–37), epileptics (Mt. 17: 14–18) and those physically maimed (Mt. 15: 30). People harassed by fevers (Mt. 8: 14–17) and tormented by demons (Mt. 8: 28–34) were wonderfully transformed. The dying were restored (Lk. 7: 1–10) and even the dead were raised to life (Mt. 9: 18, 19, 23–26; Lk. 7: 11–15, 8: 40–42, 49–55; Jn. 11: 1–44). And these miracles are to mention but a few.

Throughout this entire period of ministry, Christ was without a home (Lk. 9: 58). But His friends (Lk. 4: 38, 39, 5: 29, 9: 4–6, 10: 38; Jn. 12: 1, 2) and others (Lk. 7: 36, 11: 37, 38, 14: 1) received Him into their homes. Some generous women supported Him financially (Lk. 8: 2, 3). Money donated to the group was given to the care of a treasurer who made necessary purchases

(Jn. 13: 29). This man, Judas, proved to be totally disloyal and unworthy. He not only stole money (Jn. 12: 4–6), but he betrayed Christ in order to get more (Mt. 26: 14, 15). All through His ministry the Lord Jesus spent time with God in disciplined prayer (Mt. 14: 23; Mk. 1: 35; Lk. 6: 12), with His disciples in the work of teaching and training (Mt. 5: 1–7: 29, 10: 1–11: 1, 13: 36, 18: 1, 20: 17, 24: 3, 26: 1) and with the people in compassionate service (Mt. 15: 29–39, 19: 1, 2).

At a particular time of crisis in His life, Christ took three of the disciples up a mountain side where He was transfigured before them (Mt. 17: 1–8). When Luke recorded the details of this event he said that the two men who talked with our Lord (Moses and Elijah) 'spoke of His departure (Greek = exodus) which He was to accomplish at Jerusalem' (Lk. 9: 31). Here, as elsewhere, the Cross was uppermost in Christ's thinking. He paid several visits to Jerusalem. He approached one such occasion with a particularly heavy heart knowing it to be His last (Lk. 19: 41). He grieved over the city knowing how many times its occupants had slain God's messengers (Mt. 23: 34–37), ignored God's warnings (Lk. 19: 41–44) and abused God's house (Lk. 19: 45, 46). His disloyal companion, Judas, betrayed the Lord for money (Mk. 14: 10, 11).

Jesus arranged to have a final Passover meal with the disciples when, on breaking the bread, He told them of His now imminent death. As He poured out the wine it became a symbolic action vividly portraying the shedding of His blood for them and for many (Mk. 14: 12–25). Under no illusion about their well-meant but unreliable protestations of loyalty, He told them that they would forsake Him (Mk. 14: 26–31). They were alert enough to make empty promises, but too tired to stay awake with Him in Gethsemane as He prayed (Mk. 14: 32–42). Once arrested at the instigation of the betrayer, Christ's warning words about their disloyalty were proved true (Mk. 14: 43–50).

He was brought before the high priest, scribes and elders (Mk. 14: 53), before Pilate (Mk. 15: 1), Herod (Lk. 23: 5–11) and then taken back to Pilate (Lk. 23: 12, 13). Eager not to condemn Christ to death, Pilate did his utmost to persuade the crowd to release Him by making use of a long-standing tradition regarding the pardon of a criminal at festival time. But they asked instead for a notorious and dangerous offender named Barabbas, and Jesus was sentenced to death (Mt. 27: 15–26). He was mocked by the Roman soldiers (Mt. 27: 27–31) and led out to be crucified (Mt. 27: 32–44).

Two criminals were crucified with our Lord (Mt. 27: 38); one of whom trusted in Christ as he hung beside Him on the Cross

(Lk. 23: 39–43). When He was about to breathe His last
(Lk. 23: 46), Christ cried out, 'It is finished' (Jn. 19: 30). At that
moment the huge Temple veil was torn from top to bottom
(Mk. 15: 37, 38). Extraordinary scenes followed this event
(Mt. 27: 51–54).

Jesus was then buried by a small group of friends (Mk. 15: 42–
47). But on the first day of the next week (Mk. 16: 2) He was
raised from the dead and appeared to His disciples and to others
(Mt. 28; Mk. 16; Lk. 24; Jn. 20, 21). After spending some time
with His followers instructing them and urging them to spend
time in expectant prayer (Lk. 24: 49), He ascended to His
Father (Lk. 24: 50, 51; Acts 1: 9–11), His earthly work accomplished (Jn. 17: 4).

iv) His ministry

We have noted some of the historical details about the life and
work of Jesus Christ. What about the nature of His ministry
among men? First, it was a *dependent* ministry. He relied on God
(Jn. 5: 26) and on the Holy Spirit (Mt. 12: 28). God worked
through Him (Acts 2: 22). Moreover, it was *authoritative* (Mk. 1:
22, 2: 3–12, 11: 27–33; Lk. 4: 32, 36; Jn. 5: 30, 7: 16–18, 17: 2).
In one account a Roman Centurion revealed that he had a
penetrating insight into Christ's unique authority (Lk. 7: 1–10).

As we have seen, Jesus had a *miraculous* ministry. Apart from
the healing miracles there were other 'signs' of His divine authority and power. On more than one occasion He multiplied food
(Mt. 14: 15–21, 15: 32–38; Mk. 8: 19, 20). He walked on water
(Mt. 14: 25, 26; Jn. 6: 19). People who were sick had merely to
touch Him (Lk. 6: 19) or His clothes (Mk. 5: 25–34, 6: 56) and
they were well. In many cases Christ's miracles were used to
create faith (Jn. 11: 14, 15, 12: 9–11), and yet, for all these
merciful deeds, many people did not believe (Jn. 12: 37–41).

Although there were hundreds who were not won to faith by
Jesus' miracles, it was an essentially *God-exalting* ministry (Mt.
15: 31; Mk. 2: 12; Lk. 9: 43, 13: 10–13, 17: 15). It may not
always have persuaded men, but it glorified God. In its effect
upon those He met, Christ's ministry was *unobtrusive* (Mt. 12:
15–21) and yet *popular* (Mt. 4: 24, 25; Mk. 1: 28, 3: 7, 6: 32–34,
53–56). It was *loving* (Mt. 9: 36; Acts 10: 38) and yet *disturbing*
(Mt. 10: 34–36; Mk. 6: 14–16). It was bitterly *opposed* (Mt. 9: 34,
12: 14, 19: 3, 22: 15–22; Lk. 11: 53, 54; Jn. 5: 16, 8: 37, 40,
10: 31, 39, 15: 24, 25) yet in many respects *highly successful* (Jn.
10: 42, 11: 45). He made an immense impression upon some, but
others did not respond to His ministry and message (Mt. 11: 20–24,
13: 57, 58; Jn. 1: 11, 5: 38, 40, 6: 36, 64). It was a ministry

which was *attested by God* (Jn. 5: 31, 32, 36, 37; Acts 2: 22) and yet proved *divisive among men* (Lk. 3: 17, 12: 49–53; Jn. 7: 25–31, 40–52, 9: 16, 39, 10: 19–21). Some urged Him to stay with them (Jn. 4: 40–45) whilst others begged Him to leave (Lk. 8: 37).

It is clear that people formed entirely different estimates of Him. It was all as the aged Simeon had said on the day when he held the infant Jesus in his arms; He was for the rising of some and the falling of others and 'a sign that is spoken against' (Lk. 2: 34). He exposed the hearts of men (Lk. 2: 35) and for this reason many people set themselves against Him, ruthlessly determined to end His life and work.

v) His character

As interesting as are the events of Christ's life, even more fascinat ing is the *person* He was. The New Testament assures us that He was *sinless* (2 Cor. 5: 21; Heb. 4: 15, 7: 26; 1 Pet. 2: 22; 1 Jn. 3: 5), *compassionate* towards individuals (Mk. 10: 21; Lk. 7: 13; Jn. 11: 5, 35, 36) as well as towards crowds (Mt. 14: 14, 15: 32, 23: 37), *prayerful* (Mk. 1: 35, 6: 46; Lk. 3: 21, 5: 16, 9: 18, 10: 21, 11: 1, 22: 32, 41, 44, 45; Jn. 11: 41, 17: 1–26; Heb. 5: 7), *obedient* (Mt. 26: 36–44; Lk. 2: 51; Jn. 4: 34, 5: 30, 6: 38, 14: 31; Rom. 5: 19), *holy* (Lk. 4: 34, 5: 8; Heb. 7: 26), *gentle* (Mt. 11: 29), *faithful* (Heb. 3: 2, 6), *humble* (Jn. 13: 3–5), *submissive* (Mk. 14: 61, 15: 1–5, Rom. 15: 3, 4; 1 Pet. 2: 23), *grateful* (Mt. 11: 25; Jn. 11: 41), *meek* (2 Cor. 10: 1), *patient* (Lk. 13: 34; 1 Tim. 1: 16), *guileless* (Jn. 7: 18; 1 Pet. 2: 22), *righteous* (1 Jn. 2: 29, 3: 7) and *pure* (1 Jn. 3: 3).

Jesus Christ was absolutely perfect (Heb. 5: 9; 9: 28); a man who lived the most exemplary life (Mt. 11: 29, 30; Jn. 13: 14, 15; Rom. 15: 7; 1 Pet. 2: 21; 1 Jn. 2: 6) that has ever been known among men. Although perfectly human, He was also uniquely divine. He was unique in the sense that, with amazing perception, He knew men's thoughts (Mt. 12: 25; Mk. 2: 8; Lk. 7: 37–50; Jn. 6: 61, 64). He knew which of His disciples would suffer for their faith (Mk. 10: 39; Jn. 21: 18, 19). He knew what was said in His absence (Jn. 20: 24–29). He knew only too well that His disciples would scatter in fear (Jn. 16: 32), that He would be openly denied by one of them (Jn. 13: 36–38) and cruelly betrayed by another (Jn. 6: 46, 65, 13: 11, 21–30). He knew when His end drew near (Jn. 13: 1) and could predict the details of His own arrest and death with astonishing precision (Mt. 16: 21, 17: 12, 22, 23, 20: 18, 19, 26: 2; Mk. 8: 31, 9: 12, 13, 30–32; Lk. 9: 22, 44; Jn. 12: 32, 33). He clearly predicted other future events with remarkable detail. For example, the Fall of Jerusalem and the destruction of its Temple (Mt. 24: 1, 2, 15–28) were predicted. These events occurred approximately thirty or thirty-five years after His death.

As well as living in a way that was thoroughly blameless before men, He also lived a life that was entirely pleasing to God (Mt. 17: 5; Mk. 1: 11; Jn. 8: 29; Rom. 15: 3).

b. THE WORK OF JESUS CHRIST

In the exposition of Christian doctrine it is common to refer to the death of Christ as His 'work'. This is not meant to infer that His redemptive achievement is confined to the event of the Cross. Obviously, the preceding life and ministry of Christ is of the utmost importance for an adequate understanding of His death. Jesus often spoke of His suffering. His teaching interprets His death just as His resurrection vindicates it. But, for all that, this term 'the work of Christ' necessarily focuses attention on the greatest and most vital event of His ministry, viz. His death and resurrection. We are born to live. He was born to die (Jn. 12: 27).

When Jesus was only a baby His mother was told of the sorrow that was bound to come (Lk. 2: 35). At the beginning of Christ's ministry John the Baptist identified Him as 'the Lamb of God' (Jn. 1: 29, 36) who would take away the sin of the world. In one brief sentence John's words summarized some of the most important aspects of Christ's redemptive mission. It mentions His sacrificial vocation ('the Lamb'), His essential deity ('of God'), His effective atonement ('which takes away the sin') and His universal appeal ('of the world'). We must now note what kind of place is given to this teaching in the Bible.

i. The death of Christ

i) Its importance

The actual form and content of the New Testament Gospels is a striking indication of the importance of this theme in early Christian thought. The Gospels have been described as 'passion narratives with extended introductions'. In any other kind of biography one would hardly expect to commence reading about the closing week of the subject's life when barely half-way through the book. Yet in the Gospel narratives this is precisely the case. It is one illustration of the supreme place given to this wonderful theme in the mind and purpose of God as well as in the preaching of the early church.

ii) Its prediction

We have already noted how the Old Testament writers viewed Christ's death. Jesus reminded His disciples (Mt. 26: 31; Jn. 3: 14, 13: 18, 17: 12) and His accusers (Mt. 26: 54–56) of these Old Testament predictions concerning His sufferings. Furthermore, the gospel writers later grasped the deeper significance of many of these Old Testament sayings as they reflected on the events of Christ's atoning sacrifice (Jn. 19: 23, 24, 31–37). The New Testament letters mention these Old Testament prophetic insights about the work of Christ (1 Cor. 15: 3; 1 Pet. 1: 10–12). Old Testament sayings about the Cross were given special prominence in the apostolic preaching. When proclaiming what Christ had done for men, the apostles turned to what God had earlier said to men (Acts 3: 18, 8: 30–35, 13: 29). When reasoning with Jews in the synagogues Paul 'argued with them *from the Scriptures* explaining and proving that it was necessary for the Christ to suffer' (Acts 17: 2–3, 26: 22, 23, 28: 23).

iii) Its anticipation

Christ's death and resurrection were not only predicted in the Old Testament books but the Event was anticipated by Jesus during His earthly ministry. He spoke about it not merely in general terms but described it in specific and precise detail. He told His disciples it would occur in Jerusalem (Mt. 16: 21); that He would be delivered to the chief priests and scribes (Mk. 10: 33) or to 'the Gentiles', i.e. the 'godless' (Mk. 10: 33; Lk. 18: 32); that He would be condemned to death (Mk. 10: 33), mocked (Mk. 10: 34; Lk. 18: 32), shamefully treated (Lk. 18: 32), spit upon (Mk. 10: 34; Lk. 18: 32), scourged (Mk. 10: 34; Lk. 18: 33), crucified (Mt. 20: 19) and killed (Mk. 10: 34; Lk. 18: 33).

Jesus knew He would not die an ordinary death but would be betrayed into the hands of sinners (Mt. 26: 45). But, although He knew it was both inevitable and ghastly, He did not regard it as a horrible tragedy but as the hour of approaching glory (Jn. 17: 1). It was after Judas went out to betray Him that Jesus said, 'Now is the Son of Man glorified' (Jn. 13: 30–32). At the end He portrayed it in parabolic form (Mt. 21: 33–46; Mk. 12: 1–12; Lk. 22: 14–20). It never moved from the horizon of His thinking. Our Lord set His face steadfastly towards it (Lk. 9: 51, 53; Isa. 50: 5–7).

iv) Its context

It is highly significant that the historical context of Christ's work was the Jewish Festival of Passover. In the Synoptic Gospels there is a clear reference to the sacrificing of the Passover Lamb in the Last Supper narrative (Mk. 14: 12–25; Lk. 22: 7–23), while in John's Gospel and Peter's First Epistle the Passover is given a central place both in the story of Christ's death (Jn. 19: 14, 31–37) and its interpretation (1 Pet. 1: 18–20). When the blood of the Passover Lamb was sprinkled over the doorposts in Egypt, the Hebrew slaves knew they would be *saved* from the destroying angel.

It marked the beginning of their *redemption*. They were *released from bondage* to be God's free people. All these ideas are given rich expression in the New Testament doctrine of Christ's atoning death. When Jesus died He saved, redeemed and liberated His enslaved children.

v) Its nature

We know that Christ died on a Cross. We also know that death by crucifixion was a common enough occurrence in the Roman world. At some time or other, one is bound to enquire why Christ's death was entirely different from all others. The New Testament asserts at least seven things about its nature and character:

First, it was eternally determined. Jesus knew it was to come and the Old Testament prophets were also aware of it. But it goes back even further still. In the eternal ages past it was planned by God out of love for man. On this matter there is no uncertainty. Peter realized that there was nothing accidental about Christ's death and told those great crowds on the day of Pentecost that Jesus was 'delivered up according to the definite plan and fore-knowledge of God' (Acts 2: 23). Later, Peter wrote his First Epistle and referred to Christ's death as 'destined before the foundation of the world' (1 Pet. 1: 20).

Secondly, it was voluntarily endured. The death of Christ was no arbitrary decision on the part of God. We hardly do justice to Scripture if we drive a wedge between what God demands of Jesus and what Jesus does of His own volition. They plan in perfect unity. Jesus is charged by the Father to surrender His life, but in the same context we are told that He does it of His own accord (Jn. 10: 18). He lays down His life for the Father (Jn. 10: 18) because He loves Him, and also for the sheep because they need Him (Jn. 10: 11, 15). It is in this context that Jesus clearly says, 'I and the Father are one' (Jn. 10: 30).

Neither was Christ's death a sinister achievement on the part of sinful men. His life was not snatched hastily away from Him. It was deliberately laid down by the Lord (Jn. 10: 15, 18). Jesus told Pilate that he had very limited power in the matter (Jn. 19: 10, 11). It was not simply the cruel work of men. God was in it.

Thirdly, it was lovingly conceived. Jesus accepts the Father's will in all this knowing that the Cross will be a unique demonstration of the Father's love for the world. It is because God loved the world that He gave His Son at the Incarnation (Jn. 3: 16). And at the Cross the magnitude of that love was made evident to all (1 Jn. 3: 16). The apostles rejoiced in the assurance of God's sacrificial love revealed at Calvary. Paul asserts that 'God shows

His love for us in that, while we were yet sinners, Christ died for us' (Rom. 5: 8). John glories in the truth that our salvation begins not in the moment when we love God but because He loves us 'and sent His Son to be the expiation for our sins' (1 Jn. 4: 10).

It is important to see that the Cross is not only a demonstration of God's love but of Christ's love also. Father and Son act in perfect harmony as they manifest the wonder of the divine love. Jesus says, 'Greater love has no man than this, that a man lay down his life for his friends' (Jn. 15: 13). Paul referred to Christ as 'the Son of God who loved me and gave Himself for me' (Gal. 2: 20).

Fourthly, it was sacrificially achieved. Goethe said, 'blood is a very precious juice.' We shall never know what it cost our Lord when He died. An ancient liturgy refers to 'Thine unknown sufferings'. Jesus was aware that it was not merely an indescribably dreadful physical experience; others had gone through that. Far more important, it was a solitary and unrepeatable *spiritual* experience. He bore the sins of mankind as He died on that Cross (1 Pet. 2: 24). He did something for us that we could not possibly do for ourselves (1 Pet. 3: 18).

As Jesus anticipated that agonizing encounter with human sin, He knew only too well what it would cost Him. He knew about the intense agony of separation from a holy God who could not look upon sin. This is the real horror of Calvary. No wonder He shrank from it as He prayed in the garden (Mt. 26: 39, 42, 44). Jesus knew that, had it been possible, God would have found some other way (Mk. 14: 36). But in all this, Christ's dominating passion was to obey His Father's will rather than question His Father's purpose (Lk. 22: 42). It is not surprising that, as He hung in physical agony and spiritual desolation, He cried out, 'My God, my God, why hast thou forsaken me?' (Mt. 27: 46; Mk. 15: 34).

Fifthly, it was illegally executed. From the divine point of view the Cross was part of God's plan of redemptive love. But from a human point of view it was an act of vindictive murder. This is made clear in the Scriptures. Jesus' accusers took every opportunity to trap Him into an unwise saying (Mt. 22: 15–22; Mk. 3: 6, 12: 13; Jn. 5: 18). They hated Him because He healed sick people on the Jewish sabbath. In their view He violated the Mosaic Law (Mk. 2: 23–27; Jn. 5: 16). They opposed Jesus for claiming equality with God by addressing Him as 'Father' (Jn. 5: 18). And because His miraculous signs were causing many Jews to believe in Him (Jn. 11: 45–53, 12: 9–11) they despised Him even more.

Although it was contrary to the Jewish Law (Exod. 20: 16), the religious leaders produced false testimony in order to bring an accusation against Him (Mt. 26: 59; Mk 14: 56). But it proved contradictory (Mk. 14: 56) and therefore unconvincing. They finally accused Him of threatening to destroy the Temple (Mt. 26: 60, 61; Mk. 14: 58), a misrepresentation or misunderstanding of His actual words (Mt. 24: 2; Jn. 2: 19–21). It was a saying which obviously irritated the Jews (Mt. 27: 40; Mk. 15: 29) whatever He meant by it. Thus their hatred deepened.

The Roman authorities, however, were not in the least bit troubled that Jesus claimed to be the Son of God; that was a purely theological issue (Mt. 26: 63). After all, there were plenty of Messianic pretenders in the period and, in the view of the Romans, Jesus might merely be another such fanatic (Acts 5: 36, 37). Such religious speculations did not interest them (Jn. 19: 6, 7). So the Jews made mischievous use of Christ's claim to *kingship* (Jn. 19: 12). A title like that had political overtones (Jn. 18: 33–38) and could not be ignored by a Roman Governor however sympathetic he might be (Jn. 19: 13–16).

So Christ was accused before Rome. But He was given only a mock trial without proper witnesses; the work of mob violence from a manipulated crowd (Mt. 27: 20–23) rather than legal jurisdiction by dispassionate judges. Preaching about it, only a matter of weeks after the event, Peter said that, although Christ's death was part of God's predetermined plan, the Lord of glory had been 'crucified and killed by the hands of lawless men' (Acts 2: 23). The apostle Paul also gave expression to the injustice of Christ's accusers when he said, 'Though they could charge Him with nothing deserving death, yet they asked Pilate to have Him killed' (Acts 13: 28). His death at the hands of men was a corruption of Roman justice and a violation of Jewish law. Even the thief on the cross beside Jesus (Lk. 23: 39–41) and the soldier beneath (Lk. 23: 47) affirmed Christ's innocence. It was, in the final analysis, an act of vindictive murder.

Sixthly, it was accepted. Yet, although entirely guiltless, Christ submitted Himself to this intense agony—not as an act of inevitable surrender to vindictive men but as an expression of complete obedience to a loving God. The idea of 'obedience' is found in New Testament contexts about the Cross. 'Charged' by the Father to lay down His life (Jn. 10: 15, 18), Jesus obediently accepts it. Paul, in one of his most magnificent passages, affirms that Christ became obedient unto death, even death on a Cross (Phil. 2: 8). The Epistle to the Hebrews says that the Lord Jesus actually 'learned obedience through what He suffered' (Heb. 5: 8). At the time of the arrest in the garden Christ turned to impetuous Peter and said, 'Shall I not drink the cup which the Father has given me?' (Jn. 18: 11). He knew it had to be, and

He gladly accepted it. Paul says that it is by the act of Christ's obedience that many will be made righteous (Rom. 5: 19). The Lord's experience in Gethsemane is a superb example of perfect obedience to the Father in the shadow of the Cross (Mt. 26: 39). There was no other way by which men could be redeemed, and Jesus responded to the Father's will with obedient dedication and unwavering purpose.

Seventhly, it was necessarily accomplished. Jesus was convinced that it was within His power to be delivered from this dreadful experience if He wished (Mt. 26: 53, 54). But He consistently refused to be saved from it (Jn. 12: 27). He had a deep inner compulsion to surrender Himself to this baptism of suffering and death (Lk. 12: 50). Faced with its indescribable agony, it was natural for Him to hope it might not have to take place (Mk. 14: 32–36, 39), but He had anticipated it all through His life and would not shrink from it now. He often referred to it as His 'hour' or 'time' which was certain to come (Jn. 2: 4, 7: 6, 8, 30, 8: 20, 12: 23, 17: 1). The point is, He realized that it was absolutely essential for man's salvation.

This emphasis on the utter *necessity* of Christ's Cross is given a prominent place in the atonement teaching of the Lord Jesus. There was a 'must' about it (Jn. 3: 14). After the Resurrection Christ told His friends that it was 'necessary that the Christ should suffer these things' (Lk. 24: 26). The angels at the tomb reminded the bewildered women that during His teaching ministry Jesus had often told them that 'the Son of Man *must* be delivered into the hands of sinful men and be crucified' (Lk. 24: 6, 7). Surely they remembered the many occasions when He had made this absolutely clear to them (e.g. Mt. 16: 21; Lk. 9: 22, 17: 25).

vi) Its purpose

From a purely human point of view, the death of Christ must have seemed an appalling waste. He was only just over thirty years of age and in a very short time had exercised an astonishingly successful ministry as a Teacher, Healer and Leader. Why should such a morally blameless and spiritually perfect life be cut off in its prime? We turn now to the *reason* for Christ's death and note that:

First, it was a sacrificial death. The interpretation of Christ's sufferings is often presented in the New Testament with the aid of vivid sacrificial language. Paul says that Christ, the Paschal Lamb, has been sacrificed for us (1 Cor. 5: 7). The Lord Jesus 'gave Himself up for us, a fragrant offering and sacrifice to God' (Eph. 5: 2). The Jewish priesthood perpetually went on making their various offerings, but Christ's atoning sacrifice was 'offered for all time a single sacrifice for sins' (Heb. 7: 27, 9: 11–14, 10: 12–14).

Secondly, it was a propitiatory death. Some contemporary theologians shrink from the implications of the sacrificial language of the New Testament. It is obvious that a sacrifice is offered to God. And Paul makes this abundantly clear in his reference to Christ's voluntary offering of Himself (Eph. 5: 2). It was a propitiation.

A Holy and Righteous God was grieved by human sin, and Christ offered Himself as the one perfect sacrifice for that sin. The essential background to the Cross is not only the love of God for men but God's holy wrath toward men (Rom 1: 18, 5: 9; 1 Thess. 1: 10). Without the grim reality of our sin, Christ's death would not have been necessary. He died not only to show us how much God loves us and also how much He hates our sin. One of the earliest summaries of Christian doctrine which we possess says this about our Lord's death: 'Christ died for our sins' (1 Cor. 15: 3). His death was the *only* way of dealing with the sinister fact and destructive effect of our sin.

Thirdly, it was a reconciling death. God loves the sinner. This is wonderfully true. But He cannot tolerate man's sin. There is warfare between man and God, and they need to be reconciled. Christ's death on the Cross effects that reconciliation (Rom. 5: 10). In his own experience, Paul knew what it was to oppose God's will, deeply religious though he certainly was (Acts 9: 1–9, 22: 4–16, 26: 9–18; 1 Tim. 1: 12–16). He came to understand that the gulf had been bridged by Jesus Christ, the *only* Mediator (1 Tim. 2: 5; Heb. 9: 15, 12: 24). By His death, Jesus Christ brought both Jew and Gentile back to God and also broke down the wall of hostility which divided them (2 Cor. 5: 18–20; Eph. 2: 13–16; Col. 1: 20–22).

Fourthly, it was a substitutionary death. Here is another category of thought which has offended some recent writers on the atonement. Yet the idea of substitution, or something remarkably close to it, pervades many of the New Testament passages about Christ's sacrificial death. In dying on the Cross, He does something 'for us'. The phrase often recurs in atonement contexts (Rom. 8: 32; 2 Cor. 5: 21; Gal. 3: 13, 14). Peter says that Christ died 'for sins once for all, the righteous for the unrighteous that He might bring us to God' (1 Pet. 3: 18). Since New Testament times many have gratefully acknowledged the truth: 'in my place condemned He stood.' Like the thieves who hung on each side of Christ, we too were worthy of punishment. All have sinned against God (Rom. 3: 23), disobeyed and grieved Him. But Christ died *in our stead*.

Fifthly, it was a pardoning death. Man needs forgiveness. Overwhelmed by a sense of guilt, the truly penitent man cries out for cleansing and, by Christ's expiatory sacrifice, this pardon is assured (Eph. 1: 7; Col. 2: 13, 14). Jesus Himself emphasized this vital aspect of His redemptive work. It was to effect the eternal miracle of the forgiveness of sins (Mt. 26: 28). The Lord Jesus, says Paul, was 'put forward as an expiation by His blood' (Rom. 3: 25). The Epistle to the Hebrews reminds us that 'without the shedding of blood there is no forgiveness of sins' (Heb. 9: 22). Christ 'made purification for sins' (Heb. 1: 3) and 'put away sin by the sacrifice of Himself' (Heb. 9: 26). Moreover, it is by Christ's 'once for all' sacrifice on the Cross (Heb. 7: 27, 10: 12) that the cleansing process is continued in the life of a believer. John puts it in the most graphic way possible; it is the blood of Jesus Christ which keeps on cleansing us from all sin (Heb. 9: 14; 1 Jn. 1: 7; Rev. 1: 5, 6, 7: 14), if we come to Him in confession (1 Jn. 1: 9).

Sixthly, it was a redemptive death. In the New Testament far more than one category of thought is pressed into service in order to give adequate expression to the meaning of Christ's work. We are taken to the altar and reminded it is a sacrifice (Eph. 5: 2). We are led into the law-court and realize that by this unique offering we are acquitted, justified and made right with God (Rom. 3: 26, 5: 9). When we were helpless and godless offenders, Christ died for us (Rom. 5: 6, 8). By the shedding of His blood He paid the price (Mk. 10: 45) to obtain our release from bondage and slavery and bring us into the service of a God who loves us and longs for our fellowship (Rom. 3: 24; Gal. 3: 13, 14; Eph. 1: 7; Col. 1: 14; Tit. 2: 14).

Seventhly, it was a victorious death. Christ's sacrifice achieves something more than even the Godward and manward aspects that we have briefly considered. It was also a triumphant conquest in which the Devil was vanquished. The exciting and fortifying theme of 'Christ as Victor' is given some prominence in the New Testament. Jesus referred to it (Jn. 12: 31–33, 14: 30), and the New Testament writers went on to develop it (Col. 2: 15; Heb. 2: 14, 15; Rev. 12: 10, 11). Obviously, the Devil is still at work in the world (1 Pet. 5: 8, 9), but he is doomed. The world's most decisive battle was fought at Calvary when the conquering Christ was Victor as well as Victim.

vii) Its effects

We close this summary of the biblical doctrine of Christ's death by observing how a Christian is to respond to it.

First, he believes it. The Christian does not only think of the

Cross as an historical event. He recognizes its importance in his *own experience*. Christ died on the Cross to save him and, by faith, he fully accepts that totally undeserved work of grace and mercy. It is 'those who believe' (1 Cor. 1: 21) in the message of the Cross who are saved (1 Cor. 1: 17–24). It is a personal, dynamic experience of faith.

Secondly, he appropriates it. Real faith always appropriates. The benefits of Christ's atoning death are personally appropriated by the believer. He gratefully receives and enjoys the forgiveness (Eph. 1: 7), justification (Gal. 2: 15–21), peace (Eph. 2: 14–17), deliverance (Gal. 1: 4), power (1 Cor. 1: 18) and holiness (Heb. 10: 10, 13: 12; 1 Pet. 2: 24) that is his in Christ.

Thirdly, he proclaims it. The apostle Paul lived solely to preach the Cross of Christ (1 Cor. 1: 23, 2: 2; Gal. 3: 1). He gloried in its message and longed to proclaim its truth. This is not only the responsibility of an isolated New Testament apostle. It is every Christian's privilege. Moreover, the Cross has its own appeal. Jesus said that by it men would be drawn to Him (Jn. 12: 32), and His word was proved wonderfully true on the day Jesus died. A guilty thief made his confession of faith in the Kingship (Lk. 23: 42, 43) of the crucified Christ. Such witness is costly (Heb. 13: 12, 13; Rev. 12: 11) but rewarding (Jn. 4: 36; Jas. 5: 19, 20).

Fourthly, he shares in it. A further thing must be said about the Cross. Believers do not only stand before the Cross in adoring wonder. They remember the words of the Lord Jesus and determine, in His strength (Phil. 4: 13), to make it a reality in their own lives. Christians freely acknowledge that, as far as their salvation is concerned, the Cross is a finished work. However, as far as Christian sanctification is concerned, the Cross is a continuing personal experience. Christ is crucified for the sinner and the believer is crucified with Christ (Gal. 2: 20). The New Testament has a great deal to say about this aspect of Christ's death (2 Cor. 1: 5; Gal. 6: 14, 17; Phil. 3: 10, 11; Col. 1: 24).

Of course, it is possible for some types of sanctification-teaching to degenerate into meaningless mysticism. The New Testament doctrine of holiness is intensely practical. For example, how does the Christian react to hostility? The crucified Lord is the believer's inspiring example when undeserved persecution comes into his life (1 Pet. 2: 21, 4: 12, 13). In moments of intense hardship and bitter opposition he is urged to 'consider Him who endured from sinners such hostility against Himself so that you may not grow weary or fainthearted' (Heb. 12: 2, 3).

Fifthly, he glories in it. The Christian shares the exultant gratitude of the redeemed (Gal. 6: 14). He anticipates the worship of the saved multitude which no man can number, who sing a new song in heaven; 'Worthy is the Lamb who was slain' (Rev. 5: 6–14). They exalt the Lamb of God in words which recall the greatest event in human history: 'Thou wast slain and by Thy blood didst ransom men for God.' They rejoice in the universal appeal of this saving and victorious act, for the ransomed host come 'from every tribe and tongue and people and nation'. They share in Christ's triumphant conquest, for He has 'made them a Kingdom and priests to our God and they shall reign on earth' (Rev. 5: 9, 10).

viii) Its sequel

Two important themes must be mentioned as we consider the immediate events which followed Christ's death on the Cross: first, His mission during the 'three days' and, secondly, His appearance on the third day.

A careful examination of a passage in 1 Peter leads us to the conclusion that immediately after His death Christ visited the 'realm of departed spirits'. Peter says Christ 'preached to the spirits in prison', and this statement is made in the context of Christ's death, resurrection and ascension (1 Pet. 3: 18–22, 4: 6). This is one of the few hints we have about our Lord's redemptive mission to those who had died centuries earlier, before His atoning death could avail for them. But it is only right to say that there are a number of variant interpretations of this passage in 1 Peter 3 and the student should consult the commentaries.

The Resurrection is the further sequel to which we must refer. In Christian preaching the Cross must not be separated from the Resurrection. These are not two isolated events. Rather, they are essentially complementary. In New Testament thought they are closely related aspects of Christ's redemptive work. Without the Resurrection the Cross would be a meaningless tragedy and an appalling waste. We turn, therefore, to the biblical teaching about Christ's Resurrection.

ii. The Resurrection of Christ

On the Cross Jesus passed through the experience of intense physical and spiritual agony and eventually took His last breath (Lk. 23: 46). He died! About this important fact there is no doubt. When we come to the Resurrection, however, it is another matter. Those who have tried to oppose the Christian message have invented a multitude of tales to explain away the Resurrection story. Some have suggested He merely swooned, later to be revived. But the New Testament asserts that He died. John is particularly anxious to stress the fact (Jn. 19: 33–35)—in view of fanciful and misleading ideas—that Christ did actually pass through the experience of death. This is one of the reasons the assertion is made 'He was buried'

(1 Cor. 15: 4). It was a real and actual death. Consequently it was
a genuine, indisputable Resurrection. It is important to see that the
Resurrection of Christ was:

i) Foretold by prophets

The Lord Jesus pointed out that His Resurrection had been given
a place in the message of the Old Testament. When He expounded
the Scriptures to His disciples He said that everything written
about Him 'in the law of Moses and the prophets and the Psalms
must be fulfilled . . . Thus it is written that the Christ should
suffer and on the third day rise again' (Lk. 24: 44–46). Although
the Suffering Servant must die, He will yet live to 'see his offspring'. He will see the fruits of His sacrificial suffering in redeemed children. He shall 'prolong His days' (Isa. 53: 10, 11). The
Lord Jesus regarded Jonah's experience as a type of His own
burial and resurrection (Mt. 12: 40).

When the apostles began their preaching ministry in Jerusalem
and beyond, they made mention of the Old Testament predictions of Christ's Resurrection. They referred not only to the Old
Testament prophets as such, but to passages in the *Psalms* with
prophetic or predictive content such as Psalm 16: 8–11 (quoted
in Acts 2: 25–28 and Acts 13: 35), Psalm 110: 1 (used in support
of the Ascension of Christ and quoted in Acts 2: 34, 35) and
Psalm 2: 7 (quoted in Acts 13: 33).

From these references in the *Acts* we can see that in their
preaching, both Peter and Paul referred to the Resurrection of
Jesus as an event clearly foretold in the Old Testament. When
writing to the Corinthian Church, Paul was doubtless quoting
directly from a very early Christian confession or 'Statement of
Faith' when he used the words 'that He was raised on the third
day in accordance with the Scriptures' (1 Cor. 15: 4). From the
gospel narratives one gets the impression that the disciples had
either forgotten or not known some of these Old Testament
passages about the Resurrection of Christ (Jn. 20: 9). Moreover,
the Resurrection was:

ii) Promised by Jesus

Whenever the Lord Jesus talked about His death He usually
referred at the same time to the important sequel to His death;
the Resurrection (Mt. 12: 38–40, 16: 21, 17: 9, 23, 20: 18, 19, 26:
31, 32; Mk. 8: 31, 9: 31, 10: 34; Lk. 9: 22, 18: 33). Yet His
disciples did not always understand it (Mk. 9: 10). These and
other sayings about the Resurrection (Jn. 2: 19–22) became
known to Christ's opponents. At His trial they were misinter-
preted and misused in order to accuse Him (Mt. 26: 60; Mk.

14: 58). At His crucifixion the crowds quoted His words in jest (Mk. 15: 29, 30). After Christ's burial the religious authorities of the day made reference to His predicted Resurrection and, because of this, tried to take precautions against the possible theft of Christ's body (Mt. 27: 62–66). Another vital aspect of the event is in the fact that it was:

iii) Accomplished by God

In a host of different places the New Testament makes it abundantly clear that the Resurrection of Christ was an act of God. The early Christian preachers boldly proclaimed to their astonished congregations that it was God who raised Him up (Acts 2: 24, 32, 3: 15, 4: 10, 5: 30, 10: 40, 13: 30, 33, 34). The writers of the New Testament epistles also refer to the Resurrection as the achievement of an Almighty God (Rom. 4: 24, 6: 4; Col. 2: 12; 1 Thess. 1: 10; Heb. 13: 20; 1 Pet. 1: 21).

The Resurrection is a demonstration of 'the immeasurable greatness of God's power' (Eph. 1. 19, 20). What does God demonstrate in that He raised Christ from the dead?

First, He accepts Christ's sacrifice. The Resurrection testifies to the finished work of Christ (Heb. 10: 11–18, 13: 20).

Secondly, He declares Christ's deity. Obviously, Jesus Christ was the Son of God from all eternity, but the Resurrection announces this truth clearly to the world (Rom. 1: 4).

Thirdly, He vindicates Christ's word. During His ministry, Jesus had made definite promises about the Resurrection. God saw to it that they were gloriously fulfilled (Mt. 12: 40; Jn. 2: 19–22). And this glorious act of God was:

iv) Witnessed by men

The historicity of Christ's Resurrection is an important aspect of New Testament belief. The Risen Christ frequently appeared to His disciples and friends. He met them personally (e.g. Mary Magdalene, Jn. 20: 11–18) and collectively (e.g. the disciples in the Upper Room, Jn. 20: 19–29). He spoke to them clearly in a voice they could recognize, using their own names (Jn. 20: 16). But there were some occasions when they did not immediately identify Him (Jn. 20: 14, 21: 4). Luke suggests that their initial failure to recognize Him was not due to a change in Christ's appearance but to a purposeful act of God in order to make the experience specially meaningful to them (Lk. 24: 15, 16). Luke also says that Christ gave many proofs of His risen life (Acts 1: 3). The disciples needed proof, for they did not always believe when they were told of His Resurrection (Mk. 16: 11, 13, 14). Even when they actually saw Him for themselves, His disciples could

hardly believe their eyes, and continued to doubt (Mt. 28: 17).
One of His followers refused to accept the message of the Risen
Lord until he had seen for himself (Jn. 20: 24, 25).

This period of post-Resurrection activity (Acts 13: 31) lasted
forty days (Acts 1: 3), and Paul tells us that during this time
Christ appeared to Peter and the rest of the disciples (1 Cor.
15: 5), to James (1 Cor. 15: 7) and also to a company of five
hundred believers at one time. Some of these people were alive
when Paul wrote these words and could have supported his claim
if others had suggested it was mere fabrication (1 Cor. 15: 6).
Peter could tell the vast crowds who listened to him on the day of
Pentecost that all the disciples were witnesses of the Resurrection
(Acts 2: 32). Thus it is clear why the Resurrection was:

v) Proclaimed by the apostles
One of the most convincing aspects of early Christian apologetic
was the early Christian preaching which 'gave their testimony
to the Resurrection of the Lord Jesus' (Acts 4: 33). To have seen the
Lord was an essential qualification for apostleship. They had to be
'a witness to His Resurrection' (Acts 1: 22, 3: 15, 5: 32, 10: 40,
41). Whenever the apostles were presented with an opportunity
to expound the Christian message, they instinctively referred to the
Risen and Glorified Lord (Acts 2: 24–36, 3: 14, 15, 4: 10, 5: 30–
32, 10: 39–41, 13: 29–39, 26: 22, 23). We must not imagine that
this message was always believed (Acts 17: 30–32). No, but it was
faithfully declared whether men accepted it or not. There were
many, like Saul of Tarsus, who were converted at the moment when
the glorified Christ appeared to them personally (Acts 9: 3–6;
1 Cor. 9: 1, 15: 8–10; Gal. 1: 16). Finally, it was:

vi) Experienced by believers
Just as the death of Christ is something more than mere history
for the believer, so Christ's Resurrection is a personal experience
as well as a factual historical event. Christians are identified with
Christ's death and they share His Resurrection (Rom. 6: 15). The
historicity of the Resurrection is vital to the believer's justification
(Rom. 4: 24, 25) and sanctification (Rom. 6: 4). It is not only a
truth which Christians confess by word of mouth, important as
that is (Rom. 10: 9). It is an experience of everyday life by which
a believer proves the power (Rom. 8: 11; Phil. 3: 10) and
presence (2 Cor. 13: 4, 5) of the Risen Christ.

By the Resurrection of Jesus our inheritance is guaranteed
(1 Pet. 1: 3–5), our confidence is sustained (1 Pet. 1: 21), our
hope is confirmed (1 Cor. 15: 12–19) and our destiny is assured
(1 Cor. 15: 20–28).

iii. The Ascension of Christ

After a period in which Jesus moved among His disciples (Acts 10: 40, 41) encouraging and teaching (Lk. 24: 36–49), commissioning them (Jn. 20: 19–23) and speaking about the Kingdom of God (Acts 1: 3), He ascended to the Father (Lk. 24: 50, 51; Acts 1: 2, 9–11) and sat down at the right hand of God (Mk. 16: 19; Lk. 22: 69; Acts 2: 33, 7: 55, 56; Rom. 8: 34; Eph. 1: 20, 21; Col. 3: 1; Heb. 12: 2; 1 Pet. 3: 22). The event did not take them by surprise, for Jesus had mentioned it during His ministry (Jn. 6: 62). He told them He would return to the Father (Jn. 16: 10, 28, 17: 11), although they were puzzled by such sayings (Jn. 16: 16, 22). The apostles were persuaded that, just as the death and Resurrection of Christ had been predicted in the Old Testament, so had the Ascension (Acts 2: 33–35). In the New Testament, the Ascension points to several things about Jesus Christ.

i) His vindication

When Christ's atoning work was complete (Heb. 10: 12), 'He sat down at the right hand of the Majesty on high' (Heb. 1: 3). At the Cross men had mocked and maligned God's Son. They had despised His person and rejected His mercy. But the Ascension is the divine vindication of our Lord Jesus Christ (Heb. 1: 13). By giving Christ the favoured place at His right hand, God is saying to the host of heaven what earlier He declared to men on earth: 'This is my beloved Son with whom I am well pleased' (Mt. 3: 17).

ii) His exaltation

The Ascension idea in the New Testament is often expressed in terms of exaltation. It is the moment of supreme honour. 'God exalted Him at His right hand as Leader and Saviour' (Acts 5: 31). As the Ascended Lord, He is the Head of the Church (Eph. 1: 22, 23), the Lord of the universe (Eph. 1: 20–22; 1 Pet. 3: 22), the Donor of gifts (Eph. 4: 7–12), the Pioneer of our faith who marks out the way ahead for all believers (Heb. 2: 10, 6: 19, 12: 2). Thus He inspires us to look where He is seated, remember His victory and 'seek the things that are above' (Col. 3: 1–2).

iii) His intercession

Christ appears in the presence of God not only to receive the Father's honour but to represent the children's needs (Heb. 9: 24). The Ascended Lord is not only a conqueror, He is a priest. He enters the holy place with a complete understanding of our needs, for He too has been tempted (Heb. 2: 17, 4: 14–16). He has been appointed to this priestly ministry by God (Heb. 5: 5, 10) and this sympathetic, intercessory ministry will continue for ever (Heb. 6: 19, 20, 7: 3, 17, 23–25). Because of this gracious and unceasing intercession for us (Rom. 8: 34), Christians are invited to come with boldness to the place of prayer (Heb. 4: 16, 10: 19–22) and to go out with courage to the place of witness (Mk. 16: 19, 20). Christians know that the Ascended Christ is both praying for them (Heb. 7: 25) and working with them (Mk. 16: 20).

iv. The return of Christ

On the day when the Lord Jesus passed into the heavens, the onlookers were told that He would come back again (Acts 1: 11). There are different interpretations and various views as to the details concerning the Second Coming of Christ and related events, but we shall confine ourselves here to the basic, central issues with which there is little dispute among evangelical Christians.

i) Its time

Throughout history there have been many hundreds of people who have made highly speculative predictions about the precise moment of either Christ's return or 'the close of the age'. Even the first disciples were interested in the question and wanted to know the facts (Mt. 24: 3). Jesus was content to tell them about events which would precede His coming, but not the actual date. This information was known only to God (Mt. 24: 36; Mk. 13: 32). Because the exact time is not known to men, they are to watch, and be alert at *all times* (Mk. 13: 33, 35, 37).

ii) Its antecedents

Although it is best for men to remain ignorant of the precise moment of Christ's return, they are told about a series of dramatic events which will take place on earth prior to His coming. These 'signs' assume various forms. Some are national and political, some natural and physical, some religious, domestic or judicial, some in the earthly realm, others in the heavenly. These precursors of Christ's return are given prominence in the teaching of Jesus and include wars (Mt. 24: 6, 7; Mk. 13: 7, 8; Lk. 21: 9, 10), signs in sun, moon and stars (Lk. 21: 25), earthquakes (Mt. 24: 7; Mk. 13: 8; Lk. 21: 11), famines (Mt. 24: 7; Mk. 13: 8; Lk. 21: 11), persecution of His followers (Mt. 24: 9; Mk. 13: 9; Lk. 21: 12), increased evil (Mt. 24: 12), the emergence of false prophets (Mt. 24: 11) and Messianic pretenders and impostors (Mt. 24: 3–5; Lk. 21: 8), family disloyalty (Mk. 13: 12; Lk. 21: 16), pestilences (Lk. 21: 11), terrors (Lk. 21: 11), hatred of Christians (Mk. 13: 13; Lk. 21: 17), imprisonment (Lk. 21: 12), accusation (Lk. 21: 12–15) and death (Lk. 21: 16). There will be times of fear and foreboding (Lk. 21: 26). Entire nations will be in distress and perplexity (Lk. 21: 25), as well as individuals.

iii) Its manner

The New Testament asserts that Christ's return will be: *First,* sudden. It will be like the appearance of a thief (1 Thess. 5: 1–11). Many will not be thinking about it when, unexpectedly, He will appear (Mt. 24: 37–44). Believers are therefore urged to be ready for it (Mt. 25: 1–13; Mk. 13: 33–37; Lk. 12: 42–48) and to prepare for it by hard work (Mt. 24: 45–51), faithful stewardship (Mt. 25: 14–30) and compassionate caring (Mt. 25: 34–40).

Secondly, visible. Men will know He has returned. He will come on the clouds of heaven (Mt. 26: 64; Mk. 13: 26; Lk. 21: 27). As surely as the disciples saw Him go, so the world will see Him return (Acts 1: 11; 1 Jn. 3: 2; Rev. 1: 7).

iv) Its achievement

In that day the whole earth will recognize Him as the rejected Saviour and the unacknowledged King. Every knee will bow to Him (Phil. 2: 9–11). He will clothe every believer in a body like His own (1 Cor. 15: 49; Phil. 3: 21). Then being made like Him (1 Jn. 3: 2), they will appear with Him in glory (Col. 3: 4). Those who have died in Christ will be part of the triumphant host (1 Thess. 4: 14), and they will share in His conquest (Rev. 12: 10, 11). His reign will be eternal (Rev. 11: 15).

v) Its demands

Although there will be multitudes of unbelievers who will not expect Christ's return, Christians eagerly await His victorious appearing (1 Cor. 1: 7; Phil. 3: 20; 1 Thess. 1: 10; Heb. 9: 28). Believers have a steadfast hope in the Christ who has promised to return (1 Thess. 1: 3). They pray that He will soon come back (1 Cor. 16: 22; Rev. 22: 20). New Testament Christians greeted one another with the reminder that He is 'at hand' (Phil. 4: 5).

But God's people do not only pray for it; they work. Christians know that those they have won to faith in Jesus are their 'joy and crown' at Christ's Coming (1 Thess 2: 19). Thus they are eager in evangelism and zealous in service (Phil. 2: 16). Because they want to meet their Lord unashamed, the promise of His Coming quickens their zeal for holiness and purity of life (Phil. 1: 10; 1 Thess 3: 13; Tit. 2: 12, 13; 1 Jn. 3: 3). It encourages their endurance (Mk. 13: 13; Rev. 2: 25) knowing that Christ will keep them until that day (Phil. 1: 6; Jude 24; Rev. 3: 10). Meanwhile they may have to suffer, but even this brings joy: they know how glad they will be when He appears (1 Pet. 4: 13).

The Christian longs for all this to happen quickly. Still, New Testament believers were urged to be patient (Jas. 5: 7, 8) and not throw away their confidence (Heb. 10: 35–39). Believers know that the waiting time calls for steadfastness (Lk. 21: 17–

19). They heed the word of the returning Christ who said, 'Watch' (Lk. 21: 36). Those who love the truth of Christ's return prepare themselves for it in a twofold manner; they encourage those within the Church (Heb. 10: 25) and evangelize those outside it (Mt. 24: 14, 28: 19).

vi. The judgment of Christ

One of the leading features of New Testament eschatology, i.e. doctrines of future events, is that the role of 'Judge' has been assigned to Jesus Christ. The Father has entrusted it to Him (Jn. 5: 22, 23, 27). This truth was given an important place in the preaching of the apostles (Acts 10: 42, 17: 31). The sinless One who was judged by sinful men will one day be the judge of all. Several aspects of this theme are found in Scripture:

i) Its certainty

About the fact of Christ's future work as judge there is no doubt whatever. There are innumerable references to it throughout the New Testament. Jesus clearly taught that man is accountable to God for his life and what he does with it. He addressed the disciples and others on this subject a number of times and on different occasions (Mt. 13: 39–43, 16: 27, 19: 28, 25: 31–33).

ii) Its time

Jesus said that it will take place 'at the close of the age' (Mt. 13: 39). Obviously, we do not know when that will be, but the day has been determined by God (Acts 17: 31). The truth that He will judge men is as certain as the fact that He saves men. The hour of reaping *will come* (Rev. 14: 14–16).

iii) Its nature

Two inter-related themes are found in biblical teaching on this subject.

First, men will be judged by their response to Christ, i.e. by their faith response. This is the dominant issue. John 3: 16–18, 5: 24, are extremely important passages in this connection. The Apostle said, 'He who does not obey the Son shall not see life, but the wrath of God rests upon him' (Jn. 3: 36). Paul also writes about the judgment which awaits those who 'do not obey the gospel of our Lord Jesus' (2 Thess. 1: 8). Those who practise merely outward and formal religion will receive the greater condemnation (Mk. 12: 38–40). The truth is expressed in its most vivid form in the *Book of Revelation* when it says that the names of those who believe in Christ are written in 'the book of life' (Rev. 3: 5, 20: 15, 21: 27).

Those who have eternal life (Jn. 5: 24) will not be brought to the kind of judgment which condemns and excludes. They will be exposed to the judgment which *reproves* and *rewards* (Rom. 14: 10–12; 1 Cor. 3: 10–15, 5: 3–5; 2 Cor. 5: 10).

Secondly, men will be judged by their attitude to life, i.e. what they actually do. Jesus insisted that man will be repaid 'for what he has done' (Mt. 16: 27). Man cannot be saved by works (i.e. his own moral achievements), but he will certainly be accountable to God for his behaviour on earth. How we live among men is not a matter on which God is indifferent and unconcerned (Rev. 20: 12, 13). For example, we are accountable for our attitude and response to those in need (Mt. 25: 31–46; Lk. 14: 14).

Of course, judgment is obviously related to our opportunity. And obviously, some people have been given better opportunities than others. Opportunity clearly implies more responsibility. This is why Jesus said it would be far more tolerable for some Gentile cities in the day of judgment than for a town like Capernaum that had been given repeated spiritual opportunities but had ignored them because of arrogance and pride (Lk. 10: 13–15). A city notorious for its evil would find it 'more tolerable on the day of judgment' than the community which had persistently refused to heed the merciful and warning words of Christ's messengers (Mt. 10: 14, 15).

iv) Its universality
Nobody will escape the judgment of Christ. He will 'judge the living and the dead' (2 Tim. 4: 1). 'Every man' will be repaid (Mt. 16: 27). All nations will be judged (Mt. 25: 30; Rev. 11: 17, 18). 'Each of us shall give account of himself to God' (Rom. 14: 12). When the Lord comes it will be 'to execute judgment on *all*' (Jude 15).

v) Its finality
The teaching of the Bible on this subject certainly does not encourage belief in a 'second chance' after death. *This world* is the appointed sphere of our believing and serving opportunity. And Jesus used very definite terms when He described the experience of final judgment. He said that the righteous would go to eternal life, the unrighteous to eternal punishment (Mt. 25: 46; Mk. 9: 47, 48).

vi) Its perfection
When writing about the Coming Day, Paul described the Lord Jesus as 'the righteous judge' (2 Tim. 4: 8). Similarly, the Gospel of John contains a number of significant sayings which emphasize that Christ's judgment will be utterly just and true (Jn. 5: 30). It will not be a judgment which goes by appearances, but by realities. The omniscient God shares in it (Jn. 8: 16). The 'secrets of men' will be judged 'by Christ Jesus' (Rom. 2: 16). The hidden things

will be brought to light (1 Cor. 4: 5). Jesus said that there is nothing hidden that will not be made known in that day (Lk. 12: 2). Nobody can say it will not be fair; it will be completely just.

One aspect of this judgment emphasized in the teaching of Jesus is that there will be a number of surprises in that day. To some who clearly expect recognition the Lord Jesus will say, 'I do not know where you come from' (Lk. 13: 23–30, cf. also Mt. 25: 37–45).

vii) Its implications

The Christian views these truths with intense seriousness. The precise moment of this judgment is, of course, not known. So as far as the believer is concerned, it is always imminent; 'the Judge is standing at the doors' (Jas. 5: 9). Therefore, the judgment of Christ should do four things for us:

First, it should determine our behaviour. Day by day the believer lives in the light of Christ's return (1 Jn. 3:3) and judgment. His conduct should therefore be conditioned by the indisputable fact that one day he will answer for it (2 Cor. 5: 10). His deepest desire should be that he will be 'unblamable in holiness before our God and Father, at the coming of our Lord Jesus with all His saints' (1 Thess. 3: 13).

Secondly, it should affect our conversation. Even the Christian's speech is to be refined by this truth. He should not grumble and complain (Jas. 5: 9). He knows that many fine opportunities for edifying and God-honouring conversation are lost as valuable moments are frittered away on unprofitable gossip and destructive chatter (Mt. 12: 36, 37; Jude 15, 16).

Thirdly, it should inspire our witness. For the apostles, the greatest delight at the triumphant appearing of Christ was to bring other converts with them. They are their crown of rejoicing (Phil 4: 1; 1 Thess. 2: 19). This intensified their evangelistic concern. They also remembered the words of Christ Himself that those who acknowledge Christ before men 'the Son of Man also will acknowledge before the angels of God' (Lk. 12: 8). The reverse is also true (Lk. 12: 9). Such should be our attitude today.

Fourthly, it should demand our obedience. At the judgment, man will be reminded of the teaching of Jesus. Christ explicitly taught this; 'the word that I have spoken will be his judge on the last day' (Jn. 12: 48). Men should therefore 'listen to Him' (Lk. 9: 35). Those who rejected Christ could not bear to hear His word (Jn. 8: 43). Jesus said, 'He who is of God hears the words of God') and went on to tell his opponents, 'the reason why you do not hear them is that you are not of God' (Jn. 8: 47). It is obvious from the words of Jesus that love is the test, and love expresses itself in obedience: 'He who does not love Me does not keep My words' (Jn. 14: 24). This truth now leads naturally into our next section.

C. THE TEACHING OF JESUS CHRIST

The previous brief survey of the New Testament doctrine of the Judgment of Christ confronted us with the importance of Christ's teaching. The words of Jesus will be man's judge on the last day (Jn. 12: 48). So now it is fitting to see our Lord's role as a teacher.

Jesus was obviously in the great prophetic tradition. He was deeply conscious of His prophetic task (Lk. 4: 16–23). And He knew only too well that as the Jewish people had rejected the Old Testament prophets, so they would persecute Him (Mt. 23: 29–39; Lk. 4: 28–30).The crowds described Him as 'a great prophet' (Lk. 7: 16), and His disciples called Him 'Teacher' (Mk. 4: 38). He used similar teaching methods to those popularized by the great prophets of the Old Testament; vivid metaphors and images, and symbolic actions, sometimes called 'prophetic symbolism' (e.g. Isa. 20: 1–6; Jer. 13: 1–11, 19: 1–15, 27: 1–15; 35: 1–19; Ezek. 4: 1–5, 17).

In these 'acted sermons' the prophets were not merely using visual aids; in Hebrew thought the symbolic action was thought to *initiate* the event of which the prophet was speaking. Our Lord's action in breaking bread at the Last Supper ought to be understood in terms of prophetic symbolism. This is why He said, 'This is My Body' (Mk. 14: 22). The action was separated from the event only by hours.

Thus Jesus the Teacher gathered a group of disciples (see Isa. 8: 16) around Him in order to ensure that the truth He taught was continued. Again, this was in line with the prophetic tradition (cf. the 'sons of the prophets' in Old Testament times; 2 Kings 2: 3, 4: 1, 6: 1).

The following aspects of Christ's teaching ministry are emphasized in the New Testament:

i. Its source

Jesus openly declared that His teaching was *revealed* truth. It was a word given to Him by God for men; 'The word which you hear is not Mine but the Father's who sent Me' (Jn. 14: 24). In this sense, Christ was again in the great prophetic tradition, for the messengers of Old Testament times came with an authoritative word, 'Thus saith the Lord' (Isa. 1: 2, 10, 24; Jer. 2: 2; Ezek. 14: 4; Amos 1: 3; Mic. 6:1).

And as the truth came from God, it had to be obeyed. The true prophet had *stood* in the counsel of the Lord, *heard* His word and been *sent* by Him (Jer. 23: 18, 21, 22). Christ was uniquely conscious of this privilege and, as the only begotten Son of God, knew the authoritative word of God better than any Old Testament prophet could ever discern it. Christ had been in the presence of God from all eternity (Jn. 1: 1). He had heard God's word (Jn. 17: 8) and was sent by Him to declare it (Jn. 7: 28). The Fourth Gospel frequently records the affirmation made by Jesus that He teaches only that which He has already received from God (Jn. 8: 26, 28, 40, 12: 49, 50, 14: 24).

ii. Its form

It is interesting to see how gifted a teacher Jesus was. The Lord used a variety of effective approaches in order to communicate the message. For example, He made use of the parable on many occasions. This device had been used in Old Testament times (e.g. by Nathan before King David; 2 Sam. 12: 1–14). One of its main purposes may have been to create an acute sense of involvement. The parable forced the hearer into committing himself to a decision on the matter in question before realizing that he had passed judgment on himself.

Much of Christ's teaching is presented with the aid of vivid, yet simple word pictures, e.g. the two ways (Mt. 7: 13, 14), the two trees (Mt. 7: 16–19), the two houses (Mt. 7: 24–27), etc.

It is also interesting to note that Christ's teaching was often presented in a poetic as well as pictorial way, probably to aid memorization. C. F. Burney demonstrated many years ago that the various types of Hebrew poetry are present in the discourses of Jesus; parallelism, rhythm and rhyme. The use of these forms certainly aided the memory, and it is possible that Christ used Rabbinic teaching methods.

A more recent scholar, Professor Harald Riesenfeld, has shown that it is likely that Jesus taught and trained His disciples with the same methods as the Jewish rabbi of the day: 'In the Gospels we are shown very clearly that Jesus was a teacher, and especially in relation to His disciples. . . . He made the Twelve learn the message of the Kingdom by heart.' Good examples of Hebrew parallelism are:

> 'He that would save/his life/shall lose it:
> But he that shall lose/his life/ . . . shall save it'
>   (Mk. 8 35)

> 'There is no good tree/producing/corrupt fruit
> Nor yet a corrupt tree/producing/good fruit.'
>   (Lk. 6: 43)

In order to detect the rhythm in the teaching of Jesus it is necessary to retranslate the sayings into Aramaic, the vernacular of the first century Palestinian. Various poetical devices were used by our

Lord, and all these illustrate Christ's skill as a teacher who wanted
His words to be remembered long after His departure.

iii. Its quality

It is a mistake to think of the Lord Jesus as a 'simple' wandering
preacher and unqualified teacher. A careful study of the Gospels
shows that even His opponents recognized His skill. They were at
pains to point out that He had not been trained at the recognized
schools (Jn. 7: 15), but He amazed them all the same. They could
not deny that He knew the Old Testament extremely well and
quoted freely from all its main sections. New Testament scholars
have shown that there is evidence that He was acquainted with the
Rabbinic Hebrew such as that used in the schools of the Jewish law.
His controversies with those who set themselves against Him reveal
Him as a highly competent scholar who knew how to handle His
opponents (e.g. Lk. 20: 19–26 in addressing the Scribes and chief
priests; Lk. 20: 27–40 in discussion with the Sadducees).

iv. Its nature

We have already seen that Christ's teaching was from God. His
hearers soon recognized that it was *authoritative* (Mt. 7: 28, 29; Jn.
12: 49). Jesus claimed that His message had an eternal and abiding
value. It was *imperishable* (Mt. 24: 35; Mk. 13: 31). Furthermore, it
was *effective*. It was a word which exposed sin (Jn. 15: 22). It is
interesting to note that it was after *hearing* the teaching of Jesus
(Lk. 5: 3), as well as *seeing* the miracle (Lk. 5: 6), that Peter said,
'Depart from me, for I am a sinful man, O Lord' (Lk. 5: 8). It was a
word which produced results. Christ had only to say a word, and
what He demanded was done (Mt. 8: 8; Jn. 4: 50, 53).

Furthermore, once He had spoken man had only to hear and
believe that word fully to see a miraculous transformation in his life
(Jn. 5: 24). On hearing Him for the first time, His own fellow
townsmen at Nazareth confessed that His teaching was *gracious*
(Lk. 4: 22). But tragically, they soon rejected it when they realized
how *searching* it was (Lk. 4: 23–30; Jn. 9: 39–41).

v. Its impact

Although Jesus' teaching had these rich qualities, it was variously
received. His teaching made entirely different impressions on
different people. Some were *astonished* by it (Mt. 7: 28; Lk. 4: 32)
while others were *annoyed* by it (Lk. 4: 28, 29). Some who heard
Christ found His teaching *arresting* (Lk. 19: 47, 48), but many of His
contemporaries found it *irritating*, so much so that they made plans
to destroy Him (Jn. 11: 45–53, 18: 19–23).

The teaching naturally produced different results in people
according to their own spiritual sensitivity and obedience—or lack

of it. Jesus described some of His contemporaries as 'faithless' (Mk. 9: 19). On another occasion He linked the theme of 'unbelief' with that of ignorance when He told His hearers that they knew 'neither the Scriptures nor the power of God' (Mk. 12: 24). His congregations, therefore, had in them those who minimized what God could do and ignored what God had said (faithless)—as well as those who had faith.

There were occasions, of course, when even the disciples were baffled by what Christ taught (Mt. 16: 5–12; Jn. 6: 60). At other times they totally misunderstood His sayings (Jn. 6: 41, 42). There were occasions when those who listened to Christ failed to grasp His meaning because they constantly thought in materialistic categories. There are several examples of this in John's Gospel (e.g. Jn. 2: 20, 21, 3: 4, 4: 11, 31–33).

vi. Its content

Obviously, it is impossible to do justice to the teaching of Jesus in a few paragraphs. Sometimes a series of great theological truths can be found in a sentence or two. He did not waste words. We cannot even summarize the teaching adequately, but the following subjects will at least illustrate something of the immense variety found in it and indicate something of its astonishing range. The list is far from exhaustive. But it is important to see that the Lord Jesus had important things to say about:

Anxiety　　Mt. 6: 25–33; Lk. 12: 11, 12, 22–31.
Assurance　　Jn. 5: 24, 10: 14, 28.
Baptism　　Mt. 3: 15, 28: 19.
Behaviour　　Lk. 6: 43–45, 17: 1, 2.
Children　　Mk. 9: 36, 37, 42, 10: 13–16.
Commitment　　Mt. 7: 13, 14; Lk. 9: 57–62, 16: 13.
Correction　　Lk. 17: 3; Jn. 15: 2.
Criticism　　Mt. 7: 1–5; Lk. 6: 24–26.
Dependence　　Jn. 15: 4, 5.
Destructive speech　　Mt. 12: 33–37.
The Devil　　Lk. 10: 17, 18, 22: 31; Jn. 8: 44, 16: 11.
Discernment　　Mt. 7: 6.
Discipleship　　Mt. 8: 18–22, 10: 37–42, 13: 44–46, 16: 24–26;
　　　　　　Mk. 8: 34, 35, 10: 28–31; Lk. 9: 23, 24, 57–62,
　　　　　　14: 25–35; Jn. 12: 25, 26.
Disobedience　　Jn. 3: 36.
Divorce　　Mt. 19: 3–9; Mk. 10: 2–12; Lk. 16: 18.
Eternal Life　　Jn. 3: 14–16, 36, 5: 24, 6: 27, 40, 47, 54, 8: 51,
　　　　　　10: 27–29, 11: 25, 26, 17: 2, 3, 20: 31.
Eternal Security　　Lk. 10: 20, 12: 32; Jn. 10: 27–29.
Exclusiveness　　Mk. 9: 38–40; Lk. 9: 49, 50.

Faith   Mt. 17: 19–22; Mk. 1: 15, 5: 34–36, 9: 23, 11: 22–24;
            Lk. 17: 5, 6; Jn. 8: 24, 11: 25, 26, 12: 46, 20: 29.
Fasting   Mt. 6: 16–18; Mk. 9: 28, 29.
Forgiveness   Mt. 6: 14, 15, 18: 23–35; Mk. 2: 5–12, 11: 25;
            Lk. 6: 37, 7: 40–47, 17: 3, 4.
Freedom   Jn. 8: 31–36.
Fruitfulness   Jn. 12: 24, 15: 2–8, 16.
The Future   Mt. 22: 23–33, 24: 1–44; Mk. 13: 3–27; Lk.
            20: 27–40.
Generosity   Lk. 6: 38, 14: 12–14.
Giving   Mt. 6: 2–4; Mk. 12: 41–44; Lk. 6: 38; Acts 20: 35.
God's Word   Lk. 8: 11–21, 16: 16, 17, 21: 33.
Heaven   Jn. 14: 1–4.
Hell   Mk. 9: 43–48.
His Own Continuing Presence   Mt. 18: 20, 28: 20.
Holy Spirit   Mt. 10: 20; Lk. 11: 13, 12: 12, 24: 49; Jn. 3: 5, 8,
            7: 37–39, 14: 16, 17, 25, 26, 15: 26, 16: 7–15,
            20: 22; Acts 1: 4–8.
Human response to the Gospel   Mt. 13: 1–23; Mk. 4: 1–20; Lk.
            8: 4–15.
Humility   Mt. 18: 1–4, 20: 25–27; Mk. 9: 33–37, 10: 42–44;
            Lk. 9: 46–48, 14: 7–11, 17: 7–10, 18: 9–14, 22:
            24–27.
Hypocrisy   Mt. 23: 1–36; Lk. 12: 1–3.
Impurity   Mt. 15: 1–20; Lk. 11: 37–41.
The Kingdom   Mk. 1: 15, 10: 15, 23–27, 12: 28–34; Lk. 7: 28,
            11: 2.
The Law   Mt. 5: 17–48, 9: 14–17.
Love   Mt. 7: 12, 22: 35–40; Lk. 6: 32–36, 10: 25–37; Jn.
            13: 14, 15, 34, 35, 15: 12–17.
Marriage   Mk. 10: 6–9.
Mission   Mt. 28: 19, 20; Mk. 16: 15–18; Lk. 24: 47, 48;
            Jn. 4: 35–38, 10: 16, 20: 21.
New Birth   Jn. 3: 1–8.
Obedience   Mt. 7: 21–27, 12: 50, 21: 28–32, 28: 20; Mk.
            3: 31–35; Lk. 6: 46–49, 11: 27, 28.
Opposition   Mt. 13: 24–30; Lk. 11: 23.
Partnership   Jn. 4: 36–38.
Peace   Jn. 14: 27, 16: 33.
Persecution   Mt. 10: 16–30.
Possessions   Mt. 19: 23–26; Mk. 10: 23–27; Lk. 12: 13–21,
            18: 18–30.
Prayer   Mt. 6: 1, 5–13, 7: 7–11, 9: 38, 18: 19; Mk. 9: 18, 28,
            29, 11: 22–25; Lk. 11: 1–13, 18: 1–8; Jn. 14: 13, 14,
            15: 7, 16, 16: 23.

Pride   Lk. 16: 14, 15, 18: 9–14.
Priorities   Mt. 6: 19–24, 22: 35–40; Mk. 8: 36, 37, 12: 28–34;
              Lk. 9: 25, 12: 31–34, 14: 16–24; Jn. 6: 27.
Rebellion   Lk. 11: 47–52.
Relationships   Mt. 18: 15–22; Mk. 9: 50.
Repentance   Mk. 1: 15; Lk. 13: 1–5, 15: 7, 10.
Responsibility   Mt. 18: 5, 6, 10–14; Mk. 4: 25, 12: 13–17;
              Lk. 10: 13–16, 12: 48, 19: 11–27.
Rewards   Mk. 9: 41, 10: 29, 30.
Sabbath   Mt. 12: 1–14; Mk. 2: 23–28; Lk. 6: 1–11, 13: 10–17.
Salvation   Lk. 15: 1–32, 19: 9, 10.
Service   Mt. 9: 37, 38, 25: 14–40; Lk. 9: 62, 10: 2–12.
Sin   (i)   Its inwardness (Mk. 7: 14–23).
          (ii)   Its seriousness, e.g. the three worst offences are:
                  to attribute the compassionate works of Christ to
                  the Devil (Mt. 12: 22–32; Lk. 11: 15; Jn. 7: 20),
                  to say that Christ was possessed by the Devil (Mk.
                  3: 22), to persist in unbelief when confronted with
                  the offer of mercy (Jn. 3: 17–20). Unbelief is the
                  greatest sin (Jn. 3: 18, 16: 9).
Sincerity   Mt. 7: 15–20.
Stewardship   Lk. 16: 1–12.
Success   Mt. 13: 31, 32.
Unity of Christians   Jn. 17: 20–23.
Witnessing   Mt. 28: 19, 20; Mk. 5: 18–20, 8: 38; Lk. 9: 26.
Worship   Jn. 4: 21–24.

To study Christ's teaching is our finest education. To understand it is our highest privilege. To obey it is our greatest responsibility. To share it is to bring others to lasting joy. What a man was this one called Jesus! He was the Son of God.

3. GOD IS A SPIRIT

Of the three persons of the Godhead, it is the person and work of the Holy Spirit which is the most difficult to understand. We can appreciate the person of Jesus Christ. Even though His incarnation is something of a mystery, He is bone of our bone and flesh of our flesh. Thus we have common ground of understanding. We can conceive of God the Father, though He is 'in light inaccessible', 'whom no man can approach unto' (1 Tim. 6: 16). We have fathers of our own and may ourselves be fathers. And so again, we have some common area for our understanding, naïve though our concepts may be. But there is mystery about the Holy Spirit that leaves us baffled. We seem to 'clutch the inviolable shade'. He seems ethereal and perhaps even somewhat frightening.

Jesus underscored this mystery of the Spirit when in John 14: 17

He said, 'The Spirit . . . the world cannot receive, because it does
not see Him.' To the Christian, however, He is known. This is true
because *He is experienced.* The fact that He is invisible does not make
Him any less real. Moreover, the importance of a proper understanding of the Holy Spirit cannot be overemphasized. Here are
some reasons for that statement:

First, He is God with us here and now. The Father and the Son
are in one sense in another dimension. The Bible says, 'Our Father
which art *in heaven,*' 'Jesus, whom *the heaven* must receive' (Acts 3: 21).
They are, as we say, transcendent, i.e. beyond the time-space
dimension. But the Spirit is on earth. He is with and in us *in this life.*
Or, as we say, He is immanent (Jn. 14: 16, 17).

Secondly, it is through the activity of the Spirit that we know both
the Father and the Son. Indeed, without the Spirit we cannot
comprehend spiritual things at all. He has come from that other
dimension and He alone is competent to reveal what belongs to that
realm. Without the Spirit, we are in spiritual darkness (1 Cor.
2: 11, 12).

Thirdly, We are dependent on the Spirit for everything in our
Christian life. 'Without Me you can do nothing,' said our Lord
(Jn. 15: 5). We are but tiny branches of Christ. He is the great
Vine. We cannot live apart from Him. And the life-giving power
that flows from Him to us is the Holy Spirit. No branch can live
without that flow of power. We must, therefore, understand clearly
who this One is and what is His relation to God, to Jesus, to the
Christian and to the world.

a. THE NATURE OF THE HOLY SPIRIT

i. The Holy Spirit is a person

It might not always appear from the Old Testament that the Holy
Spirit is a person. The word 'spirit', both in Hebrew and Greek, is
the same as the word 'wind' or 'breath'. So the Spirit of the Lord
might be translated as 'the breath of the Lord.' Thus the Spirit
might seem to be only a Divine quality or influence. Some groups
regard the Spirit as being just this. Yet there are certain Old
Testament passages which clearly point to the Spirit as being
personal and distinct from Jehovah himself (Isa. 63: 10, 14).

But it is when we come to the New Testament that we see made
explicit what is only implicit in the Old Testament. *First,* the Holy
Spirit is always referred to as 'him' and not as 'it'. Although the
words 'the Spirit' are neuter in New Testament Greek, the pronoun
used for the Spirit is always in the masculine and so must be translated 'he' and 'him' (Jn. 14: 16, 17, 26, 15: 26, 16: 7, 8, 13, 14).

Secondly, the Spirit is continually shown as acting in a personal
manner. For example, He lives with us and in us; He teaches,

witnesses, reproves, speaks, guides and prays for us (Jn. 16: 13; Rom. 8: 14, 26). He glorifies Christ (Jn. 16: 14). These are not things done by a mere influence.

Thirdly, the Spirit is acted upon as a person. He can be lied to, grieved, resisted. On the other hand, He can be received and known (Jn. 14: 17, 20, 22; Acts 5: 3, 7: 51; Eph. 4: 30).

ii. The Holy Spirit is a divine person

This truth is evident from the *titles* used for the Spirit. He is called the 'Spirit of God' in contradistinction to the 'spirit of man'. He is the 'Spirit of Christ' (Rom. 8: 9), the 'Spirit of life in Christ Jesus' (Rom. 8: 2). He is the 'Eternal Spirit' (Heb. 9: 14). He is the 'Spirit of God' (1 Cor. 2: 11). He is 'the Spirit of Him who makes alive our mortal bodies' (Rom. 8: 11). He is the 'Holy Spirit' (Rom. 9: 1). These are obviously titles of deity or pertaining to deity. Thus they point to the fact that the Spirit is actually in the Godhead.

It is also evident from the close association of the Spirit with the Father and the Son that He is deity. It is quite false to say that trinitarian formulæ do not appear in Scripture. As we have seen earlier, they appear in the baptismal words of Matthew 28: 19, where the Spirit is placed in unity with the Father and Son in the one 'Name'. And as previously pointed out we also see this principle set forth in the benediction of 2 Corinthians 13: 14; where the three persons are on the same level of divinity.

This association is clear in our Lord's references in John 14: 17, 21 and 23. The Spirit comes to indwell the believer, but this involves both Christ and the Father indwelling. So close is the association that where the Spirit is, there is the entire Godhead.

Again, the Father is said to send the Spirit in the Son's name. But the Son is also said to send the Spirit from the Father. We therefore speak of the Spirit as proceeding from the Father and the Son, so as to realize their Presence with us. In Revelation 1: 4, 5 the Holy Spirit in His sevenfold activity is the author of grace and peace together with both the Father and the Son.

To lie to the Spirit is tantamount to lying to God (Acts 5: 3, 4), and to hear the message of Christ to the churches is to hear what the Spirit says to them (Revelation chapters 2 and 3). This is sufficient evidence that the Bible teaches both the personality and deity of the Spirit and His coequality with the Father and the Son.

b. THE WORK OF THE HOLY SPIRIT

The Bible is full of the activity of God, and this activity always involves the work of the Holy Spirit. This truth appears from Genesis to Revelation. Scripture does not so much define the *being* of the Spirit as it recounts His *activities*. God the Almighty is seen as active through His Spirit in creation (Gen. 1: 2) and in all historical and natural processes. In the biblical view, things do not happen by chance or blind processes. All is seen as the result of Divine initiative and activity; 'of Him and through Him and to Him are all things' (Rom. 11: 36). And the divine agent or executive in the activities of God in the universe is the 'Spirit of the Lord'.

i. The work of Holy Spirit in the Old Testament

i) The role of the Spirit in creation

Scripture does not tell us by what natural process things were created. But it does tell us by what power. 'In the beginning *God* created' (Gen. 1: 1). The power behind the entire universe is God. Involved were the three persons of the trinity; God the Father-Creator (Gen. 1: 1); God the Son-Creator (Jn. 1: 3; Col. 1: 16; Heb. 1: 2), and God the Spirit-Creator (Gen. 1: 2; Job 26: 13). The Spirit is seen like a bird, hovering or brooding or like a great wind, that moves on the inchoate mass of matter to bring to it order and life. Moreover, the creation of human life is attributed to the activity of the Spirit, as well as the maintenance of all natural life (Job 33: 4; cf. Gen. 1: 26, 2: 7; Psa. 104: 30).

ii) The work of the Spirit in redemption

In Exodus 3 God appears in the form of the 'angel of the Lord' who has 'come down to deliver' the enslaved people (Exod. 3: 2, 8). Subsequent chapters show Him bringing them out of Egypt and through the Red Sea, leading them in the wilderness by a pillar of cloud and fire. This manifestation of God is the 'angel of His presence' (Isa. 63: 9). And God's Presence is to be equated with the Holy Spirit. It is He who brings them out of the sea, leads them and causes them to rest (Isa. 63: 11, 14).

iii) The role of the Spirit in inspiration

Throughout the Old Testament the Spirit is shown as enduing individuals with special powers and gifts. Examples are Joseph (Gen. 41: 38), Moses (Num. 11: 17), the elders of Israel (Num. 11: 25, 26), Joshua (Num. 27: 18; Deut. 34: 9), Bezaleel (Exod. 31: 2, 3, 35: 30, 31), the judges (Jdgs. 3: 10, 6: 34), the prophets and the kings (1 Sam. 3: 19, 10: 10, 16: 13).

The people of Israel were the people of God. Their kingdom was a theocracy and God dwelt among them as their King. The Holy Spirit was, therefore, active amongst them; not only in a general sense but in special ways and through special people. They were to be a people formed, led and taught by the Holy Spirit. Thus their leaders were to be men *filled* with the Spirit. This applied particularly to the prophets who were anointed and inspired for their work. (Isa. 61: 1; Ezek. 2: 2, 8: 3, 11: 24, etc; 2 Pet. 1: 21).

iv) The role of the Spirit in the Messiah and the Messianic Kingdom (Isa. 11: 1, 2, 42: 1)

The age-long vision of the Jewish people and the prophets of Israel was of the advent of one on whom the Spirit of the Lord would rest in a special manner. He was seen as one who would be the King-Deliverer, possessing in the highest degree the qualities and offices of both Prophet and Priest. It would be the Holy Spirit who would endow Him with such gifts. The very name 'Messiah' means 'Anointed One' and refers to the anointing of the Spirit. This also pointed to a universal outpouring of the Spirit (Isa. 32: 15, 44: 3; Joel 2: 28; Acts 2: 16, 17). It is spoken of as being primarily upon the 'house of Israel' (Ezek. 39: 29), although finally 'it will come upon all flesh' (Joel 2: 28–32).

ii. The Holy Spirit in the New Testament

In addition to what has been said above, the New Testament reveals the Holy Spirit in a threefold relationship;

First, to Jesus Christ—the Messiah.

Secondly, to the believing community over which Christ is Lord.

Thirdly, to the world which is unbelieving and does not acknowledge Jesus as Lord.

i) The relation of the Spirit to Jesus Christ

In fulfilment of the Old Testament—and as of one who is God manifest in the flesh—our Lord Jesus appears in a special relationship to the Holy Spirit. This is evident through His incarnate life in the following ways;

First, He was conceived by the action of the Spirit. (Mt. 1: 20; Lk. 1: 35). John the Baptist was filled with the Spirit in his mother's womb, but the Messiah was conceived as a human being by direct action of the Spirit coming upon the Virgin Mary. Jesus was, therefore, God incarnate. No human father was involved and Jesus did not acknowledge Joseph as His father (Lk. 1: 34, 2: 48, 49).

Secondly, He was anointed with the Spirit for His ministry (Lk. 3: 22). Divine Son of God though He was, He needed to be anointed with the Spirit for three reasons:

(1) To fulfil the prophecy of Isaiah 61: 1 as anointed Messiah.

(2) To declare the unity of the Godhead and His dependence as a true man on the Divine power.

(3) To be an example for all believers who would follow Him.

Thus we have His reference to anointing in His sermon at Nazareth (Lk. 4: 16–21) and God's attestation of favour towards Him (Acts 2: 22, 10: 38).

Thirdly, He lived and worked in the power of the Holy Spirit.

Jesus was 'led by the Spirit' (Lk. 4: 1, 14). He spoke in the authority of the Spirit (Lk. 4: 32; Acts 1: 2). He acted in the power of the Spirit (Mt. 12: 28). We thus see absolute co-operation between Father, Son and Spirit in every detail of the life of Christ and an interpenetration at every point of the human activities of Jesus by the Divine Spirit.

Fourthly, He offered Himself as the sacrifice for sin through the energy of the Spirit (Heb. 9: 14). This is a mysterious truth. The sacrifice was one of the whole personality of the Son, penetrated and energized by the Spirit of God.

Fifthly, He rose in the power of the Spirit (Rom. 1: 4, 8: 11). The Divine energy that made possible the resurrection was that of the Holy Spirit.

Sixthly, He lives to impart the Spirit to others. The prophecy was given by John the Baptist (Lk. 3: 16). The symbol was shown in the upper room after the Resurrection when Jesus breathed upon them (Jn. 20: 22). It was confirmed by Christ's own promise (Acts 1: 5). It was expounded by His teaching while on earth (Jn. 14: 16, 26, 15: 26). By our Lord's own words we understand that the Spirit is sent not only by the Father but also by Christ the Son.

Indeed, the relation of Christ to the Spirit is the key to vital Christianity. It brings the believer into living union with Christ (1 Cor. 6: 17; Eph. 3: 16, 17) and joins the believing fellowship to Christ as a body to a head (1 Cor. 12: 12, 13) and as a building to a foundation (Eph. 2: 20–22). The Spirit is thus shown to be the uniting and animating presence between the risen Christ in heaven and believers on earth.

The relation of the Spirit to Christ is part of the mystery of the inner unity of the Holy Trinity spoken of in John 17: 21, 22. It is a unique relationship, a mystery beyond human comprehension. But since the Son becomes Man and is the Messiah, this relationship both fulfils the Old Testament prophecies and lays the basis for the relationship between the Spirit and the messianic community which is the Church.

ii) The relation of the Spirit to the Christian believer

'The Holy Spirit is the only means of guaranteeing religion as personal communion with God. He is the unique and ultimate Fact and Force in Christianity' (W. Griffith Thomas).

In the work of the Spirit in relation to Conversion there is a sixfold activity:

1) *The convicting work of the Spirit* (Jn. 16: 7–11). What is meant here is that He brings to light certain facts hitherto unrealized and presents them to the mind and conscience in such a way that

they cannot be ignored. The particular issues are sin, righteousness and judgment. This was evident on the day of Pentecost (Acts 2: 37) and is the basis of every true conversion.

2) *The enlightening work of the Spirit*. Natural man is in spiritual darkness, i.e. in ignorance of and separated from God. He cannot know God nor understand the things of God. They are foolishness to him. The work of the Spirit is to enlighten one and bring him to the knowledge of God. The darkness of the natural man is emphasized over and again in the New Testament (Rom. 1: 21; 2 Cor. 4: 4 and Eph. 5: 8, and especially 1 Cor. 2: 14, 16).

The enlightening work of the Spirit is described as similar to what He did at creation (Gen. 1: 2, 3; 2 Cor. 4: 6). But this time it is in the darkness of the human mind that He works (1 Cor. 2: 10–14; Eph. 1: 17, 18; 1 Thess. 1: 5). This enlightening usually comes through the preaching of the Gospel, and in fulfilment of our Lord's words, involves a supernatural work by which the Father and Son are revealed to us (Jn. 16: 14). Without this enlightenment no one can be saved.

3) *The regenerating work of the Spirit*. The state of the unregenerate man is plainly stated in Scripture. He is described as 'dead in trespasses and sins' (Eph. 2: 1, 5; Col. 2: 13), as alienated from the life of God, without God and without Christ (Eph. 2: 12; Col. 1: 21).

The need of the unregenerate man is clear (Jn. 3: 3, 7). A new birth is essential if he is to enter the kingdom of heaven or ever 'see' it. Jesus stated the manner of regeneration (Jn. 3: 5, 6). It is a work of the Holy Spirit analogous to physical generation. This comes through the Word spoken by God to us, which has both a cleansing and quickening effect; 'Faith comes by hearing and hearing by the Word of God' (Jn. 6: 63; Rom. 10: 17; Tit. 3: 5). The Old Testament also implies and illustrates this act of regeneration (Ezek. 36: 25–27; 37: 8–10).

4) *The sealing work of the Spirit*. Jesus spoke of Himself as having been 'sealed' by the Father (Jn. 6: 27). This evidently refers to His reception of the Spirit at His baptism and heavenly testimony to His sonship. Christians also are spoken of as being 'sealed' (Eph. 1: 13). It is interesting to note that sacrificial lambs were sealed with the temple seal after careful inspection to certify them fit for sacrifice or food. Moreover, in New Testament days merchandise when bought was stamped with the purchaser's seal pending transportation to its final destination. These two procedures provide the background for New Testament truth about the sealing of the Holy Spirit.

Sealing involves three things in the New Testament;

Faith (Eph. 1: 13). When a person hears the 'word of truth' and it results in that person believing in Christ, it immediately results in the sealing of the Spirit. Sealing is the committal of the Father to a person when he makes his committal to the Son. Further, it involves the gift of the Spirit. This results in assurance (Rom. 8: 16).

Holiness (Eph. 4: 30; 2 Tim. 2: 19). The sealing is the presence of the Spirit. Sin is the grieving of the Spirit, which mars the seal. As holiness is the nature of the Spirit, it becomes the hallmark of one who possesses the Spirit. The seal on the forehead of the Old Testament High Priest had the inscription: 'Holiness unto the Lord'.

Guarantee. The term 'seal' is connected with the word 'earnest' (2 Cor. 1: 21, 22; Eph. 1: 13, 14). By the sealing of the Spirit the believer is given a divine 'deposit' against the day of final purchase. The Spirit is the guarantee of divine ownership and preservation unto glory.

5) *The baptism of the Spirit.* This truth is first referred to by John the Baptist (Mt. 3: 11). Then it was confirmed by our Lord (Acts 1: 4, 5) with reference to the initial enduement of the Spirit at Pentecost. Basically, it is *the receiving of the Spirit* by the believer (Acts 2: 38; 1 Cor. 12: 13). It is analogous to 'being made to drink into the one Spirit'. *It is thus experienced by all true believers.*

It is also *the act and experience whereby the believer is united with Christ* and incorporated into the Body of Christ (1 Cor. 12: 13; Gal. 3: 27, 28). Further, it involves *reception of power*, since the Spirit is the powerful presence of God in us (Acts 1: 5, 8). It occurs at conversion to *all* believers.

6) *The re-creating work of the Spirit.* The New Birth gives the believer a new nature and a new life in which we are re-created in the image of God. This is the direct work of the Spirit (Rom. 8: 1, 2, 9, 10; 2 Cor. 5: 17). The gift of the Spirit imparts a new principle of life which delivers one from sin and death and opens the way to a 'new creation'.

iii) The work of the Spirit in relation to communion or fellowship

First, fellowship with God is made possible by the work of Christ, but made vital by the work of the Spirit. 'Our fellowship is with the Father and with His Son Jesus Christ' (1 Jn. 1: 3). How close and intimate this is can be seen from our Lord's teaching; 'My Father will love him and we will come unto him and make our abode with him' (Jn. 14: 23). This fellowship is only possible, however, because of the Spirit who abides in the believer and

makes real to him the presence of God the Father and the Son
(Jn. 14: 16, 18; 1 Jn. 3: 24). Access to God is through Christ, i.e.
access into favour and acceptance with God (Rom. 5: 2). And by
the Spirit we have access into the very presence of God in *personal
communion* (Eph. 2: 18). The intimacy of this is marvellous (Rom.
8: 15).

Secondly, fellowship with one another is based on our fellowship
with God and is of the same kind (Jn. 14: 20, 17: 21, 22). The
type of union that exists in the Triune Godhead—and also the
kind of union that prevails between Christ and believers—is to
exist between believers as well. And this is made possible only by
the indwelling of the Holy Spirit (2 Cor. 13: 14; Phil. 2: 1). This
was evident at Pentecost where the filling of the Spirit resulted in
believers being of one heart and one soul (lit. 'one flame') and being
'together' in fellowship (Acts 2: 1–4, 38, 42, 44, 4: 31, 32).

The fellowship of the Spirit within believers is therefore:

(1) *Like the fellowship of the godhead* (Jn. 17: 21);
(2) *Supernatural*, from heaven 'It sat upon each of them' (Acts
    2: 3);
(3) *Abiding*, 'They continued steadfastly in the fellowship'
    (Acts 2: 42);
(4) *Universal*, i.e. involved all the redeemed (Acts 10: 45–47,
    11: 16, 17; 1 Cor. 12: 13);
(5) *Indivisible* (1 Cor. 1: 12, 13; Eph. 4: 3–6).

This great uniting work of the Spirit is the power that creates
the Body of Christ (1 Cor. 12: 13).

iv) The work of the Spirit in relation to Christian life and character

First, the Spirit indwells believers. In contrast to our Lord, who
was only *with* His disciples, the Spirit is both *with* us and *in* us. In
contrast to external influences or objective truths, the Spirit
indwells both the personalities and bodies of all believers. This is
a mystery, but is the secret of dynamic and experiential Christianity. Note:

(1) *The Gospel statements*. 'He shall be in you' and 'I in you'
    (Jn. 14: 17, 20).
(2) *The Acts experience*. The entire Book of Acts implies the fact
    of the Spirit's indwelling and filling (Acts 2: 4).
(3) *The Epistolary teaching*. The body of the Christian is a shrine
    in which the Holy Spirit lives. The Christian fellowship is a
    temple of the Spirit (Rom. 8: 9–11; 1 Cor. 3: 16, 6: 19;
    2 Cor. 6: 16; Gal. 4: 4–6).

The Spirit is sent forth into our hearts as the Son was sent forth into the world. The effect of this is marked (Jas. 4: 5; 1 Jn. 3: 24). The Spirit dwells in us as custodian. He gives assurance of the presence of Christ. The personal indwelling of the Spirit is the dynamic of the Christian life.

Secondly, the Spirit assures believers. One of the great emphases of the first epistle of John is that 'we know' (1 Jn. 4: 13). The New Testament evidence of true Christian experience was the gift of the Holy Spirit. Hence the question asked of the disciples of John the Baptist in Acts 19: 2.

(1) *The assurance is inward.* The witness of the Spirit with our spirit (Rom. 8: 15, 16).
(2) *The assurance is outward.* This is the confession that Jesus is Lord and the 'manifestation of the Spirit, given to every man' (1 Cor. 12: 3, 7). This fulfils the promise of our Lord in reference to His ascension and the gift of the Spirit when He said, 'In that day you shall *know.*'

Thirdly, the Spirit sanctifies believers. Sanctification means 'setting apart', and it must be seen as twofold. It is initially *Positional and Instant*, i.e. the setting apart of the redeemed person to belong to the Lord for His possession and use. In this sense it has affinity to the 'sealing' of the Spirit, who by His indwelling marks and possesses us for the Lord (1 Cor. 6: 11; 2 Thess. 2: 13; 2 Tim. 2: 19; 1 Pet. 1: 2). This sanctification has nothing to do with inherent holiness. It is the position of the believer through grace alone. But secondly, sanctification is *Personal and Progressive*. The work of the Spirit is to make us in character what we already are 'in Christ'. So He continually convicts and enlightens concerning sin, enables repentance, wars against indwelling sin, applies forgiveness, delivers us from the power of our carnal self and creates within us new desires and a new nature. This, of course, depends on our co-operation (Rom. 8: 1–10, 12–14; Gal. 5: 16–25; Eph. 5: 8, 9).

Fourthly, the Spirit empowers believers. The word for 'Spirit' suggests 'powerful wind or breath'; and since the Spirit is the breath of the Almighty God, His presence is always associated with power. This appears in the Old Testament as well as in the ministry of Christ. (Micah 3: 8; Lk. 4: 14; Acts 10: 38.)

(1) *The promise* of this power is clearly given in Luke 24: 49 and Acts 1: 8.
(2) *The experience* of this power is described in Acts 2: 4, 12, 37, 43; 4: 31, 33; 6: 10; etc.

(3) *The exposition* of this power is given in such passages as
   Romans 8: 11, 15: 13, 19; 1 Corinthians 2: 4; Ephesians
   1: 19, 3: 16, 20.

The power of the Spirit is given for effective witness, but also for
spiritual grace, knowledge, victory in spiritual conflict, help in
physical weaknesses and for the fullness of spiritual living.

Fifthly, the Spirit teaches and guides believers. The specific
promise of this was given by our Lord in His teaching about the
Spirit (Jn. 15: 26, 16: 13, 14). The sequence is that He shall
speak, shall teach, shall bring to remembrance all Christ has said,
shall guide into all truth, shall show things to come, shall 'receive
of mine and show it to you' and 'shall testify of me'. All this the
Spirit did inspiring the apostles in the writing of Scripture and
teaching believers in every age.

The nature of this work is described in Ephesians 1: 17–19.
He is the Spirit of wisdom and revelation, who enlightens the
eyes of our heart so that we can 'know' spiritual truths. This is
basic to all Christian growth and is essential because of the inability of our natural minds to understand the 'things of God'
(1 Cor. 2: 9–16). The Spirit is called 'the anointing which we
have received from God' who 'teaches us all things and is truth'
(1 Jn. 2: 27). In the Old Testament (Isa. 11: 2) the Spirit who
rests on the Messiah is the Spirit of wisdom and understanding.
The Messiah imparts that same Spirit to believers as an 'anointing' in order to teach them (1 Jn. 2: 20, 21, 27). So He is called
'the Spirit of Truth' as opposed to the 'spirit of error' (Jn. 14: 17,
16: 13; 1 Jn. 4: 3, 6).

Sixthly, the Spirit prays for and in believers. Christ prays for us
in the heavenly realm (Heb. 7: 25). He is the advocate with the
Father (1 Jn. 2: 1). The Spirit prays for us on the earthly plane,
matching His intercessions with those of Christ. He is the advocate
with us (Jn. 14: 16). The word 'comforter' is the same as 'advocate' meaning 'one who stands alongside to help'. He prays *for* us
because of our human frailty and ignorance. Actually, we do not
know how to pray. But God, who searches hearts, knows the mind
of the Spirit and the Spirit prays for us according to God's will
(Rom. 8: 26, 27).

He prays within us. Since He dwells in us, He prays in us, and
by His mighty intercessions He absorbs our frail prayers so that
we learn to pray not in the flesh but in the Spirit, i.e. under His
powerful influence and control. Hence the phrase 'praying in the
Spirit' (Rom. 8: 15, 27; Eph. 6: 18; Jude 20).

Seventhly, the Spirit renews believers. What is begun at conversion is continued throughout the Christian life. Regeneration is the

imparting of new life. Sanctification is the increasing and perfecting of this new life, by the 'renewal of the Holy Spirit'.

(1) *Renewal is the renewing of our mind* (Rom. 12: 1, 2). By nature
our way of thinking is different, indeed contrary, to God's way.
We have a 'carnal mind' which is darkened and perverted.

(2) *Renewal is the renewing of the whole man.* 'A new heart will I
give you, says the Lord.' Our nature is corrupt through deceitful
desires. Every part of the personality is affected by sin (Rom.
3: 10–18). Thus we need to be re-made throughout. Such renewing involves the putting away and constant mortification of the
old nature, i.e. the repudiation of self and the acceptance of
Christ as our new life.

(3) *Renewal is the renewing of the Divine Image* which has been
marred by sin, and the progressive transformation of the believer's character into the likeness of Christ. Renewal is the basic
process of sanctification (Jer. 17: 9; Ezek. 36: 26, 27; Mt. 15: 19;
Rom. 1: 28, 8: 7, 12: 2; 2 Cor. 3: 18, 4: 16; Eph. 4: 21–24, 5: 27;
Col. 3: 4–10; Tit. 3: 5). We will see this in more detail later.

Eighthly, the Spirit leads and guides believers. Jesus was led by
the Spirit (Lk. 4: 1). Even as the incarnate Son of God, He did
nothing of Himself but was subject to the direction of the Father
through the Spirit. It is the hallmark of the 'sons of God' that they
too are subject to the leading of the Spirit. Prophets in the Old
Testament were controlled in their actions and movements by the
Spirit. So too were the apostles in the New Testament. Both
Ezekiel and Philip are described as being caught away and carried by the Spirit. In the Acts we find the Spirit restraining or
constraining the apostles and so directing their movements. They
were in submission to His inward control. We also find the
gathered church directed in their decisions by the Spirit (Ezek.
3: 14, 24; Acts 8: 26, 29, 39, 10: 19, 20, 16: 6, 7; Rom. 8: 14).

Ninthly, the Spirit enables believers in worship. God is a Spirit
and worship is essentially an activity of the human spirit. We
must worship in spirit and in truth, draw near in heart as well
as with lips, sing with the spirit and with the understanding. For
this we obviously need the aid of the Holy Spirit (Jn. 4: 23, 24;
1 Cor. 14: 15, 16; Eph. 5: 18–20; Phil. 3: 3; Jude 20; Rev.
1: 10–17). It is interesting to note the connection between being
filled with the Spirit and singing with melody in the heart to the
Lord. Also the connection between 'in the Spirit' and seeing the
Son of Man so as to worship Him, is an essential fact to grasp.

Tenth, the Spirit exercises custodianship over believers. The
Spirit is called 'Lord'. He is also the Spirit of the Lord and His
concern is to make real the Lordship of Christ in the Christian
experience. He is also concerned to take possession of the believer

as one purchased by the sacrifice of Christ. He desires that one be kept spotless from the defilement of the world and presented spotless to Christ. His presence is the guarantee of final redemption. Furthermore, He yearns jealously over us with a love that can brook no rivalry and so is in opposition to the 'world' which ever seeks to alienate us from Christ our true bridegroom (1 Cor. 6: 19, 20; 2 Cor. 3: 17; Eph. 1: 13; Jas. 4: 4, 5).

In the eleventh and final place, the Spirit quickens the bodies of believers. It was in the power of the Spirit that Christ's body was made alive. If then He dwells in our bodies they will be affected. If Jesus lived a human life 'in the power of the Spirit' (Luke 4: 14), then we too can do so. Physical vitality and healing can be gained through the powerful activity of the Spirit within (Rom. 8: 11).

v) The relation of the Spirit to the unbelieving world

The 'world' is a different concept in Scripture from the 'earth'. To the latter the Spirit stands in relation as Creator and Sustainer of all natural life. To the former He is in a different relation. The 'world' as a system of life is spoken of as being 'without God', separate from Christ and governed by the 'god of this world', viz. the Devil. It is in a state of enmity with God.

The unbeliever, while in the relationship of a creature to the Creator-Spirit, is not in a right spiritual relation to Him. He is a 'natural man who does not receive the things of the Spirit of God' (1 Cor. 2: 14). Furthermore, he 'walks after the flesh' and 'minds the things of the flesh'. He is 'carnally minded', 'dead in trespasses and sins'. He cannot please God and does not know God.

Our Lord described the 'world' as that which 'receives not the Spirit of God, neither knows Him'. Its attitude to Him is reflected in its attitude to His followers and His Holy Spirit (Gen. 6: 3; Rom. 8: 1, 5, 7; 1 Cor. 2: 12, 14; Eph. 2: 2, 3, 12; 1 Jn. 2: 16, 17; Jude 19).

The activity of the Spirit in the world is twofold.

First, general activity. God is always active in the world in the natural processes of life as creator and sustainer. He is also active in the historical processes. His sovereign power is behind the great events of men and nations. He raises up and casts down. He works all things according to the purpose of His will. He will subdue all to Himself (Psa. 139: 7; Isa. 40: 13, 59: 19; Ezek. 1: 20, 21; Rev. 1: 4, 5: 6). Note: the 'seven Spirits' is a form of speech for the Holy Spirit in sevenfold activity, possibly based on Isaiah 11: 2, or using seven as the figure of perfection.

Secondly, specific activity. The Spirit has come to reprove the world, i.e. to present the world with certain facts in such a way that it cannot plead ignorance of them. The word 'reprove' can mean 'convince' or 'convict'. This happened, for example, on the day of Pentecost and continues to this day. By this means believers are gathered out from the world, and the unbelieving world is condemned. He convicts of three things; sin, for not believing on Christ, righteousness, because He, having died, has returned to the Father, and judgment, because Satan—the prince of this world—has been finally judged in the Cross and the Resurrection (Jn. 16: 7–11).

vi) The infilling of the Holy Spirit
The Holy Spirit is given to 'fill' believers.

First, the relation of baptism in the Spirit to filling of the Spirit. The prophecy of John the Baptist was that Jesus would baptize in the Spirit as distinct from baptizing in water. This was a reference to the Pentecostal effusion of the Spirit and immersion in the Spirit (Mt. 3: 11; Acts 1: 5, 11: 16). As pointed out, baptism in the Spirit is the dramatic initiatory action in which, at conversion, the believer receives the Spirit from the ascended Lord and is baptized into the Body of Christ, the Church. This includes *every* believer in every age who receives the Spirit by faith (1 Cor. 12: 13). The effect of being initially baptized in the Spirit is to be initially filled with the Spirit (Acts 2: 4). But subsequent *fillings* occurred again and again in apostolic experience (Acts 4: 8, 31, 13: 9, 52). It is also seen to be the experience of chosen people for special work (Exod. 31: 3, 35: 31; Judges 6: 34; 1 Sam. 10: 10; Acts 9: 17). The pattern of the Acts appears to be that of *one* baptism, at conversion, but *many* fillings of the Spirit throughout the Christian life.

Secondly, the relation of the filling of the Spirit to the Lord Jesus Christ. The Spirit was not sent to fill believers until Christ was ascended. He is associated with the glory of Christ and comes to make the glory real within the Church. The indication of the filling of the Spirit is therefore the exalting of Christ in the life (Jn. 7: 39, 16: 14; Acts 2: 33).

The words 'filled' and 'fullness' relate both to the indwelling of the Spirit and also to the Christian's relation to Christ. The Church is Christ's 'fullness', i.e. that in which Christ finds His completeness. At the same time, Christ is the Church's fullness, the One in whom we find our completeness. And this is realized by the fullness of the Spirit, both in Christ the Head and in Christians as members of His Body. And Christ also desires to fill all believers (Eph. 1: 22, 23, 5: 18; Col. 1: 19, 2: 3, 9, 10). The order is clearly given in Ephesians 5: 18. The strengthening (and infilling) of the Spirit makes real the abiding presence of

Christ, which leads to 'being filled with all the fullness of God' (Eph. 3: 16–19).

It is thus true to say that 'the filling of the Spirit is the realization of the Lordship of Christ' in the heart through surrender and faith. The believer must submit himself wholly to Christ and trust God to fill him with the Spirit (Lk. 11: 13).

Thirdly, the necessity for the filling of the Spirit.

(1) *We must be filled with something*. Nature abhors a vacuum. Ecclesiastes is the record of the attempt of man to fill his life by every means and yet the discovery that he is still empty. Hence the Lord's call and promise; 'If anyone *thirst*, let him . . . *drink*. Out of his heart shall *flow* rivers of living water' (Jn. 7: 37–39). The Spirit is the answer to man's inner thirst. 'We have been all made to drink into one Spirit' (1 Cor. 12: 13). Hence the contrast in Ephesians 5: 18 between being 'drunk with wine' and 'being filled with the Spirit'.

(2) *It is the will of God*. This is clear by the command 'Be filled with the Spirit', and again 'Walk in the Spirit' (Gal. 5: 16; Eph. 5: 18).

Fourthly, the results of the filling of the Spirit. The filling of the Spirit results in certain qualities of life, powers, virtues and expressions. The first of these in Acts was *power*, as explained above. Another is *joy*. The disciples were filled with joy and the Holy Spirit. Another is *love*, which is 'poured out in our heart' by the Holy Spirit (Rom. 5: 5). Another is *praise and worship*. At Pentecost the filling resulted in declaring the wonderful works of God in ecstatic utterances. Another is *fearlessness*; they 'spoke the Word of God with boldness'. All this is in keeping with the Lord's words that 'out of the heart the mouth speaketh'. To be filled with the Spirit is to be filled with truth, power, love, joy and every grace (Acts 1: 8, 2: 11, 4: 31, 13: 52; Rom. 5: 5; Eph. 3: 16–19, 5: 19, 20).

Fifthly, the moral effect of the filling of the Spirit. In Galatians chapter 5 there is described the warfare between the 'flesh' and the 'Spirit'. The 'works of the flesh' are the moral results of living in the power of our fallen human nature. The 'fruit of the Spirit' is the result of our living under the power of the Spirit. A tree filled with sap will bear fruit, and a life filled with the Holy Spirit will bear spiritual fruit. The ninefold 'fruit of the Spirit' (Gal. 5: 22, 23) are moral characteristics of Christ produced in the believer by virtue of that union with Christ which the Spirit makes real in his life. They are not 'works' which we strive to produce, but 'fruit' which the Spirit produces. They are the great evidences of a life filled with the Spirit. 'Victory' in the

Christian life, as it is called, is the result of the Spirit enthroning Christ as Lord within our personalities. It is His conquest over us in the war between 'flesh' and 'Spirit'. It is his 'fruit' in us displacing the 'works of the flesh', and His power in us overcoming the world, the flesh and the Devil (Rom. 8: 2–4; 1 Jn. 2: 14, 4: 4, 5: 4). It is therefore vital that through faith and commitment to Christ's Lordship we are daily filled with the Spirit.

vii) The spiritual gifts of the Spirit

It is important to distinguish between the *Gift* of the Spirit and the *gifts* of the Spirit. The Spirit is Himself the divine gift to the believer (Lk. 11: 13; Jn. 7: 39; Acts 2: 38, 10: 45). The basis on which the Spirit is given is repentance, faith and obedience (Lk. 11: 13; Acts 2: 38, 5: 32; Gal. 3: 2). This occurs at conversion to Christ when one is baptized with the Spirit.

The gifts of the Spirit are those abilities and activities by which the Spirit works and shows Himself through believers. They are described as manifestations, operations and administrations—the working of God. Nine 'charismatic' gifts are enumerated in 1 Corinthians 12. They are not natural capacities, but special endowments given by the Holy Spirit ranging from 'wisdom' to 'interpretation of tongues'. Seven 'ministry' gifts are given in Romans 12. These are again endowments of the Spirit, with less of the miraculous element in them than those in 1 Corinthians 12: 8–10. Four (or five) other gifts are given in Ephesians 4: 11, which are 'leadership' or 'office' gifts.

Gifts of the Spirit are essential for the wholesome working of the Body of Christ. The biblical principles of scriptural gifts are:

(1) Every Christian may have some gift (1 Cor. 12: 7, 14: 31).
(2) All Christians do not have all the gifts (1 Cor. 12: 29, 30).
(3) Gifts are given by the sovereign will of God (1 Cor. 12: 11).
(4) Gifts are for building up the church not for dividing it (1 Cor. 12: 25; Eph. 4: 12, 13).
(5) Gifts must be held in humility and not in envy or rivalry (Rom. 12: 3).
(6) Gifts differ in importance and value (Rom. 12: 6; 1 Cor. 12: 31, 14: 15).
(7) Gifts must be used under spiritual discipline and only if of value to the church or individual (1 Cor. 14).
(8) All gifts must be subordinate to the overriding factor of love. This is the import of 1 Corinthians 13 which comes between the two chapters on spiritual gifts.

We shall see this in more detail in the doctrine of the Church.*

* See pages 157 ff and 177 ff.

viii) The outflow of the Spirit
The effect of all this is that the Spirit should flow out. of the life
of the believer. The promise of Jesus was 'out of His inner being
shall flow rivers of living water'. The fruits of the Spirit all have
an outward reference to others. The filling of the Spirit results in
witness to others in an outflow of power and truth and love and
grace. The personality of the Christian is set free to show forth
the life of Jesus so that He is glorified through the church. This is
the great work of the Spirit (Jn. 7: 38, 39; Acts 4: 31; 2 Cor.
4: 11).

CONCLUSION TO BOOK ONE

It is now evident that the God in whom we live and move and have
our being is a great God indeed. To know Him is life's greatest
attainment; to serve Him is life's greatest achievement; to be with
Him forever is life's greatest goal. The heart of all mankind should
cry out with the Psalmist:

> As a hart longs for flowing streams,
> so longs my soul for thee, O God.
> My soul thirsts for God, for the living God.
>
> (Psa. 42: 1, 2)

BOOK II

WHAT THE BIBLE SAYS ABOUT MAN AND HIS SALVATION

The great God of the Universe, in His person and work, is incomparable. So glorious is our God that it may seem rather presumptuous to give an entire section to the doctrine of mere man. Yet man is presented in the Bible as the crown of God's creation. Moreover, as incomprehensible as it may seem, God in a very real sense became man in the person of Jesus Christ. Therefore, it is quite proper to move into this subject. We begin with:

I. THE CREATION OF MAN

1. CREATION FOR MAN'S SAKE

The Old Testament gives an importance to man quite out of proportion to his physical stature. When confronted by the vastness of the universe, the Psalmist could not but express his astonishment that in a world so immense God should nevertheless take note of him (Psa. 8: 3, 4). It is significant that while there are passages of Scripture which bear testimony to God's power and wisdom in creation, the emphasis is given not to the vastness of God's universe but to the personal care and concern which God shows to the individual.

It is true that He tells the number of the stars, but more important still He heals the broken in heart (Psa. 147: 4). It is true that He formed the mountains and created the wind, but much more He declares to man what is His thought (Amos 4: 13). It is true that He created the heavens and stretched them out, but furthermore, He gives breath to the people upon the earth and spirit to those who walk within it (Isa. 42: 5). He did not make the world a void, but formed it to be inhabited (Isa. 45: 18). Thus the story of creation reaches its climax in the creation of man (Gen. 1: 26). Clearly, the wonders of creation were not for their own sake but in order to provide a setting within which the goodness and mercy of God towards man might be displayed.

2. MAN MADE IN GOD'S IMAGE
In some respects man is like the beasts who perish (Psa. 49: 12).
There is a similarity in their characteristics. They show the same
appetites, yet there is a marked differentiation and men are essentially of a different kind. Genesis 1: 26 speaks of the divine intention
to make man 'in our image, after our likeness'. Such terms are not
intended to point to an absolute identity between God and man
(Psa. 8: 5). Rather, they point to the possibility of communication
between man and his Creator. In the fullness of his whole being,
man shares the image and likeness of God. This is the manner of
man. He was created without blemish (Ezek. 28: 12). Such was his
perfection that God who had already pronounced His creation to
be good now added the superlative as He contemplated the man
whom He had made (Gen. 1: 31).

Furthermore, it must be remembered that while the perfection
was marred it can be said of those who followed, as it has been said
of the first man, that he was made in the image and likeness of God.
Thus Adam begat a son, Seth, correspo.iding to his image and likeness even as he had first been begotten of God (Gen. 5: 3). Note,
as we must, Adam's sin involved *all* who followed. But this must not
blind our eyes. True, his descendants shared in his sin, but they still
shared in his heavenly nature with all the potentiality for converse
with the divine.

3. WALKING WITH GOD
Such potentiality is seen both in Adam and in Enoch. God walks
in the garden in the cool of the evening. His call to Adam 'Where
art thou' becomes, in view of Adam's sin, a divine interrogation.
Of course, apart from his sin, it might well have become a gracious
invitation to share God's walk and thus His fellowship. So Enoch
at a later time truly walked with God. And such was the intimacy
of their conversation that it was continued in a wider context, for
God took him and opened up to him a further and a fuller life in
spheres beyond those which hitherto he had known (Gen. 5: 24).
So too for those who followed, the earthly sphere need no more be
reckoned as setting the limits of the life of man.

4. MAN IS OF THE EARTH
The Genesis story emphasizes the close relationship between man
and the earth from which he was formed. In Hebrew the words are
cognate, *adam* (man) and *adamah* (earth). Apart from God, the
distinction could never have been made. And apart from Him, it
could not be sustained. So man is destined to return to the ground
from which he was taken, for he is a living soul only by virtue of the
divine inbreathing. When the life-spirit of God is withdrawn, his
life is no more (Gen. 2: 7, 3: 19, 18: 27, cf. 1 Cor. 15: 47). Of

this the Psalmist was only too painfully aware (Psa. 104: 29), and from this Job shrank back instinctively (Job 34: 14).

5. MAN AND WOMAN

We have spoken already of man's unique relationship with God. We turn now to his relationship with others within the created order. The differentiation of the sexes is central in original creation (Gen. 1: 27; Mk. 10: 6). Men and women are complementary each to the other. Consequently, marriage is stamped as honourable and blessed of God (Heb. 13: 4). Sexuality is thus inherent in the creation (Gen. 2: 24), and procreation is the fulfilment of God's purpose (Gen. 1: 28). Not for one moment is there the slightest suggestion of shame in such sexual relationships (Gen. 2: 25), for it is all part of the created order which God pronounces to be good (Gen. 1: 31). It is only the corruption of the divine plan that brings God's displeasure.

6. MAN AND CREATION

Man's relationship with the animal creation, although so different, is equally ordained of God. He is to exercise dominion over the animals (Gen. 1: 28; Psa. 8: 6–8). This is implied by the very act of God permitting Adam to name all the animals. This was not merely an interesting linguistic exercise to see how Adam would differentiate one species from another. To name a person or thing is to show evidence of the power which is wielded over them (2 Kings 23: 24).

Lastly, the inanimate creation is equally to serve man's needs (Gen. 1: 29). He is not to become slave of material things, for if he does God will no longer be his master (Mt. 6: 24). On the other hand, he is not to be unmindful of the material world. The preserving of the resources of nature is man's responsibility. The importance of the ecology crisis is biblically centred. He has work to do within creation that is appointed by God (Gen. 2: 15). Labour is not a curse imposed upon him as a punishment, for at this point, remember, Eden has not yet been invaded by sin. Work is a privilege, and a true son of God will be able to say, 'My Father worketh hitherto and I work'. In everything man is God's vice-regent. Through him, in this ideal setting, all things are to be kept in subjection to their Creator. Man has great responsibilities.

II. THE FALL OF MAN

An observer would be quick to note that the conditions of man's life in the succeeding years have never at any time corresponded to those described above. Therefore, any discussion of the doctrine of man must inevitably take account of the radical change which has come about. The close relationship of Genesis chapters 1 and 2 to chapter 3 serves to emphasize the change. Genesis 1 and 2 leave no room for doubt as to the beneficent character of God's creation. Genesis 3 is equally clear in attributing the change that entered the human family to action of a totally different kind on the part of man. Responsibility is fixed fairly and squarely upon man's shoulders.

It must be first noted that the prohibition relating to the tree of the knowledge of good and evil (Gen. 2: 17) does not introduce an alien element into an otherwise perfect situation. The prohibition is in accord with the true nature of the created order. It requires obedience, not for the sake of testing man's place in the divine economy but in order to emphasize what is intrinsic to his state. He owes his life to God. He has no existence apart from God's creative word and spirit, and all that is required of him is that he walks humbly within the limits of God's order and does not try to step out beyond them.

Now it is just here that the arrogance of sin is set forth. Most significantly, sin is not represented so much as a stooping to things which are base as it is seen as a reaching up to things which are forbidden. It is a stepping out of the sphere to which man rightly belongs and an attempt to enter into that sphere which belongs only to God. Yet the higher and the lower are not unrelated. The whole man was involved in this act of rebellion. In the temptation is an appeal to the sensual in that the tree seemed good for food, and to the æsthetic for it was a delight to the eyes, and to the spiritual for it was to make men wise as gods (Gen. 3: 6). Thus in the moment that man reaches up to heights which are not his, he sinks to depths which otherwise he would never have known. So does spiritual pride go along with sensual degradation, and in the very moment when he hopes to become like God he becomes aware of his shame (Gen. 3: 7).

1. SIN'S CONSEQUENCES
Far, however, from gaining more, Adam was involved in disastrous loss. In place of fellowship with God, he experiences the fear of God (Gen. 3: 10). Instead of the joy to be found in community life, there is mutual blame (Gen. 3: 12) and recrimination. Rather than enjoying the marvellous communication of life to a new generation, there is the pain and travail now characteristic of childbirth— henceforth to become proverbial (Jn. 16: 21). The service which was to be received from the animal kingdom gives place to a fierceness showing only too well that man's rebellion against the authority of God is matched by the rebellion of the creature against the authority of his master. This is expressed in the narrative by the enmity set between the serpent and the woman for all generations (Gen. 3: 14, 15).

Not even then are the full results of the fall enumerated, for they are not confined to man himself. They overflow into the environment. Man's close relationship with the soil, to which reference has already been made, is now re-emphasized in that the ground shares his penalty. Toil had not previously been a hardship. Now it is accompanied by frustration (Gen. 3: 17, 18), and the land which might have yielded plentifully is now to bring forth thorns and thistles.

Above all, there falls across the path of life the shadow of an impending death, all the more certain because its harbingers are already here (Gen. 3: 19). How greatly such unmistakable signs were to be multiplied is the burden of the chapters which follow as they trace the developing consequences of sin. Disorder in the universe and disturbance in human relationships go hand in hand. Jealousy, suspicion, hatred and murder not only arise but are perpetuated in succeeding generations. Even nature itself leaves its beneficence behind, and in the flood combines to bring upon all mankind the destruction and doom already so clearly foreshadowed.

2. THE SECOND ADAM

Genesis chapters one to three are not to be regarded as mere myth retold from generation to generation. It is not written as only an ancient legend. Rather, it is experienced in all of life. Every assessment of man's situation must take account of what is written here. It is the essence of what has occurred in the human situation. It is the starting point of all thought if it is to be marked by a sense of reality (Rom. 5: 12). Moreover, if mankind, in all its need, ever grasps a real message of hope, it must be hope of a kind which takes full account of all that is involved in Adam's fall. Adam truly fell, and all mankind has fallen with him.

But there is a message of hope—a true, thrilling message. Hope is found in the fact of a second Adam who overcame temptation in the place where the first Adam had succumbed (Mk. 1: 13). Once again the perfect image of the divine was manifested (Col. 1: 19), viz. in Jesus Christ, the Second Adam. Through Him there is given the sure and certain hope that those who are incorporate in Him will be changed into the same image from glory to glory (2 Cor. 3: 18). This we shall see in considerably more detail later as we study what the Bible says about the 'atonement'.

III. THE ESSENTIAL NATURE OF MAN SINCE THE FALL

'What is man?' (Psa. 8: 4). The question has intrigued the human race in every generation. The Bible does not set out to present a systematic treatment of the subject, nor does the theme necessarily occupy a central place in Scripture. But many important things are said, and an understanding of the biblical doctrine of man will enable us better to appreciate the Christian doctrine of salvation.

In contemporary Christian preaching there is a pressing need for a return to the biblical understanding of man. Much modern arrogance concerning man's independence—not to mention the modern existentialists' despair concerning man's value—would be dispelled if we honestly faced the biblical estimate of man.

We can consider the teaching of Scripture under six main headings:

1. MAN'S UNIFIED NATURE

The idea that man consists of two incompatible elements—a physical body which constantly opposes an immaterial spirit—is utterly foreign to biblical thought. Man is an integrated being; a being with a physical and a spiritual part to his nature, both of which are essential and interrelated features of his real manhood. The body is dead without the spirit (Jas. 2: 26), but man's spirit is 'unclothed' without a body (2 Cor. 5: 1–4). Man cannot live by bread alone (Mt. 4: 4); he needs spiritual food as well as material nourishment (Jn. 6: 27, 48–51, 58).

a. MAN'S PHYSICAL NATURE

The Greek philosophies of biblical times had a disparaging notion of man's physical nature. They saw the body as the prison-house of the soul. To them redemption consisted in being freed at death from the fetters of the body. Actually, they saw the whole material world as somewhat evil in itself. The Bible has a far more exalted doctrine of the body—and of all creation for that matter.

New Testament writers are at pains to stress that the Son of God took a human body in His Incarnation (Jn. 1: 14; Phil. 2: 7; Col. 1: 22; 1 Tim. 3: 16). To deny this fact is to be guilty of deception (2 Jn. 7). Jesus was without sin (Heb. 4: 15), yet partook of our nature of flesh and blood (Heb. 2: 14, cf. 10: 5). This Christological teaching in Hebrews must dispel beyond any doubt the idea that the body is evil.

The importance of man's body is stressed also in Christ's ministry. He ministered to the needs of the whole man, e.g. His concern about the physical refreshment and comfort of His disciples (Mk. 6: 31), His healing of the sick and maimed (e.g. Mk. 3: 1–6, 5: 25–34; Lk. 17: 12–14; Jn. 5: 5–9, 9: 1–7) and His feeding of the hungry (Mk. 8: 1–3; Lk. 9: 12–17). All these incidents confirm Christ's concern for man in his physical as well as spiritual needs.

The Apostle Paul emphasizes:

i. The dignity of the body

Far from disparaging the body as essentially opposed to man's spiritual nature, Paul views the body as a potentially effective instrument for expressing man's spiritual life. The body of the redeemed man is the temple of the Holy Spirit (1 Cor. 6: 19). Therefore, man is urged to glorify God in his body (1 Cor. 6: 20) and to offer his entire self to God as a grateful thank-offering (Rom. 12: 1). The Apostle longs that Christ will be honoured in his body (Phil. 1: 20). Paul also writes with equal conviction, however, about:

ii. The degradation of the body

Although the body is not essentially evil, the Bible will not allow us to forget that the fleshly part of our nature is often used as an instrument of sin. The body can be dishonoured (Rom. 1: 24) and made to serve the lusts of the flesh rather than the righteousness of God (Rom. 6: 12). It needs constantly to be disciplined (Rom. 8: 13; 1 Cor. 9: 27) and yielded positively to the service of Christ (Rom. 6: 13). Pious, ascetic practices in themselves cannot check man's indulgence of the flesh (Col. 2: 23). The sum of Paul's teaching is that the body can best be used when it is surrendered willingly and gratefully to God (Rom. 12: 1, cf. Heb. 10: 5–7 where the writer links the idea of obedience to the will of God with the body, the instrument of that obedience).

b. MAN'S PSYCHOLOGICAL NATURE

The question is often posed whether man's nature is bipartite or tripartite; whether man consists of body and soul or body, soul and spirit. With equal integrity and sincerity, Christian people have arrived at different conclusions concerning the biblical teaching on this question. The Bible does not set out to present its readers with a precise and detailed statement about man's psychological nature. In the Old Testament terms like 'soul' and 'spirit' are used almost interchangeably to describe either emotional (Gen. 34: 3) or religious experiences (Deut. 4: 29; Psa. 42: 2). 'Spirit' is used frequently to give expression to sensory perception as well as religious experience (Psa. 51: 17; Ezek. 11: 19, 18: 31).

Those who turn to the New Testament for a tripartite understanding of man cite verses such as 1 Thessalonians 5: 23 and Hebrews 4: 12. Others, preferring a bipartite understanding of man's nature, are persuaded by general tendency of Scripture to refer only to man's body on the one hand and man's soul or spirit on the other. In this thinking, 'soul' and 'spirit' are used interchangeably, describing the psychological or 'spiritual' aspect of man's nature (Rom. 8: 10; 1 Cor. 5: 3; Heb. 13: 17; Jas. 2: 26).

However one chooses to define the constituent elements in man's nature, the Bible nevertheless constantly reminds us of the supreme importance of man's *spiritual* nature. Jesus insists that there is nothing worth having in exchange for the spiritual life of man (Mt. 16: 26).

2. MAN'S MORAL FREEDOM

Although the course of every man's life is influenced by a variety of factors such as parentage, upbringing, circumstances, friendships, etc., the Bible insists that man is morally free. In his relationships with God and his fellows, he is capable of making real choices.

The Bible presents us with teaching on various aspects of the theme of man's moral freedom.

a. ITS PURPOSE

'Man's chief end is to glorify God' (Westminster Confession). This idea is rooted in Scripture: man is to love God (Deut. 6: 4–5). But the appeal of love obviously implies that man is free either to love or not love. Man's love for God would have little value if he were no more than a puppet. He must be capable of real choice if the relationship between God and man is to be meaningful.

Man's right use of his freedom is illustrated at many points by the biblical writers. To employ this gift for its true purpose means delighting to do God's will (Psa. 40: 8), serving the Lord (Josh. 24: 15), choosing faithfulness (Psa. 119: 30), loving the Lord's testimonies (Psa. 119: 31, cf. 119: 173) and choosing the things that please the Lord (Isa. 56: 4). The necessary help to choose the right way will be given to the man who fears the Lord (Psa. 25: 12).

Man is always at the point of real choice. He is urged to choose life rather than death (Deut. 39: 15, 19), to serve the Lord rather than other gods (Josh. 24: 15, 23), to follow the Lord rather than false deities (1 Kings 18: 21), to enter life by the narrow rather than the broad gate (Mt. 7: 13, 14), to build life on a firm foundation rather than on one which is insecure (Mt. 7: 24–27) and to serve God rather than mammon (Mt. 6: 24).

The tragedy of man's condition is that he so often uses his freedom for the wrong purpose. He rejects God's revelation of Himself in Jesus Christ (Jn. 1: 10, 11), loves darkness rather than light (Jn. 3: 19), refuses to come to the light (Jn. 5: 40), yields his members to impurity (Rom. 6: 19), deliberately ignores the fact of God's creative activity (2 Pet. 3: 5) and worships the creature rather than the Creator (Rom. 1: 25).

b. ITS CONSEQUENCES

Man's moral freedom has serious consequences. In the teaching of the Bible man is personally responsible for his actions and ultimately accountable to God for them.

i. Man's responsibility

The biblical doctrine of man insists that each individual is responsible to God for the way in which he chooses to act. Every man must bear the consequence of his *own* sin (Deut. 24: 16). In every age men have tried to escape responsibility by blaming either their contemporaries or their forefathers. The Old Testament prophets emphasized that man cannot blame his ancestors (Jer. 31: 29). They insisted on man's personal responsibility: 'Each man who eats sour grapes, his teeth shall be set on edge' (Jer. 31: 30; cf. Ezek. 18: 4). David illustrates his acceptance of this truth. Admitting his own wilful choice of sin, he clearly accepts responsibility for it (Psa. 51: 3, 4).

ii. Man's accountability

God is not arbitrary or petulant in His dealings with men. Something of the divine nature and glory of God has been revealed to all men (Rom. 1: 20). To ignore or reject this revelation is to incur guilt before God.

Man is inexcusable. God has revealed Himself in creation (Rom. 1: 20; cf. Psa. 19: 1–4) and supremely through His Son (Jn. 1: 14; Heb. 1: 2). Man is therefore accountable to God because he has wilfully rejected God's self revelation and refused to glorify Him as he ought.

Many of the Old Testament statements concerning judgment are uttered against the background of man's stubborn rejection of God's mercy and covenant-love (Deut. 29: 24–28; 2 Kings 17: 15–18; 2 Chron. 36: 15, 16; Prov. 1: 24–29; Isa. 1: 28, 65: 11, 12, 66: 3, 4; Jer. 7: 13).

The New Testament also emphasizes the serious consequence of man's wilful rejection of God's grace in Christ. Man is condemned because he rejects the Light (Jn. 3: 17–19).

C. ITS LIMITATIONS

While the Bible makes it plain that man is morally free and responsible, it also leaves the reader in no doubt that man's moral freedom is severely limited by his captivity to sin. Man cannot exercise his freedom to be what God intended, because over him various tyrants hold sway and he has willingly submitted to their rule. Man's will is fettered and consequently his freedom to act as he ought is severely limited.

This was Paul's experience; when he wished to do good, he discovered his utter inability to act as he desired (Rom. 7: 15, 18, 19). Like other men, he was a slave to sin (Rom. 6: 16, 17, 20, cf. Jn. 8: 34). Man's state is also described as being 'confined under the law' (Gal. 3: 23), 'in bondage to beings that by nature are no gods' (Gal. 4: 8), 'slaves of corruption' (2 Pet. 2: 19), subject to the desires of the flesh which prevent a man from doing what he would (Gal. 5: 17, cf. Rom. 7: 5; Eph. 2: 1–3; Tit. 3: 3), slaves of the devil (2 Tim. 2: 26, cf. 1 Jn. 3: 8; 5: 19) and in slavery to the elemental spirits of the universe (Gal. 4: 3, 9). By voluntarily submitting to the tyranny of sin man forfeits his freedom to yield his allegiance and life to God (Mt. 6: 24; Rom. 6: 12, 13, 19).

3. MAN'S SINFUL CONDITION

For many modern writers any discussion of man's sinfulness is regarded as an unnecessary exercise in morbid self-analysis. For the Christian, however, the magnitude of God's grace and mercy can be fully understood only against the background of an honest appraisal of what the Bible teaches about man's sinfulness and need. To read that God loves us is wonderful enough, but such love will inspire an even deeper devotion when we remember that 'God commends His love to us in that while we were yet sinners Christ died for us' (Rom. 5: 8).

The condition which we call man's sin is described in Scripture in various ways. Positively, it is transgression of the law (Psa. 51: 1; Dan. 9: 5; 1 Jn. 3: 4), wrongdoing or acting wickedly (Dan. 9: 5; 1 Jn. 5: 17), devising folly (Prov. 24: 9); negatively, it is failing to do what we know is right (Jas. 4: 17) and falling short of God's standard (Rom. 3: 23).

The Bible says a number of important things about man's sinful condition. Although we have viewed some of these concepts in a generalized manner in the previous section on 'The Fall of Man', now we must approach the theme in some detail.*

a. UNIVERSAL CONDITION

At the bar of Scripture *all* men are condemned because of their sin. The Old Testament leaves no room for any smug display of self-righteousness. Its most serious condemnation is that men do not honour God as He deserves (Psa. 53: 1–3). A recurring theme is that no man is righteous before God (Psa. 130: 3, 143: 2; Prov. 20: 9; Eccles. 7: 20). David reflects that there is none that does good (Psa. 14: 2, 3), and it seems that he passed on this insight to his son, Solomon (1 Kings 8: 46). Isaiah also emphasizes the universal sinfulness of men (Isa. 53: 6, 64: 6).

The New Testament echoes the same truth. Though Jesus does not make any formal statement on the theme, it is clear that He assumes that all men are evil (Mt. 7: 11, cf. Jn. 8: 7) and need to repent (Mk. 1: 14, 15). Paul insists that all men, both Jews and Greeks, are under the power of sin (Rom. 3: 9–12, 3: 23, 5: 12) and are accountable to God (Rom. 5: 19). John asserts that the

* Also see page 91ff.

man who denies the fact of sin in his life is guilty of appalling self-deception (1 Jn. 1: 8).

b. INWARD CONDITION

The Bible contends that man's sinful condition is not derived solely from environmental factors such as circumstances and relationships. Man's sinfulness stems rather from a sickness of the heart (Jer. 17: 9, cf. Eccles. 8: 11; Isa. 1: 5). Ezekiel makes implicit reference to this inwardness of man's sin when he records that God's gift to His needy people would be a new heart (Ezek. 36: 26). Jesus also exposed the inner root of man's sinfulness. It is what comes out of a man that defiles him (Mk. 7: 20–23), and He endorses the point in discussion with the Scribes and Pharisees (Mt. 23: 25–28). To recognize the need for a clean heart is, therefore, the first step to a new and right relationship with God (Psa. 51: 10–13).

c. VISIBLE CONDITION

Although sin has this 'inward' character, it does manifest itself visibly in evil deeds (Col. 1: 21, cf. Rom. 7: 5). The New Testament, in particular, describes the visible marks of the man who is 'still of the flesh' (1 Cor. 3: 3). Paul, on several occasions, gathers these visible signs of human sin and lists them (Rom. 1: 29–31; Gal. 5: 19–21; Col. 3: 5–8). By such deeds men deny that they know God (Tit. 1: 16). Jesus spoke about recognizing men for what they are by the fruit which they bear: 'the bad tree bears evil fruit' (Mt. 7: 17, cf. Mt. 3: 10, 12: 33–35; Lk. 6: 43, 44).

d. RADICAL CONDITION

Every aspect of man's life is affected by sin. This is not to deny that there is some trace of God's image left in man's nature as we saw earlier. Still, man's mind, will and affections are all tainted by his rebellion against God.

i. Man's mind is corrupted

Man is incapable, because of sin, of thinking in the right way about himself and about God. Early in man's history God saw that the mind and imagination were the seat of sin (Gen. 6: 5, cf. 8: 21; Prov. 15: 26). The mind of the man who is separated from God through sin (Isa. 59: 2) may deny the very existence of God (Psa. 10: 4, cf. 14: 1), be set on iniquity (Isa. 59: 7) and harbour evil thoughts (Jer. 4: 14).

The Apostle Paul has some serious things to say about the thoughts of the unredeemed man and indicates a number of characteristics of the unregenerate mind. It is dark (Rom. 1: 21), base (Rom. 1: 28), unable to grasp spiritual truth (1 Cor. 2: 14), hostile (Col. 1: 21), futile (Rom. 1: 21; Eph. 4: 17), sensuous (Col. 2: 18), corrupt (2 Tim. 3: 8; Tit. 1: 15;), veiled (2 Cor. 3: 14–16), blinded by the god of this world (2 Cor. 4: 4), set on the flesh (Rom. 8: 7), depraved (1 Tim. 6: 5) and set on earthly things (Phil. 3: 19). Man, therefore, desperately needs a renewal of his mind (Rom. 12: 2, cf. Col. 3: 10).

ii. Man's will is fettered
The fact that the will is also subject to sin's tyranny is, as we have already seen, clearly asserted in Scripture.

iii. Man's affections are perverted
Man loves the wrong things. Not loving God as he should (Deut. 6: 5), he loves evil more than good (Psa. 52: 3, cf. Prov. 2: 14; Mic. 3: 2), darkness rather than light (Jn. 3: 19, cf. Job 24: 13–17), the ways of sin more than the ways of God (Jer. 14: 10, cf. 2 Pet. 2: 15) and pleasure more than God (2 Tim. 3: 4). Equally serious is that man outside of Christ lacks any real sense of gratitude, which is a mark of love (Rom. 1: 21). The root of his problem is that his affections are turned inward toward himself (Phil. 2: 21, 2 Tim. 3: 2) rather than outward as they ought to be, toward God and his fellow men (Lev. 19: 18, 34; Mt. 22: 35–40; Lk. 6: 27–31, 10: 36, 37; Gal. 5: 14).

e. TRAGIC CONDITION
Man's sinful state is actually tragic. The Bible describes in graphic metaphors the pathetic results of man's rebellion against God.

i. Man is lost
This is the testimony of the Psalmist (Psa. 119: 176) and the Prophets (Isa. 53: 6; Jer. 50: 6). Jesus depicts man's condition as like a coin which is lost to a housewife, a sheep which is lost to the shepherd and a son who is lost to the Father (Lk. 15: 3–24). Christ had compassion on the crowd who were like aimless and helpless sheep (Mt. 9: 36) and conceives His mission to the world in terms of seeking and saving the lost (Lk. 19: 10).

ii. Man is blind
Because of sin and the rule of 'the god of this world', man is robbed of spiritual insight (2 Cor. 4: 4) and is incapable of seeing or understanding spiritual truths (1 Cor. 2: 14, cf. Eph, 4: 18). Man walks in darkness (1 Jn. 1: 6, 2: 11) and needs to be called out of this condition to be saved (1 Pet. 2: 9); until this happens he is under the dominion of darkness (Col. 1: 13). In Old Testament expectation, the ministry of the Messiah was to bring sight to the blind (Isa. 29: 18, 35: 5). Jesus drew attention to the fulfilment of this promise in His own ministry (Mt. 11: 5, 15: 31). Alongside His ministry to the physically blind (Jn. 9: 1–7), Jesus saw Himself as the Light to overcome man's spiritual blindness (Jn. 8: 12, cf. 9: 5).

iii. Man is estranged

Another tragic result of man's condition is that there is an estrangement between God and man (Isa. 59: 2. cf. Gen. 3: 8). God's face
is hidden from men because of their sin (Mic. 3: 4, cf. Deut. 31: 17,
18). Paul asserts that this estrangement has been caused by man's
hostility to God (Rom. 5: 10, 8: 7; Col. 1: 21). Such estrangement
means separation from the life of God (Eph. 4: 18) and, consequently, hopelessness (Eph. 2: 12). Christian preaching involves an
appeal to estranged men to be reconciled to God through faith in
His Son (2 Cor. 5: 18: 21, cf. Col. 1: 20–22; Rom. 5: 10).

iv Man is dead

On account of man's trespasses and sins, the Bible describes him
as spiritually dead (Eph. 2: 1–5; Col. 2: 13). Jesus stresses this
feature of man's condition in the parable of the Prodigal Son. The
Father rejoices that his returned son, though once 'dead', is now
alive (Lk. 15: 24). The raising of Lazarus from physical death is
recorded by John as a 'sign'. He who called the physically dead man
out of the tomb (Jn. 11: 43) offers to men spiritual life (Jn. 11: 25,
26). The condition upon which this life is given to needy men is
faith (Jn. 5: 24, 6: 40, 47).

4. MAN'S INHERENT MORTALITY

The Bible does not only teach that man is dead spiritually but that
he is subject to death physically. It is characteristic of man that he
dies.

a. THE FACT OF DEATH

On two occasions in the Old Testament we are told that a man
escaped the experience of death. Both Enoch (Gen. 5: 24) and
Elijah (2 Kings 2: 11) were translated. As a general principle,
however, death is a universal and incscapable fact of human and
animal experience (Psa. 49: 12; Eccles. 3: 19). Man is powerless to
stave off this unwelcome visitor (Psa. 22: 29, 49: 7–9, 89: 48;
Eccles. 9: 12). It is appointed for men to die once (Heb. 9: 27).
Jesus impressed the same truth upon His hearers in the parable of
the Rich Fool. Wealth, ease and merriment could not deflect death
from its mission (Lk. 12: 19, 20). The Bible sees death as a fact to be
reckoned with by all. It is the great leveller, a universal feature of
the human race (2 Sam. 14: 14; Job 30: 23) and no respecter of
persons (Psa. 49: 10; Eccles. 2: 16).

b. THE CAUSE OF DEATH

Thoughtful reflection forbids us to believe that death is intrin-
sically natural to man and God intended it to be so. It is hard to
imagine that death, as something dark and forbidding, was an

original part of the experience of the man God created and then pronounced good (Gen. 1: 31). Our feelings are confirmed when we turn to Scripture, for there it is made undeniably plain that man's mortality is one of the results of sin. Early in man's history death is pronounced by God as the inevitable consequence of sin and disobedience (Gen. 2: 15–17). His warning having been disregarded, the prediction is eventually, though not immediately, fulfilled (Gen. 3: 19). From this point onwards death enters the arena of human history as an alien and dreaded enemy. Unfaithfulness (1 Chron. 10: 13), violence (Prov. 1: 19), all manner of wickedness (Rom. 1: 29–32), sins (Ezek. 18: 4) and rebellion against the Lord (Jer. 28: 16) are all singled out as resulting eventually in death, though the Bible affirms that it is man's state of sinfulness itself, rather than isolated sins, which leads to death (Rom. 6: 23). It is Paul to whom we need to turn for the most explicit statements concerning the cause of death. Adam's transgression is directly responsible (Rom. 5: 12, 17). By this one man came death and in Adam all die (1 Cor. 15: 21, 22).

But in its presentation of the doctrine of sin, the Bible stresses man's personal responsibility. Because of the solidarity of the human race, we all somehow and in some sense share the guilt of Adam's rebellion. But death comes to *all* because *all* men sin (Deut. 24: 16; Ezek. 18: 20; Rom. 5: 12, cf. Jer. 31: 30). The rabbis had a saying: 'Every man is the Adam of his own soul'. In every individual case, death is the result of 'sowing' to the flesh (Gal. 6: 7, 8) and is the grandchild of desire (Jas. 1: 14, 15).

C. THE EXTENT OF DEATH

Death operates only in the sphere of the physical body. Scripture gives no support to any theory of total annihilation. It is man's *body* which is subject to corruption and mortality, but his soul, or human personality, continues to live on beyond death.

Luke 23: 46 notes that when He breathed His last, or physically died, Jesus commended His spirit, His enduring self, to God His Father. Paul considers it better to die, that is to put off his flesh, so that his spiritual self might be with the Lord (Phil. 1: 23, cf. 2 Cor. 4: 16; 2 Pet. 1: 13, 14). To the unbeliever this biblical truth comes as a serious warning. When we die, each of us is still responsible to God (Mt. 10: 28, cf. Lk. 12: 4, 5; Rom. 14: 10–12); we must all give an account of deeds done in the body (2 Cor. 5: 10, cf. Mt. 12: 36).

d. THE METAPHORS OF DEATH

Many vivid and colourful metaphors are employed in God's Word to remind the reader of the reality of death and the brevity of a man's life in the body. Life is like a shadow (1 Chron. 29: 15, cf. Psa. 39: 6), a flying shuttle (Job 7: 6), a swift runner (Job 9: 25), a weaver's cloth (Isa. 38: 12), a vanishing mist (Jas. 4: 14), water (2 Sam. 14: 14), grass (Psa. 90: 5, 6, 103: 15, 16; Isa. 40: 6, cf. Isa. 51: 12; Jas. 1: 10; 1 Pet. 1: 24), a few handbreadths (Psa. 39: 5), a flower of the field (Psa. 103: 15) and a breath (Job 7: 7, 16).

e. THE LORD OF DEATH

Just as it is God who gives (Gen. 2: 7; Psa. 104: 30, 119: 73; Acts 17: 25) and sustains life (Job 12: 10; Acts 17: 28), so it is He who takes it. He is sovereign in the ordering of death (Deut. 32: 39; 1 Sam. 2: 6; Job 1: 21, 10: 8, 14: 5). It is He who turns men back to the dust (Psa. 90: 3), who takes back man's spirit to Himself (Job 34: 14) and removes man's breath (Psa. 104: 29). No man has authority over the day of death (Eccles. 8: 8), but our times are in the Lord's hand (Psa. 31: 15).

5. MAN'S CORPORATE ENVIRONMENT

Some important truths are stressed in the Bible concerning man's relationship with his fellows. John Donne's conviction that 'No man is an island, entire of itself' is abundantly illustrated throughout the entire Bible. God's Word addresses itself to men who are social beings and who, because of their creation by the same Maker (Mal. 2: 10; Acts 17: 26, cf. Prov. 22: 2), are ultimately related to one another.

In God's loving purpose for man, it was not good that he should be alone (Gen. 2: 18). From the outset of human history, God places man in a social context where he may both give and receive companionship and love.

God's design for the world was that man should multiply and fill the earth (Gen. 1: 28, 9: 1, 7), thereby creating a great family of men. The tragedy is, man's sinful pride led to the racial fragmentation of this divinely ordained family (Gen. 11: 1–9).

The redemptive purpose of God for mankind was initiated through Abraham. God promised to make of him a great nation (Gen. 12: 2, 15: 5, 17: 4, 5, 18: 18), establish His covenant with Abraham's descendants (Gen. 17: 7, 8) and bring blessing to all the families of the earth by him (Gen. 28: 14). In Israel's early history, God's blessings were mediated to tribe or nation. Salvation for the individual was closely and inseparably related to his belonging to the people of God (Gen. 17: 14).

Jesus, in His life and teaching, stresses the importance of man's corporate environment. This is seen, for example, in His relationship with the disciples. He calls twelve to be with Him (Mk. 3: 14). Then He sends them out not singly but two by two (Mk. 6: 7) and urges them to serve each other in a spirit of loving concern (Jn. 13: 14, 15, 34). Christ stressed that to follow Him would involve men not in a selfish individualism but in a fellowship of love and service (Jn. 17: 20–23).

The New Testament teaching concerning the Church reflects the corporate nature of man. The Church is conceived in terms of the redeemed society. It is described in images which involve the holding together of different parts in one whole. The vine has its several branches (Jn. 15: 1–5), the body its various members (1 Cor. 12: 12–30; Rom. 12: 4, 5) and the building its many stones (1 Pet. 2: 4, 5).

Because man is a gregarious creature, the Bible insists that he cannot avoid certain implications:

a. THE REPERCUSSIONS OF SIN

No man sins to himself. He cannot escape the consequences of other men's sins and cannot himself avoid infecting the community around him by his own sinfulness. Jesus impressed upon His hearers the seriousness of causing someone else to stumble through our sin (Matt. 18: 6). The Apostle Paul warns his readers about the same danger (Rom. 14: 12, 13; 1 Cor. 8: 13). David's lust was made all the more tragic because of its social consequences. Others, including Bathsheba, Uriah and Joab, suffered because of the sin of one man (2 Sam. 11: 2–27). Achan's greed led to defeat and disappointment for all the people of God (Josh. 7: 20, 21, 25). This passage illustrates the strong sense of solidarity which existed among the Hebrew people. Israel as a whole is addressed as being guilty of Achan's sin: 'Israel has sinned . . . they have stolen and lied' (Josh. 7: 11, 12). This is one important principle to grasp, especially in the light of our Western ideas of individualism.

It is in the context of this Hebrew concept of the solidarity of the race that Paul's teaching about the involvement of all men in the sin of Adam must be considered. The whole human race became polluted by Adam's rebellion against God (Rom. 5: 12; 1 Cor. 15: 22) and shares the guilt of Adam's transgression (Rom. 5: 18, 19).

b. THE RESPONSIBILITY OF SERVICE

Because God has placed him in a social environment, man is intended to find his greatest fulfilment both in perfect love for God *and* in complete devotion to the service of others. God's design and purpose for man in his corporate environment is clearly defined by Jesus (Mk. 12: 31) and witnessed to by the Apostles (Gal. 5: 14, cf. Jas. 2: 8). This obligation of man towards his fellows is enshrined within the Old Testament covenant idea and is spelt out in the Ten Commandments. A man who belongs to the covenant people has responsibilities man-ward (Exod. 20: 12–17) as well as God-ward (Exod. 20: 1–11).

Both the Law and the Prophets contain important teaching about man's responsibilities as a social being. Leviticus reminds the worshipper of obligations towards his neighbour (Lev. 19: 18) and includes an immense amount of legislation concerning various aspects of Hebrew social life (e.g. Lev. 18, 19, 25, etc.). Many passages in the writings of the prophets draw attention to social obligations and the peril of neglecting such duties (e.g. Isa. 1:17, 58: 6, 7; Jer. 22: 3; Amos 1: 3–2; 3, 4: 1, 5; 11, 8: 4–6; Mic. 6: 8).

6. MAN'S UNIQUE VALUE

In making an honest appraisal of man's sinfulness, care should be taken that we never forget the biblical teaching concerning man's value. As we discussed previously, man is not just an animal. God gave man 'the breath of life' (Gen. 2: 7). Man is made in God's image (Gen. 1: 27). This vital principle is constantly referred to in the Scriptures. For example, James makes use of it when he writes about the seriousness of cursing a man (Jas. 3: 9). There needs to be a renewed assertion of this important biblical truth in our own day. The computer age ought to be reminded of the infinite value of each individual. At times economic, social and political considerations tend to obscure the needs of the individual. Life is constantly becoming more 'depersonalized'. But as Jesus indicated, *every* life is of supreme worth; 'What can a man give in return for his life?' (Mk. 8: 36).

Evidence to support this aspect of the biblical doctrine of man is found supremely in the life and ministry of Christ. To read the Gospels is to be made aware of the great compassion of Jesus for all. The value He placed on men's lives is revealed in two ways:

a. JESUS DEMONSTRATED IT IN HIS LIFE

His condescension in 'being born in the likeness of men' (Phil. 2: 7, cf. Jn. 1: 14) indicates His high estimate of man's value. 'The incarnation of the Son of God is itself a declaration of the worth which God attaches to man. It is a declaration that human nature, despite its corruption by sin, is worth redeeming and is capable of being redeemed.' (Maldwyn Hughes *Christian Foundations*, pp. 77–8.)

The deep concern of Jesus for men and women in need illustrates the value He placed on them. Although He had compassion on the great crowds, He often turned to focus His care and sympathy on the need of the individual: the despised tax-gatherer (Lk. 19: 1–10), the bereaved mother (Lk. 7: 11–15), the sick woman (Mk. 5: 25–34), the distracted father (Mk. 5: 22–24) and the seeking Pharisee (Jn. 3: 1–21). People obviously mattered to Him.

b. HE AFFIRMED IT IN HIS TEACHING

Jesus had a great deal to say concerning man's value and worth to God:

i. Man is the object of God's providential care

He makes the sun rise and the rain fall on all men, the just and the unjust (Mt. 5: 45). Jesus used an intentionally extravagant metaphor to suggest the extent of God's knowledge of and concern for men (Mt. 10: 30). If birds of the air (Mt. 6: 26) and flowers of the field (Mt. 6: 28) are cared for, then God will all the more care for men.

ii. Man is the object of God's special interest

Jesus also stressed the unique interest which God attaches to man. His needs are of greater importance than rules about the keeping of the Sabbath or the recovery of a sheep (Mt. 12: 12, cf. Mk. 2: 27). A man's value far outweighs that of many sparrows (Mt. 10: 31). He is made in God's image and for fellowship with God. Therefore, he cannot live by bread alone (Mt. 4: 4) but needs spiritual sustenance.

iii. Man is the object of God's relentless search

The three parables in Luke 15 illustrate the fact that Jesus saw man as infinitely worth seeking and finding. As the sheep is important to the shepherd (Lk. 15: 3–7), as the coin is valuable to the housewife (Lk. 15: 8–10) and as the son is precious to the Father (Lk. 15: 11–24), so each individual man or woman matters to God. Jesus describes His mission as one of seeking and saving the lost (Lk. 19: 10). God's great love for the world prompted the mission of His Son and His death upon the Cross (Jn. 3: 16, 17). It is to this tremendous theme we now turn.

IV. GOD'S PROVISION FOR MAN'S NEED

1. ATONEMENT

The word 'atonement' in Christian theology denotes both the restoration of harmonious relations between God and sinners, and the action taken by God to achieve this. The consequence of sin is that man is spiritually separated from God, the Holy One (Gen. 3: 23, 24; Isa. 59: 2). He lives under the wrath of God (Psa. 90: 4; Jn. 3: 36). As we have seen, the Bible teaches that physical death as now experienced by man is the judgment of God upon his sin (Rom. 5: 21; 1 Cor. 15: 56). And eternal separation will be his lot unless something is done (Mt. 25: 41). But something has been done! God has acted, for God loves His human creatures and seeks to restore them to the relationship with Himself which they lost in the 'fall'. It will be well to look at all the great terms relating to salvation, first from the Old Testament perspective then from the New Testament. This shall be the procedure for the next several pages.

a. ATONEMENT IN THE OLD TESTAMENT

While sacrifice is not the only aspect of the atonement known to the Old Testament, the Hebrew verb for 'make atonement' (*kaphar*) is used in connection with sacrifice in the majority of cases. *Kaphar* means either to 'cover over' or to 'wipe away' sin, so that it no longer constitutes a barrier between God and man (Psa. 65: 3, 78: 38; Isa. 6: 7). It thus denotes something which God does to man. This meaning is conveyed by some modern speech translations of the Bible when they use the word 'expiate' to translate *kaphar*.

i. The meaning of sacrifice in the Old Testament

The Old Testament contains little direct explanation of why sacrifice was effective. We may safely say that for many worshippers in Israel, the value of sacrifice lay in the mere fact that it had simply been ordained by God. They did not attempt to develop a rationale for the command. 'The whole conception of sacrifice falls under the category of revelation; this is the way God has commanded sacrifice to be offered, and when it is offered in this prescribed way the worshipper effectually draws near to God.' (H. W. Robinson, *Religious Ideas of the Old Testament*, London). We may, however, look in the following directions for further light on the meaning of sacrifice.

Sacrifice was regarded as a gift to God. This idea was especially prominent in the case of the burnt offering, in which the entire sacrifice was consumed on the altar (Lev. 1). And no doubt it was probably at least an element in all sacrifice. The gift expressed the penitence of the giver and his desire for the renewal of fellowship with God.

i) Sacrifice was a means of communion of man with God

In this manner fellowship with God was experienced, and thereby it was restored. This aspect of sacrifice appears most clearly in the case of the peace-offering which partook of the nature of a social act; part of the offering being eaten by the offerer and his friends (Lev. 3). It also serves to reveal the connection between the sacrificial ritual and the covenant, i.e. sacrifice was God's gift to a people in covenant relation with Himself. The establishment of this relationship had been accompanied by sacrifice and a meal

(Exod. 24: 3–11). By such means fellowship was maintained and repaired (Psa. 50: 5).

ii) Sacrifice was the release of life

In Leviticus 17: 11 God declares that 'the life (soul, i.e. the vital force) of the flesh is in the blood; and I have given it for you upon the altar to make atonement for your souls; for it is the blood that makes atonement, by reason of the life.' By means of death, the life of the sacrificial animal was released so that it could return to God. 'The life which atones is a life which has passed through death.' (A. G. Hebert, *The Throne of David*, London, p. 202.) The true worshipper identified himself with this offering, thus rededicating his life to God.

iii) Sacrifice included a penal element

We have spoken of the God-ward reference of biblical atonement. This is not to say that by means of sacrifice men placated a vindictive God and made Him favourable to them. There was no place for such pagan ideas in the religion of Israel. Sacrifice was God's gift to Israel, expressive of His love, and it was effective only because He was willing to accept it. But the whole scope of biblical teaching on the subject indicates that the process of atonement also included the expression of God's judgment. At the heart of sacrifice lay death! And death, as we have seen, is part of God's judgment upon sin; actually, as in the case of a human being, symbolically, as in the case of a sacrificial animal. Thus God's wrath and His mercy were conjoined at the sacrificial altar. There His holiness was established and His grace was conveyed.

Some dispute whether Old Testament sacrifice included the idea of the victim's dying as a substitute for the one who offered it. We believe that the substitutionary element was certainly present, but perhaps not the prominent point in sacrifice. We take this position because the principle of substitution appears clearly in Isaiah 52: 13–53: 12. This is the last of four passages in Isaiah which are known as 'The Servant Songs' (the other three are 42: 1–4; 49: 1–6, 50: 4–9). These songs record words spoken by, or to, a 'servant of the Lord'. They describe His call, His mission, His preparatory experiences and His sufferings. Finally, in the last song, His humiliation and death and probably His Resurrection after death are described.

The technical language of sacrifice is used in Isaiah 53: 10, where it is said that the Servant makes Himself a guilt-offering (*asham*, cf. Lev. 5: 14ff). Beholding His patient acceptance of undeserved suffering and death, and perceiving that it was on their behalf, the spectators are moved to penitence and faith in God. In some of the songs, at least, the writer appears to be des-

cribing his own people, the Jews and their suffering during the
Exile. But Christians have always believed that the Servant Songs
find their ultimate fulfilment in the redemptive sufferings, death,
and the resurrection of Jesus Christ. Isaiah 52: 13–53: 12 contains the supreme statement of the principle of sacrifice in the
Old Testament. And this passage *clearly* includes the element of
personal, spiritual substitution. These verses obviously, ultimately
speak of our Lord Jesus Christ as God's great Substitute for the
sin of the whole world (Acts 8: 26–39).

ii. The value of sacrifice in the Old Testament

Reference has been made at several points in the foregoing discussion to the necessity of repentance and surrender on the part of an
offerer if his sacrifice was to be acceptable to God. For Israel's
spiritually minded people, sacrifice was never regarded as mechanical
or magical in its operation. Where it was sincerely offered it was a
true means of atonement. Nevertheless, it was an imperfect means;
one which lacked finality—a point forcefully made in the Epistle
to the Hebrews (7: 27, 9: 25, 10: 1–4). Atonement in the Old
Testament always pointed forward to a perfect sacrifice which lay
in the future. And, of course, this was effected in the death and
resurrection of Jesus Christ.

iii. The prophetic offer of forgiveness

There are passages in the Old Testament which appear to indicate
that the prophets of Israel were totally opposed to sacrifice (Jer.
7: 21ff; Amos 5: 25). These must be read, however, against the
background of the abuse of sacrifice which was all too common in
their day (Isa. 1: 12–17). There is no reason to believe that the
pre-exilic prophets, who were the most outspoken on this point,
would not have lent their support to sacrifice which expressed a true
and sincere desire for reconciliation with God. Both the sacrificial
system of the priest and the preaching of the prophet were gifts of
God. Nevertheless, like sacrifice, the prophetic offer of divine forgiveness was somewhat deficient. For it was not grounded in the
full and ultimate demonstration of God's righteous dealing with sin
as is seen finally in the person of Jesus Christ.

b. ATONEMENT IN THE NEW TESTAMENT

In the New Testament, as in the Old Testament, atonement is
the work of God. But here it is accomplished in and through Jesus
Christ. The point upon which Christ's atoning work turns is His
death and resurrection. Now these great events must not be treated
in isolation from His life in the flesh and His eternal high-priestly
ministry. It is the entire 'Christ Event' that must be grasped. We
shall consider five aspects of the work of Christ.

i. The work of Christ as God's gift

Christ is God's ultimate gift to man. His Cross is the supreme revelation of God's love for sinners; a love which proved stronger than human sin, evil, and death (John 3: 16; Romans 5: 8).

ii. The work of Christ as a sacrifice

The New Testament regards the death of Jesus Christ as a sacrifice. This is clear in the passages which speak of Him as Saviour from sin (Mt. 1: 21; Lk. 1: 77; Jn. 1: 29; Acts 13: 38; etc.). It is also implied in passages which interpret the work of Christ in terms of the Servant of the Lord portrayed by Isaiah (Mt. 3: 17, cf. Isa. 42: 1; Acts 8: 32–35; 1 Pet. 2: 24–25; etc.). Some of the Servant passages are sayings of Jesus Himself (Mk. 10: 45; 'many', cf. Isa. 53: 11, 12; Lk. 22: 37), others are found in apostolic writings. It may also be affirmed that the numerous references to the sufferings, death and resurrection of Christ as taking place 'for', i.e. 'on behalf of', men are sacrificial as well as substitutionary in their significance.

iii. The work of Christ as a penal offering

It is frequently stated in the New Testament that Christ 'bore sin', died 'for sins', etc. (1 Cor. 15: 3; Gal. 1: 4; 1 Pet. 2: 24). In what sense did Christ bear human sins? The answer of the New Testament is that He, the innocent One, bore the divine judgment which rests upon human sin (Rom. 8: 3). He entered on our behalf, and in our place, into the death which is its penal consequence (Rom. 5: 12, 6: 23; Heb. 2: 9). We may speak of Christ enduring the wrath of God in the sense that His identification with sinners was such that He endured God's wrath for us and in our place.

In following up this profound subject, careful attention must be given the following passages: Romans 3: 21–26; 2 Corinthians 5: 21; Galatians 3: 13; 1 Peter 2: 24, 3: 18. These passages teach that the death of Christ was a substitutionary or vicarious sacrifice of the kind foreshadowed in Isaiah 53. Further, they draw out the implications of Christ's own words in Mark, 10: 45. The Bible clearly teaches that in the atonement, God has provided Christ as our great substitute. He bore *our* sin upon the tree (1 Pet. 2: 24).

Romans 3: 21–26 is deserving of special consideration, for verse 25 in this passage declares that Christ Jesus has been 'put forward as an expiation by His blood, to be received by faith' (R.S.V.). The Greek word translated 'expiation' is *hilasterion*. This interesting word is used either as a noun or an adjective. It serves as a noun in Hebrews 9: 5 where it is translated 'mercy seat'. If this meaning is adopted in Romans 3: 25 it means that Christ crucified is for the world what the Mercy Seat was for Israel—the place where God's forgiveness meets man's sin.

If *hilasterion* is treated as an adjective, the word means that Christ has been put forward 'in expiatory power'. But regardless of how we use it, both renderings point to the fact that in the death of Christ the sacrifices of the Old Testament were consummated. The conclusion of verse 25 and verse 26 explain that the sacrifice offered by Christ was the vindication of God's justice. His long-suffering towards sinners prior to the mission of His Son might suggest that sin is of small account to Him. But now 'the exceeding sinfulness of sin' in God's eyes has been demonstrated, and His grace in forgiveness as 'faithful and just' (1 Jn. 1: 9).

Thus in the New Testament as in the Old Testament the work of atonement is both subjective and objective. It meets the need of men, and it satisfies the love and holiness of God. In Christ, God was dealing with the sin which separates men from Him; judging it and 'accepting and bearing its penalty in His own heart'. (J. S. Whale, *Victor and Victim*, Cambridge, p. 75). The consequence is that His love for mankind now finds unhindered expression. Man can be reconciled to God through Christ.

iv. The work of Christ as an offering of obedience

As well as being God's gift to man, sacrifice is man's offering to God. We are God's creatures, made in His image, existing only in and through Him. Thus, our chief vocation is to offer Him the tribute of steadfast, loving obedience. Sacrifice is meant to be the symbol of this. But since we are unable to fulfil this vocation perfectly, Christ offered on our behalf the obedience of a fully righteous life; an obedience that was consummated in His death. This sacrifice was pleasing to God the Father (Eph. 5: 2) and was accepted by Him. The Resurrection fully proved that fact (Acts 17: 31; Rom. 1: 4).

So, those who are 'in Christ' are accepted by God for Christ's sake (Eph. 1: 6). As imperfect as our worship and obedience is, 'in Christ' it becomes acceptable (Heb. 9: 14). As on the Day of Atonement when the High Priest, standing in the Holy of Holies and sprinkling the blood on the Mercy Seat, was the link between God and Israel (Lev. 16), so the ascended Christ, the High Priest of mankind, unites His people with God (Heb. 9: 11, 14, 24). Their access to God is through Him (Heb. 4: 15, 16, 10: 19–22), and He is engaged in a ministry of eternal intercession on their behalf (Heb. 7: 25).

v. The work of Christ as the instituting of a covenant

As we have seen, the first covenant, by means of which Israel came into fellowship with God, was sealed with the blood of sacrifice (Exod. 24). This covenant was an interim provision, involving a bond essentially between God and one nation only. Of course, God intended Israel to proclaim His name among the nations. But

Israel's disobedience prevented her from fulfilling this destiny which the covenant included (Exod. 19: 6); but the Prophets dreamed of a *new* covenant which God would establish (Jer. 31: 31–34; Ezek. 37: 26). Jesus declared that this covenant—this universal covenant —was being instituted by means of His own death and resurrection (Mt. 26: 28; 1 Cor. 11: 25; Heb. 8: 8–13, 10: 16, 17). Now men and women of *all* races and nations, entering into this new relationship with God through faith in Jesus Christ, constitute the new People of God (Eph. 2: 11–22; 1 Pet. 2: 9).

Thus we may speak of the atonement wrought by Christ as 'finished'. It opened for all sinful mankind a new and eternal way to the pardon and presence of God (Mk. 15: 38; Heb. 4: 16, 9: 8, 10: 5–14). At the same time the atonement has a continuous aspect, because to the end of the day of grace Christ will continue to gather in the world-wide harvest of His sacrifice. Moreover, in Christ we also have:

2. FORGIVENESS

Forgiveness is the removal of a barrier. There is a tendency in Christian circles to use the word 'forgiveness' so broadly as to denote the *total* experience of human reconciliation with God. In the Bible, however, forgiveness is primarily the removal of barriers which sin erects against fellowship with God. Thus it is the precondition of reconciliation in its fullness. This is indicated by the verbs which the Bible uses. The Old Testament words are: *kaphar*, meaning 'cover' or 'wipe away' (Psa. 78: 38; Jer. 18: 23); *nasa*, meaning 'lift up, carry away' (Gen. 50: 17; Psa. 25: 18); *salach*, which possibly means 'let go' (1 Kings 8: 30; Psa. 103: 3).

The verbs most frequently used in the New Testament are *aphiemi*, 'send off', 'let go', and *charizomai*, which has the primary meaning, 'be gracious to'. The former word occurs, with only a few exceptions, in the Gospels and Acts, while the latter word is a favourite with Paul. It is clear that all these words depict forgiveness as the process by means of which sin, as an element which separates God and man, is removed.

a. FORGIVENESS IN THE OLD TESTAMENT

God alone forgives sin (Isa 43: 25, cf. Mk. 2: 7). Under the Old Covenant He gave the sacrificial system by means of which Israel, when penitent, could receive forgiveness. The priests were the mediators of the forgiveness conveyed. The prophets preached about a pardon unmediated by sacrifice if Israel would only repent and turn to God. The ministry of priest and prophet could not meet man's deepest need, however. Yet it did point to a perfect provision which was to come, viz. Jesus Christ.

b. FORGIVENESS IN THE NEW TESTAMENT

Jesus bestowed the divine forgiveness upon sinners during His ministry on earth (Mk. 2: 10, Lk. 7: 48). The New Testament also traces the intrinsic connection between forgiveness and His death and resurrection. Jesus Himself made this connection in His words at the Last Supper (1 Cor. 11: 25; 'the new covenant in my blood', cf. Jer. 31: 31, 34). The Epistles also present the same principle. They view the sacrifice of Christ as the ground of the divine forgiveness (Eph. 1: 7; 1 Jn. 1: 7; Rev. 1: 5). Sin as a barrier excluding men from God is removed by Him who is both sacrifice and priest (Heb. 9: 11–14).

It is of great significance that the followers of Jesus Christ abandoned sacrifice as a means of forgiveness immediately after His resurrection. The Jewish nation ceased to offer animal sacrifice only because with the destruction of the Temple it had become an impossibility. Christians abandoned it because it had been superseded. The ultimate sacrifice was made by Jesus Christ.

i. Forgiveness in human relations

Forgiveness can be shared. Jesus laid the greatest emphasis upon the necessity of a forgiving spirit if men would experience God's forgiveness (Mt. 6: 12 ff, 18: 23–35; Mk. 11: 25; Lk. 17: 3 ff). Where this spirit is lacking there can be no divine forgiveness, because there is no repentance. We must also note the commission to forgive and retain sins which the risen Christ gave to His disciples (Jn. 20: 23; cf. Mt. 16: 19, 18: 18). Jesus confers upon His servants the right and privilege to declare to men the fact and the conditions of the forgiveness of sins.

ii. The unforgivable sin (Mt. 12: 31–32 and parallels)

Jesus warned the Pharisees that they were in danger of committing 'blasphemy against the Holy Spirit'. The context reveals that by this He meant the deliberate branding as evil that which is manifestly of God (Mt. 12: 24). Perseverance in such a sin produces so great an insincerity of character that repentance becomes impossible. An unbelieving man who continually hardens his heart against the conviction of the Holy Spirit, as the Spirit draws him to Christ, is on dangerous ground. He may become so depraved and rebellious against God that he will finally, with clear understanding of what he is doing, utter the awful blasphemy that the obvious acts of God are the work of the Devil. This blasphemy, which clearly grows out of a terribly depraved state, is the sin that cannot be forgiven. Repentance on the part of such a sinner becomes impossible. And without repentance, God cannot forgive.

3. JUSTIFICATION

a. JUSTIFICATION IN THE OLD TESTAMENT

Justification in the Bible is the process by which sinners are declared to be, or made to be, righteous before God. We must begin by asking what it means to be righteous in this sense. It is of the utmost importance that we go to the Scriptures for the answer to this question, for the word 'righteousness', at least in its primary sense, has a different meaning in the Bible from that which it bears in modern English usage.

The Hebrew words for righteousness (*tsedeq, tsedaqah*) and their derivatives refer primarily to relationships. When used of human conduct, they indicate that the conduct thus described meets the standards and obligations involved in the relationship concerned. Since for the Hebrews life consisted of covenant relationships—between married partners, parents and children, rulers and subjects, etc.—one may say that righteous conduct was conduct in which the obligations of a covenant were honoured. In 1 Samuel 24: 17, Saul declares that David is more righteous than he, because he has fulfilled the duties implicit in the covenant between king and subject, whereas Saul has not (see also Gen. 30: 33; Deut. 24: 13; Prov. 12; 10; etc.). Job 29 contains a graphic picture of a righteous man. He is seen as benevolent and enjoying harmonious relationships with all the members of his community.

The foregoing helps us to understand God's activity in justifying His people, i.e. as it appears in the Old Testament. The righteousness of God is His faithfulness in the fulfilment of the promises attached to the covenant which He has initiated with Israel. It is expressed in His activity towards her, both in judgment and deliverance. In the pre-exilic prophets, the righteous God appears as the Champion and Deliverer of the oppressed poor (Isa. 11: 4; Amos 2: 6, cf. Psa. 103: 6; 146: 7 ff). Hosea, through his experiences with his wife, was able to glimpse the steadfast love of God seeking His erring but penitent partner Israel and bestowing upon her the gift of righteousness—the restoration of covenantal relationship with Himself (2: 18–20). Finally, in Isaiah we see God, who in His righteousness has condemned and punished Israel, seeking her in the exercise of this same righteousness in order to save and justify her (Isa. 45: 25; 46: 13, 51: 5–6).

b. JUSTIFICATION IN THE NEW TESTAMENT

The justification of which the New Testament speaks is 'witnessed by the law and the prophets' (Rom. 3: 21). We will briefly examine the classic statement of the doctrine made by Paul in Romans 3: 20–26.

In the previous section of the Roman Epistle, Paul has demonstrated that both Gentiles and Jews are sinners, under the wrath of God (1: 18; 2: 2; 3: 23). Human good deeds *cannot* put men back on right terms with God, not even 'the deeds of the law' as the Jews of Paul's day believed (3: 20; Phil. 3: 6). But now, God's righteousness—His righteous activity—has been manifested in the Gospel (1: 17; 3: 21). By the death of Jesus Christ as a propitiation for, or expiation of, human sin, God has provided a means whereby sinners may come into harmonious relationship with Himself. This is God's free gift. It becomes a reality for men when they put their faith in Jesus Christ. Then, being justified, they have peace with God (Rom. 5: 1). This new standing before God is the ground of their entire experience as Christians.

Thus, in the act of justifying them, God makes sinners righteous in their relationship with Himself, and He 'declares' their righteousness. This is the *essential truth* to grasp. And this 'declared righteousness' becomes a reality to the believer by means of the inner witness of His Spirit (Rom. 8: 15, 16).

But what of their 'righteousness' in the sense which the word bears in modern speech, i.e. good character and conduct? It is true that at the moment of his turn to the Lord in repentance, the sinner has no acceptable achievement to offer a holy God. Yet his submission to God's judgment upon his sin, together with his new standing 'in Christ', are the promise and guarantee of God making him experientially righteous in thought, word, and deed. And though he may not be 'perfect' in this life, his life is genuinely different after he becomes a Christian. It is for this that he has been saved (Eph. 2: 10).

Finally, we must note that the biblical doctrine of justification by faith was wonderfully set forth by Jesus in His teaching (Lk. 15: 21–24; 18: 9–14) and in His gracious dealings with sinners.

4. REDEMPTION

The English word 'to redeem' means, literally, 'to buy back, or to recover by expenditure of effort'. The idea of purchase or costly effort is attached to the biblical words which are translated 'redeem', 'redemption', etc.

a. REDEMPTION IN THE OLD TESTAMENT

We need to give particular attention to two Hebrew words.

i. Padah

This word actually means 'ransom by payment of a price'. It was used of the redemption of the firstborn (Exod. 13: 13ff) and of slaves (Exod. 21: 8). It was then used figuratively for deliverance from trouble, danger, death, etc. (2 Sam. 4: 9; Psa. 26: 11) and for

God's deliverance of His people from Egypt (Deut. 7: 8; 2 Sam.
7: 23; Psa. 78: 42).

ii. Ga'al
This has a distinctive meaning: the redemption or reclaiming of
what is one's own. It has a special use in the context of family law
and family relationships where it may often be translated 'act as a
kinsman'. The Hebrew kinsman was under obligation to avenge the
honour of a member of his family who had been killed (Deut. 19: 6),
to marry the widow of a deceased relative (Ruth 4: 5) and to buy a
relative out of slavery (Lev. 25: 48 ff). This verb is used to describe
God's action in delivering His people, both from bondage in Egypt
(Exod. 6: 6; Psa. 106: 10; etc.) and from the Exile (Psa. 107: 2; Isa.
43: 1; 48: 20, etc.).

When used as a noun, this term means 'kinsman-redeemer'
(Ruth 3: 12). It is the word used when God is called 'Redeemer'.
This use is frequent in Isaiah (Psa. 19: 14; Isa. 41: 14; 49: 7;
etc.). God's kinship with Israel is presented as one of His motives
for redeeming her. But this must not be unduly pressed, for God
was not *obligated* to save Israel. He acted in sheer grace. And His
action in redeeming Israel gave Him the right of ownership over
her.

iii. Further Old Testament thoughts
The idea of the payment of a price is not always prominent in Old
Testament passages where the vocabulary of redemption is used.
The meaning in some cases is adequately conveyed by such words
as 'deliverance', 'salvation', etc. But even here it is frequently
suggested that God's action involved Him in great effort. For
example, mention is made of His strength (Prov. 23: 10, 11; Jer.
50: 34), or it is said that He will redeem 'with a stretched out arm'
(Exod. 6: 6).

b. REDEMPTION IN THE NEW TESTAMENT
Here again, 'redemption' in some passages carries the general
meaning of 'salvation' (Lk. 1: 68; 2: 38; 24: 21). More frequently,
however, it means liberation at a price. There are two groups of
New Testament words which call for special consideration.

i. Lutron (*meaning 'ransom'*)
This word in first-century non-biblical Greek was used in connection
with the ransoming of prisoners and slaves. Obviously, it would have
conveyed this meaning to these first-century hearers. Related to it
are *apolutrosis* and *lutrosis*, meaning 'redemption', and the verb
lutroo, meaning 'I redeem'.

ii. Agorazo and exagorazo (*both of which mean 'I buy in the market'*)

iii. Conclusions from these words

The most important of all the New Testament passages is Mark 10: 45 (cf. Mt. 20: 28) where Jesus, speaking of Himself, says: 'For the Son of man came not to be ministered unto, but to minister, and to give His life a ransom for many'. Jesus is saying that He will lay down His life voluntarily. He will give Himself 'for many'. There is an echo here of Isaiah chapter 53, where the words 'for many' are found at least twice (vs. 11, 12). His surrendered life will be their ransom (*lutron*); the payment which will secure their liberation. The preposition 'for' is stressed and this bears a substitutionary meaning—'in place of many'.

Nothing is said about the bondage from which the death of Jesus liberates men, but it may be assumed that it is the bondage of sin. Neither is anything said about the one to whom the ransom is offered, but the saying strongly supports the interpretation of the death of Christ as a sacrificial offering to God, whereby the cost of reconciliation between God and sinners was met. This understanding of redemption is supported by Romans 3: 24, 25. Here Paul says that Christ Jesus, 'whom God put forward as an expiation by His blood', provided redemption on the ground of which sinners, who put their faith in Him, are justified. These passages supply the clue to the meaning of redemption elsewhere in the New Testament (e.g. Gal. 3: 13, 4: 5; 1 Pet. 1: 18, 19; Rev. 5: 9).

Among the results of redemption are: (i) the forgiveness of sins (Eph. 1: 7) and freedom from all iniquity (Tit. 2: 14); (ii) deliverance from futile ways of life (1 Pet. 1: 18); and (iii) a place as priests in God's kingdom (Rev. 1: 5, 6). The experience of being redeemed results in our belonging to a holy God, and it thus imposes on men an obligation to seek holiness of life (1 Cor. 6: 18–20, 7: 23; 1 Pet. 1: 14–19). In contrast with the redemption offered under the former covenant, redemption through Christ is eternal (Heb. 9: 12). Like other aspects of God's wonderful salvation, redemption is consummated in the life to come (Rom. 8: 23; Eph. 1: 14, 4: 30).

5. RECONCILIATION

Reconciliation, in the sense of the mending of a broken relationship between God and man, is one of the central themes of Scripture. From Genesis chapter three onwards, the Bible shows God at work to remove the barriers which human sin has erected. The prophets compare God in His grace towards sinful Israel, to a husband who seeks an erring wife in order that he may offer her a new marital relationship (Isa. 54: 6–8, 62: 4–5; Hosea 2: 14–20). The Parable of the Prodigal Son is the greatest story of reconciliation in world literature (Lk. 15: 11–32).

In spite of this, the actual words 'reconcile' or 'reconciliation' occur very seldom in the Bible in connection with the divine–human relationship. But, of course, the thought is there in many passages. The words which concern us are: *katallaso* (2 Cor. 5: 18, 19) and *apokatallasso* (Eph. 2: 16) both of which mean 'I reconcile'; and *katallage* (Rom. 5: 11; 2 Cor. 5: 18, 19) meaning 'reconciliation'.

The initiative in reconciliation is taken by God alone (Rom. 5: 8; 2 Cor. 5: 19; 1 Jn. 4: 10), for only He can meet its cost (Psa. 49: 7, 8). Paul's teaching indicates that the divine work of reconciliation was accomplished by means of the death and resurrection of Jesus Christ. Romans 5: 10 speaks of sinners being 'reconciled to God by the death of His Son'. In 2 Corinthians 5: 18–21 it is said that 'God was in Christ reconciling the world to Himself', and this statement is amplified by the words: 'For our sake He made Him to be sin who knew no sin, so that in Him we might become the righteousness of God' (v. 21, R.S.V.). It was by means of the death of His Son as a sacrifice for sinners that God reconciled the world to Himself.

There has been much discussion as to whether the enmity which had to be overcome in reconciliation was solely that felt by sinners towards God, or whether there was also an enmity on the part of God towards sin and sinners which He dealt with when making reconciliation. Is the word 'enemies' in Romans 5: 10 and Colossians 1: 21 to be understood as active or passive? Paul's teaching concerning the wrath of God and the expiatory sacrifice of Christ renders it certain that he believed there was an enmity on both sides. The Cross is the supreme offer of the divine love to sinners. By its means God seeks to remove the enmity which men feel towards Him and replace it by trust and love.

But at the Cross, God was also dealing with sin in such a way that the barriers which it presented to the free outflowing of His holy love were removed. Something happened in the death and resurrection of Christ which changed the relationship of God with sinners, prior to, and apart from, any response on their part. In accordance with this, Paul speaks of the work of reconciliation as already accomplished from the side of God. It was done for us 'while we were yet sinners' (Rom. 5: 8). By means of repentance and faith we 'receive our reconciliation' (Rom. 5: 11, R.S.V.; 2 Cor. 5: 20). The 'ministry of reconciliation' (2 Cor. 5: 18) is not the conciliatory and reconciling word, but the marvellous declaration of the *already accomplished* reconciliation.

Moreover, Paul points to reconciliation between man and man as the natural outcome of reconciliation with God. This is a second vital aspect of reconciliation. In his own day this was taking place between Jews and Gentiles (Eph. 2: 11–22). There cannot be barriers between men when the barrier between God and man is torn down. Colossians 1: 20 gives us a glimpse of Christ's reconciling work extending beyond the human race into the sphere of spiritual beings and into the entire universe. Reconciliation involves fellowship with God— and *our fellows* (1 Jn. 1: 3).

Further, in a very real sense, man is not only reconciled to God and his fellows, he is also reconciled to himself. Life is built on a threefold relationship; to God, to our fellows and to ourselves. Realizing God accepts us 'in Christ' and now being reconciled to our fellows in love, we can accept ourselves as God's children and find personal reconciliation. This produces deep peace in one's inner experience (Phil. 4: 7).

Of the three terms which Paul uses to describe human salvation— justification, reconciliation, and redemption—reconciliation appeals most strongly to the mind of today, because it belongs to the sphere of personal relations. For this reason it well serves the purposes of the evangelist and Christian witness. But care must be taken not to detach the offer of reconciliation from its ground in the atoning work of Christ, and not to present it without making plain that it calls for the response of repentance and faith on the part of men.

6. REGENERATION AND ADOPTION

The New Testament uses several phrases to describe the complete and decisive change which takes place when a man becomes a Christian. He is said to become a new creation (2 Cor. 5: 17), to have been raised from the dead (Eph. 2: 5, 6) and to have been born of God. The name given to the last-named experience is regeneration. The word occurs only once in the New Testament in connection with personal salvation; in Titus 3: 5. But the phrases 'born of God', 'children of God', etc, occur in a number of places. The vocabulary of regeneration indicates that as a consequence of repentance and faith in Jesus Christ, a man's original nature, which is opposed to God's will (Rom. 8: 7), is replaced by a new nature which is aligned to that will (1 Pet. 1: 14, 15, 22). Thus having previously been a child of disobedience and wrath (Eph. 2: 2, 3), he is now God's 'dear child' (Eph. 5: 1).

a. REGENERATION IS SOLELY THE WORK OF GOD

Such a change can be effected only by God, acting in His sovereign freedom (Jn. 1: 13, 3: 8; 1 Jn. 3: 9). The phrase 'born again' can also be translated 'born from above'. This points to the divine source of regeneration as well as to its revolutionary character. God regenerates by means of His Spirit (Jn. 3: 5–8; Rom. 8: 15, 16; Gal. 4: 6) who is given to those who exercise faith in Christ (Jn. 1: 12; Gal. 3: 26).

Regeneration is associated with baptism (Tit. 3: 5); a conjunction which was natural at a time when the confession of faith in Christ was normally followed at once by baptism. The New Testament, however, knows nothing of baptism which conveys regeneration. Rather, baptism is the symbol and seal of salvation by grace through faith. The instrument of the Spirit in regenerating is the Word of God (Eph. 1: 13; 1 Pet. 1: 23; Jas. 1: 18). From this it follows that although regeneration is a supernatural work, it is also a divine gift which calls for human reception (Rom. 8: 15; Gal. 4: 5).

b. REGENERATION IN JUDAISM AND THE GOSPELS

There is some anticipation of personal regeneration in the Old Testament (Psa. 51: 10, 11), but most Old Testament references are to national renewal (Ezek. 18: 31; 36: 26, 27). The starting points for the teaching in the New Testament are to be sought in three places: (i) Judaism; the Rabbis likened a Gentile newly converted to Judaism to a newborn child. (ii) The teaching of Jesus (Mt. 5: 9, 45; 18: 3). (iii) The life and character of Jesus; the Synoptic Gospels present the picture of the perfect Son of God (Lk. 2: 49, 22: 42), and their lines are etched even more deeply in the Fourth Gospel (Jn. 4: 34; 6: 38, etc.).

c. THE SONSHIP OF JESUS CHRIST, THE PATTERN FOR OURS

The sonship of Jesus Christ is in one sense, normative for that of all God's sons (Rom. 8: 14–16; Gal. 4: 6; Heb. 2: 10). God gives to men the Spirit of His Son who reproduces in them a filial attitude akin to that of Jesus Christ. (Compare Rom. 8: 15 and Gal. 4: 6 with Mk. 14: 36: 'Abba! Father!') The fact that Jesus Christ is the Image of God (2 Cor. 4: 4; Col. 1: 15), and that believers are 'being changed into His image (likeness)' (Rom. 8: 29; 2 Cor. 3: 18), indicates that the goal of God's process of regeneration is a race of men fulfilling the purpose for which they were created (Gen. 1: 26, 27). This goal will be finally and perfectly attained only in the life to come (Rom. 8: 17, 23; 1 Jn. 3: 2, 3).

d. ADOPTION AS AN ASPECT OF REGENERATION

Paul makes only allusive references to the new birth. Its place is taken by a concept found nowhere else in the New Testament except in his writings; that of Adoption (Rom. 8: 15; Gal. 4: 5; Eph. 1: 5). Under Roman law, an adopted child had all the rights and privileges of a normal child in his family. All links with his former family were severed, so that by adoption he became a new person. Paul therefore means by adoption what John means by the new birth. The word 'adoption', however, points to the difference between the divine sonship offered to men and the Sonship possessed by Jesus Christ—a difference which must never be overlooked. Our sonship has a beginning; His is eternal. 'We are sons by grace; He is so by nature.' (J. B. Lightfoot, *Epistle to the Galatians*, p. 169.) Now all this comes to a person through his personal repentance and faith.

7. REPENTANCE

We begin by considering repentance as a spiritual attitude and activity which conducts one into the state of salvation. As such, it is inseparable from faith to which it is related as the negative to the positive pole.

a. REPENTANCE IS BASICALLY A TURNING TO GOD

The New Testament word for human repentance is, with one exception, *metanoia*, which means 'a change of mind'. Biblical repentance includes this element, but it has a much wider range also. Behind the Greek word lies the Old Testament idea of repentance as turning, or returning, to God; the Hebrew verb is *shub*. It is used by the prophets when they call upon Israel to turn back to God from her state of rebellion against Him and to yield to Him the obedience which belongs to her standing within the Covenant (Jer. 3: 12, 18: 11; Ezek. 18: 30). This repentance must be whole-hearted (Joel 2: 13).

Normally, the prophets addressed their calls to the nation, but Jeremiah speaks to the individual (18: 11, 25: 5). The prophetic summons reached its climax in the ministry of John the Baptist. It was his task to prepare the way of the Lord by calling Israel back to God and the Covenant in preparation for the advent of the Messiah.

b. REPENTANCE IN CHRISTIAN EXPERIENCE

The ministry of Jesus began where that of the Baptist ended. His call to repentance was linked with an invitation to enter by faith into the Kingdom of God which, in Himself, had drawn near to men (Mk. 1: 15). Jesus deepened the understanding of repentance, because He gave a new inwardness to the meaning of sin. God's goodness, which in all its manifestations is meant to lead men to repentance (Rom. 2: 4), was given its supreme expression in the gift of His only-begotten Son. During His life in the flesh, Jesus quickened human repentance by His words and deeds and by the influence of His personality (Mt. 11: 23; Lk. 11: 32). In similar manner, the Spirit uses the preaching of Christ crucified and risen to effect repentance and saving faith in sinners (Acts 2: 37, 38, 5: 31).

The word 'repentance' on Christian lips thus denotes the action in which a man turns from his sin to God, in order to put his faith in Christ and Him crucified. It involves a change of attitude involving the entire personality: the intellect, which recognizes and accepts responsibility for its sin; and the will, which turns decisively from sin. This turning is followed by the re-alignment of the personality with the will of God. The Parable of the Prodigal Son clearly illustrates all these aspects of repentance (Lk. 15: 11–24).

'Godly grief', which 'produces a repentance that leads to salvation', is contrasted with 'worldly grief', mere remorse and fear of the consequences of sin, which include no reference to God (2 Cor. 7: 10, 11 R.S.V.). It is of vital importance that all remember that there can be no entrance into the experience of Christian salvation except by way of repentance and faith. Finally, it is to be noted that repentance is a permanent attitude and activity of the Christian life. 'And they who fain would serve Him best are conscious most of wrong within.'

8. FAITH

A glance at a concordance will reveal that the words 'faith', 'belief', 'trust', etc. represent one of the distinguishing themes of biblical religion in all stages of its development. So characteristic is the attitude of faith that the New Testament Christians are called 'believers' (Acts 2: 44, 5: 14). It is important to remember, however, that faith, in the biblical sense, does not mean blind belief in the absence of evidence or rational thought.* It denotes a *personal relationship;* in the Old Testament, with God, and in the New Testament, with God as He is manifest in Christ Jesus.

a. FAITH IN THE OLD TESTAMENT

The Hebrew noun *emunah* is usually translated as 'faithfulness', 'stability', 'truth', etc. The one place where it is translated as 'faith' is Habakkuk 2: 4: 'The just shall live by his faith' (cf. Gal. 3: 11; Heb. 10: 38, 39). Here the word means rather 'faithfulness', stead- fastness', i.e. a passive quality of character. But since this quality is the fruit of confidence in God and His promises, the active quality 'faith' is implied. The verb 'to believe' occurs in many places, one of the most important of these being Genesis 15: 6: 'And he (Abraham) believed the Lord; and he reckoned it to him as righteous- ness.' The meaning is that Abraham relied on God and His promises and committed himself to God to serve His purposes. This is the basic meaning of faith in the Old Testament (Psa. 27: 13; Isa. 7: 9, 28: 16, etc.). It is also expressed by the verb 'to trust' which occurs in many places (Psa. 56: 3, 84: 12; Isa. 26: 3). In addition, the nature of faith as trust appears in many of the narratives of the Old Testa- ment which depict God's servants acting in obedience to His word (Heb. 11).

b. FAITH IN THE NEW TESTAMENT ('Faith': *pistis;* 'I believe': *pisteuo*)

Faith is one of the themes which bind together the writings of the New Testament. While there is unity in the treatment of the theme, there is also variety and development. In the *Synoptic Gospels* Jesus

---

* Of course, this does not mean that all that can be known of God is purely rational. God is above rational limitations. But surely faith is not irrational or void of empirical evidences, even if God cannot be 'proved' by these methods.

urges His followers to have faith in God and to fling away all anxiety (Mt. 6: 25–34). In this, as in other respects, He is Himself 'the Pioneer and Perfecter of our faith' (Heb. 12: 2). Yet the summons which He addressed to men to leave all and follow Him anticipated the relationship of faith in Christ which men have experienced since His death and resurrection. In *Acts*, faith in Christ crucified and risen conveys salvation (2: 21, 4: 12, 10: 43).

It is in the *Pauline Epistles*, however, that saving faith receives its classic treatment. For Paul, faith is the committal of one's entire self to Christ. The Christian life from start to finish is a life of faith (Rom. 1: 17: 'through faith for faith', R.S.V.). The gift of salvation is received by faith (Eph. 2: 8). The Christian life is throughout one of fellowship with Christ mediated by faith (Gal. 2: 20). Faith points to future fulfilment and, in the form of a personal bond uniting the believer with Christ, it outlasts this life (1 Cor. 13: 13). Moreover, faith is a creative ethical force: it works 'through love' (Gal. 5: 6).

The writer to the *Hebrews* does not speak explicitly of faith in Christ. Still, he shares the New Testament conviction that salvation is by faith alone (10 : 22, 38 ff, 13: 7). He defines faith in a distinctive way: it is 'the assurance of things hoped for, the conviction of things not seen' (11: 1). Yet the difference, if there be any, between this view of faith and that of Paul is not great at all. For the unseen world of which Hebrews speaks is 'a world in which Christ holds the central place'. (J. Denney, *The Death of Christ*, p. 239).

In the *Gospel and Epistles of John* the noun 'faith' occurs only once (1 Jn. 5: 4), but the verb 'to believe' is used frequently. God's purpose in giving His Son is that men might believe in Him and enter into life (Jn. 3: 16, 36). To believe on the name of Jesus Christ is to receive power to become children of God (Jn. 1: 12; 1 Jn. 5: 1). God's total requirement of men can be expressed in terms of belief in His Son (Jn. 6: 29). Human sin reached its climax in man's refusal to believe in Jesus (Jn. 16: 9), and such refusal exposes men to condemnation (Jn. 3: 18). The signs given by Jesus had as their object the creation of faith (Jn. 2: 11). John tells us that the whole of his Gospel was composed with the same object in mind (20: 31).

In certain passages of the *Pastoral Epistles* and *Jude*, 'faith' denotes the body of accepted Christian doctrine (1 Tim. 4: 6; Jude 3). In *James* chapter two it is explicitly denied that salvation is by faith alone (v. 24). But the writer is speaking not of faith as Paul understands it, i.e. total self-committal to Christ, but of faith in the sense of barren orthodoxy of creed. One is never saved by simply accepting certain intellectual creeds. This is James' point. One must *commit* himself to Christ. This is faith that saves.

An important question is: are *repentance* and *faith* human activities or divine gifts? The fact that we are summoned to both suggests that repentance and faith are ours to exercise. On the other hand, repentance (Acts 5: 31, 11: 18; cf. Jer. 31: 18) and perhaps even faith (Phil. 1: 29) are described as gifts of God. In this, as in other matters, Christian thinking must take account of human freedom and divine election, for both are factors in Christian experience. We are free to repent and believe, but only because the grace and power of God constrain us (Jn. 6: 44).

V. HOW MAN RELATES TO GOD

1. IDENTIFICATION WITH CHRIST: 'IN CHRIST'

Under this heading we consider the teaching of the New Testament on the spiritual union of Christ and His people. The nature of this union is indicated by a phrase frequently used by Paul: 'in Christ'. With variants such as 'in Christ Jesus', 'in the Lord', and 'in Him', this occurs no fewer than a hundred and sixty-four times in the writings of the Apostle Paul. Thus it must have tremendous significance.

Not all of these cases, of course, are relevant to the present purpose, but the following passages are among those in which the phrase bears its distinctive meaning: Romans 8: 1; 2 Corinthians 5: 17; 1 Thessalonians 1: 1, 3: 8. The expression 'in Christ' describes 'the most intimate fellowship imaginable of the Christian with the living spiritual Christ' (A. Deissmann). As implied, it points to one of the experiences central to Paul's religion and theology. According to some interpreters, it was the heart and key of both. We will consider Paul's twofold use of the phrase.

a. INDIVIDUAL UNION

The believer lives in Christ as in an 'atmosphere'. Christ is in him and he in Christ. Christ and the believer become 'one' (Jn. 15: 5). This union is effected from the divine side by grace. It is received and maintained from the human side by faith. It is also supported by prayer and communion with Christ. It is likely that the starting point of Paul's doctrine of union with Christ was baptism; certainly the two are closely linked in his thought. As Romans 6: 3–5 and Galatians 3: 27 indicate, a convert passes 'into Christ' by baptism.* These passages should be read carefully so the impact of being 'in Christ' is fully appreciated. By baptism, converts pass into Christ and become His. They become one. All that Christ experienced we experience 'in Him'. This is a marvellous truth.

* Again, this is not to say one is saved by the mere act of water baptism. See pages 154ff.

b. CORPORATE UNION

Since Christ is the Head of the Church which is His body (Eph. 1: 22, 23), it follows that union with Him involves union with His people. This union is a spiritual reality in the case of all His people (Rom. 8: 1; Gal. 3: 28), and it calls for visible and practical expression. It also lays upon Christians the duty of living in a manner worthy of members of the body of Christ. Paul teaches that the communion of the believer with his Lord outlasts death: 'In Christ shall all be made alive' (1 Cor. 15: 22). This does not mean that all men share in the Resurrection unto life, but that all who are 'in Christ' do so.

c. THE SOURCES OF PAUL'S TEACHING

Paul may have coined the phrase 'in Christ', but the roots of his thought can be traced far back in the Bible. The Hebrews conceived of the closest unity between Israel and the representatives appointed by God to lead her: the king (Psa. 28: 8; 89: 38), the Son of man (Dan. 7: 13, 14) and the Messiah. Jesus laid claim to a similar identification with God's people in sayings like Matthew 18: 20 and when He spoke of Himself as the Son of man (Mt. 25: 31–46). Compare also John 11: 25, John 15: 1–8 (The Vine and the Branches) and Acts 9: 4.

The union with Christ which Paul experienced and taught is sometimes called 'mystical'. This description should be used with care as it is liable to suggest an absorption of the human spirit into Christ so as to lose its individual reality. The Bible always preserves a sharp distinction between the human and the divine. It is better to speak of 'faith-union'. Still, this marvellous truth is the basis of communion with God and the experiential foundation of Christian victory (Rom. 6: 1–14). Faith in the fact of complete identification with Christ, i.e. being 'in Christ', is what Paul presents as God's way to overcome the power of sin and temptation in one's life. In Christ, one is 'dead to sin' and 'alive to God'.

2. SANCTIFICATION

In most Protestant theology, the noun 'sanctification' denotes three principles; viz. the act of making holy, the process of becoming and the state which results from these. Among evangelical Christians it is commonly used to describe the development of the believer towards spiritual maturity. There is abundant Scriptural support for these uses of the word, of course. But the teaching of the Bible on this subject is more complex than may at first be realized.

a. HOLINESS AND SANCTIFICATION IN THE OLD TESTAMENT

A sentence in Heber's hymn takes us to the heart of the Old Testament teaching: 'Only Thou art holy' (cf. Rev. 15: 4). God is

the 'Holy One' in an absolute sense (Psa. 71: 22; Isa. 1: 4; Hosea
11: 9). Holiness is His essential nature. All His attributes and
activities are merely aspects of it. God is therefore the sole source
of holiness; man and things become holy by being separated *unto*
Him. Such separation, and the status which it confers, are both
called 'sanctification'.

Various sections of the Old Testament speak of 'holy garments'
(Exod. 28: 2), 'holy vessels' (1 Kings 8: 4), 'holy places' (Psa. 24: 3),
etc. But the holiness of persons is clearly of greater importance for
future developments (Exod. 19: 6; 2 Kings. 4: 9). The moral
perfection of God's nature became the basis of an ever-enlarging
place in man's thought of God's utter holiness (Isa. 6: 3, 5). Israel
thus came to see that separation to God demanded purity and
uprightness of life: 'Be holy, for I am holy' (Lev. 11: 44, 45). Rightly
used, the words 'holiness' and 'sanctification' always contain a
direct reference to God.

b. SANCTIFICATION AS A STATUS

'Sanctification' and 'justification' are both words which indicate
an act or process by which sinners are put into right relationship
with God. It might, therefore, appear that they are interchangeable
terms. The writer to the Hebrews does, in fact, give to 'sanctification' the meaning which 'justification' bears in the writings of Paul
(Heb. 2: 11, 10: 10, 14). By 'sanctification' Paul most commonly
means the process by which a man, once justified, grows up as a
Christian.

But it is important to realize that, from one point of view, sanctification can be seen as a status conferred by God on the believer at
the beginning of his new life. In the New Testament Christians are
called 'saints', i.e. 'separated people'. Paul writes to the Corinthians,
'you were sanctified' (1 Cor. 6: 11). A sharp line of distinction cannot, therefore, be drawn between justification and sanctification. If
justification is a man's entrance into a righteous standing before
God, sanctification is his progressive realization in character and
conduct of all that this standing involves.

c. SANCTIFICATION AS A PROCESS AND A TASK

Christians are urged to 'grow in grace and knowledge of our Lord
and Saviour Jesus Christ' (2 Pet. 3: 18). They are to 'make holiness
perfect in the fear of God' (2 Cor. 7: 1) and to 'yield their members
to righteousness for sanctification' (Rom. 6: 19). The divine appeal
of the Old Testament is repeated in the New Testament: 'Be holy,
for I am holy' (1 Pet. 1: 16). The holiness here envisaged is personal
and ethical. It shows itself in new conduct (Rom. 8: 1 ff.), new
thinking, feeling and willing (Phil. 4: 8), new speaking (Col. 4: 6),
etc. In this work of sanctification the holy God is active in the per-

son of Jesus Christ His Son (Jn. 17: 19; 1 Cor. 1: 2, 30), in the person
of the Holy Spirit (2 Thess. 2: 13) who indwells God's people (Eph.
3: 16) and by means of the word of His truth (Jn. 17: 17).

d. SANCTIFICATION AS A GOAL

Sanctification is God's will for His people (1 Thess. 4: 3). Their
complete holiness is the ultimate purpose of Christ's redeeming
work (Eph. 5: 25 ff). This goal will have been reached when the
Christian is conformed to the image of Christ Himself (Rom. 8: 29).

The idea of sinless perfection in this life finds no support in the
Scriptures. While it is true that God offers us His 'fullness' here and
now (Eph. 3: 19), and that faith in the indwelling Christ spells
victory in the Christian life, our reception of God's gifts is always
incomplete and intermittent. To the end of our life on earth we are
indwelt by sin; we must be on our guard against it and seek forgiveness for it (1. Jn. 1: 8, 9). Nevertheless, the New Testament will
not allow us to accept any standard lower than perfection (Mt.
5: 48; Eph. 5: 1), and it urges us to make this the object of our
striving (1 Cor. 9: 24; Phil. 3: 13–15).

3. LOVE TO GOD AND MAN

The biblical teaching on man's love for God and for his fellow human
beings can be understood only in the light of the New Testament
words: 'We love, because He (God) first loved us' (1 Jn. 4: 19).
Love, whatever its direction, does not originate in human nature.
It is the response to God's love.

a. THE OLD TESTAMENT CONCEPT

i. Man's love for God

The Old Testament leaves us in no doubt that the love of God—
described also as His steadfast love, grace, loving kindness, mercy,
etc.—is prior to any love which men may feel towards Him. His
love is the ground on which God appeals for Israel's love and
loyalty (Exod. 19: 4–6; Deut. 4: 5–40). Moreover, it is the recognition of it which quickens the answering love of the Psalmists
(Psa. 18: 1 ff, 116: 1 ff.).

It is instructive that two of the words used in connection with
God's love for Israel, the verb *aheb* (love) and the noun *chesed*
(covenant-love), are used of Israel's love for God: *aheb*, Deut. 6: 5,
Joshua 22: 5; *chesed*, Hosea 4: 1, 6: 4. The use of the latter word is
particularly revealing, because of the emphasis which it places on
loyalty and faithfulness. By His *chesed*, God has bound Himself to
Israel within the covenant. And she must respond with a like
loyalty. While Israel's love for God was not lacking in warmth of
feeling, as is evidenced by the devotion of the Psalmists, the quality
which God sought beyond all others was obedience (Exod. 20: 6;

Deut. 5: 10; cf. Mic. 6: 8). Thus man's love for God under the Old Covenant was an aspect of his righteousness.

Finally, we notice how the content of this love is analysed in the words, which for the Jews was the heart of their faith, 'You shall love the Lord your God with all your heart, and with all your soul, and with all your might' (Deut. 6: 5). Man's entire personality—intellect, emotion, will and body—is to be engaged in the love which he offers to God.

ii. Man's love for his fellows

Again, the same Hebrew words are used: *aheb*, Leviticus 19: 34; Deuteronomy 10: 18; *chesed*, Genesis 20: 13; 1 Kings 2: 7. It was the duty of the Israelite to extend to others a love similar to that which passed between God and himself. The *chesed* of human relationships was to be expressed in practical, humanitarian ways, as is evident in the Book of the Covenant (Exod. 20: 22–23: 33).

b. THE NEW TESTAMENT CONCEPT

Although the New Testament is aware of breadths and depths in human love which are unknown to the Old Testament, there are, nevertheless, striking parallels in the teaching of both Testaments on this subject.

i. Man's love for God

The New Testament makes explicit what is implicit in the Old Testament: 'God is love' (1 Jn. 4: 8, 16) and 'We love, because He first loved us' (1 Jn. 4: 19). Behind these and similar statements stand the supreme proofs of God's love: (a) the cross and resurrection of Christ (Jn. 3: 16; Rom. 5: 8); (b) the manifold blessings of Christian experience.

It is no disparagement to the saints of the Old Testament to say that the love of Christ crucified has elicited from believing men a devotion which far exceeds in its fervour and self-abandonment anything known prior to His advent. There are no Old Testament parallels to passages such as 2 Corinthians 5: 14; Galatians 2: 20; 1 Peter 1: 8. The fact that Christian love was something new in human experience appears in the fact that the New Testament writers used for it the new word which they had taken over from the Septuagint—the Greek language version of the Old Testament—to denote the love of God: *agape*. Like *chesed*, this indicates far more than feeling; it includes the steady alignment of the human will with the will of God. If we love Him, we will keep His Commandments (Jn. 14: 15).

Thus the New Testament also lays great emphasis upon obedience as the expression of man's love for God. In point of fact, the New Testament does not have volumes to say about man's love for God *per se*. It calls rather for faith in Him, because without faith we cannot love God. Actually, faith finds spontaneous expression in loving obedience (Jn. 21: 15–17; Gal. 5: 6). This is where the primary emphasis lies.

ii. Man's love for his fellows

The teaching of Jesus Christ concerning the whole duty of man is of great importance here (Lk. 10: 27, and parallels). Our first duty is to love God. Humanitarian service alone can never be a substitute for this. But love for God is real only where it bears fruit in love for one's fellows. The word *agape* is used in this connection also. Here it means 'a gracious, determined, and active interest in the true welfare of others'. (G. B. Caird, *St. Luke*, p. 104.) Such a love is described in 1 Corinthians 13. It is a completely 'selfless' love.

The New Testament presents more than one motive for such love: first, the love of God for us (1 Jn. 3: 16–18); secondly, the fact that Christ died for all men (Rom. 14: 15; 1 Cor. 8: 11); thirdly, the fact that Christ draws near to us in other people and their claims (Mt. 25: 31–46). Christian love thus appears as unique; a flame kindled at the fire of God's love. At the same time, we are not called upon to deny the value of love and goodness in those who make no profession of Christian faith. Although defective, these qualities are to be traced to God as the ultimate Source, because all men are made in His image.

The Bible begins by calling for love within the fellowship of faith. But it certainly does not end there. For all its concern with God's love for Israel, the Old Testament is well aware of His wider mercy. In the same way, although the New Testament has much to say concerning love within the Church (Jn. 13: 34; Heb. 13: 1; 1 Pet. 1: 22), Jesus teaches us to minister to our neighbour in every way (Lk. 10: 36, 37), and to exercise love in a sphere which has no bounds (Mt. 5: 38–48). These truths are enforced by the universal Gospel preached by the Apostles and illustrated by their missionary enterprise. Moreover, love constrains one to:

4. WORSHIP

a. THE IDEAL OF WORSHIP

One of the most striking features of The Book of Revelation is the large place which it gives to worship. The word itself occurs twenty-four times—more frequently than in any other book in the Bible. We are given glimpses of vast companies of angels and redeemed men and women worshipping with their faces turned towards God on His throne.

Nor is the worship of God confined to them. In chapter four of *Revelation* we read that 'round the throne, on each side of the throne, are four living creatures' (v. 6) of whom H. B. Swete has written:

'The four forms represent whatever is noblest, strongest, wisest and swiftest in animate Nature. Nature, including Man, is represented before the Throne, taking its part in the fulfilment of the Divine Will, and the worship of the Divine Majesty.' (H. B. Swete, *The Apocalypse of St. John*, p. 70.) When we come to the description of the New Jerusalem, we notice that it contains no temple; 'for the Lord God Almighty and the Lamb are the temple of it' (21: 22). In heaven, therefore, worship is unceasing and shared by the whole of creation.

Since we are taught to pray, 'Thy kingdom come, Thy will be done, in earth as it is in heaven', we may assume that the Apocalypse, i.e. the Book of Revelation, reveals God's ideal for worship. It needs no demonstration that this ideal is far from realization on earth. Man, though fallen, has retained some sense of God and has always offered worship of some kind (Acts 17: 22). But, being a sinner, he does so without clear knowledge of God's nature and will (Acts 17: 23), without awareness of his sin and the need for repentance, and without purity of motive (Rom. 1: 18–25).

b. GOD'S PROVISION OF WORSHIP

i. The Old Testament
God's activity to deliver man from his darkness of mind and perversion of will began with the calling of a servant nation: Israel. To them He gave a special revelation of His nature and purpose and a system of worship which corresponded with it. The latter included sacrifice, the priesthood, the sabbath, the annual festivals, the Law, the Temple, and latterly the synagogues, etc. The worship of Israel, although unique in the pre-Christian world in respect of purity and spirituality, was provisional only. It foreshadowed that which was to come.

ii. The New Testament
Jesus did not condemn the religious practices of His race. He respected and supported them (Mt. 8: 4; Lk. 4: 16). He taught, however, that the day was at hand when they would be replaced by a more spiritual worship. God, who is spirit, was seeking those who would worship Him 'in spirit and truth' (Jn. 4: 24). To 'worship in spirit' has been understood in two ways. First, God is spirit and cannot be represented by material images. Human worship must be the yielding of mind, heart and will to Him. Secondly, God is creative: a life-giving power. Thus human worship must be supported and energized by His Spirit. We are not called upon to choose between these. Both meanings are true—and both are probably intended. To 'worship in truth' means to worship the true God as He is revealed in Christ.

Such worship could not begin until after the glorification of Jesus Christ, for it was only then that the Spirit could be given in His Pentecostal fullness (Jn. 7: 39). His coming marked the beginning of Christian worship. From the outset, this was marked by joy and profound gratitude to God for His redeeming work in Christ (Acts 2: 47; 1 Thess. 1: 6; 1 Pet. 1: 8). The new song of heaven had begun on earth (Rev. 5: 9). Christian worship is offered 'in the name of Christ' (Eph. 5: 20), even if this phrase is not always used.

There is some evidence that worship was offered to Christ in New Testament times (2 Pet. 3: 18; Rev. 1: 5, 6), but the normal practice of the New Testament is to offer worship to God the Father through Christ. This is a pattern which Christians are advised to follow. The New Testament also speaks of worship 'in the Spirit' (Phil. 3: 3). Some conception of the worship of the primitive Church can be formed from Acts and the Epistles. We find that the first day of the week had replaced the Jewish sabbath. Christians met for worship then, and at other times usually in homes; Psalms and Christian hymns were sung (Eph. 5: 19), baptism was administered and the Lord's Supper was regularly celebrated.

C. THE WORSHIP OF THE ENTIRE LIFE

The Bible reveals, therefore, that even in this age of the Spirit some pattern and organization are necessary for corporate worship. But God's people must never lose sight of the ideal for worship which is realized in heaven; 'a life made up of prayer in every part' (cf. Jas. 1: 27). This profound truth is enforced in the New Testament by the use of two words: *latreuo* (verb), 'I serve' (Rom. 1: 9) and 'I worship' (Phil. 3: 3); *latreia* (noun), 'service' (Jn. 16:2) and 'worship' (Heb. 9: 1). In classical Greek these words are used in connection with a man's daily work or with some other undertaking or interest to which he gives his whole life. Biblical usage confines them to the service and worship of God.

Paul uses the noun *latreia* in Romans 12: 1 where he urges his readers to present their 'bodies' as a living sacrifice to God 'which is your spiritual *latreia* (worship or service)'. The Apostle is surely calling upon Christians to offer to God in worship all the activities of their bodily lives. So far as this is true of them, so far have they fulfilled God's ideal for human life. Outward forms of worship are valuable only as they serve to promote this.

5. PRAYER

a. PRAYER IS THE DISTINCTIVE HUMAN RESPONSE TO GOD

Prayer must be seen in the light of the fact that God is man's Creator and Redeemer. As His creature, man is made in the 'image' and 'likeness' of God (Gen. 1: 26). Thus he is capable of responding to Him. Prayer lies at the heart of this response. The Bible is aware of the fact that among heathen people there is some practice of prayer and sense of its value (Gen. 20: 7; Dan. 4: 34; Jonah 1: 6, 14). These are only passing glimpses, however, since the prayer with which the Bible is primarily concerned is that offered by men and women who are conscious of God as their Redeemer.

b. PRAYER IN THE OLD TESTAMENT

Such prayer begins under the Old Covenant. The prayer of Abraham for Sodom (Gen 18: 22–33) and the prayer of Moses for Israel (Exod. 32: 30–32) are among the most moving intercessions of all time. The prophets were men of prayer (1 Sam. 12: 19; Amos 7: 1–6 and the 'Confessions of Jeremiah', chapters 11–20). Nor was the prayer of Israel confined to her outstanding representatives. A glance at the Psalter reveals the spiritual depth and comprehensive range of the prayers in which the ordinary worshipper joined when he took part in the Temple worship. The words of Isaiah 56: 7, 'my house shall be called a house of prayer for all peoples', declare God's ultimate purpose in granting to Israel a special revelation. Furthermore, they point to the fulfilment of this purpose in Christ and the Church.

c. THE PRAYER LIFE OF JESUS

The Gospels reveal that prayer occupied a supremely important place in the life of Jesus (Mk. 1: 35; Lk. 3: 21, 11: 1). His prayers were marked by a reverent intimacy in attitude to God which was without precedent. Here, our Lord's use of the Aramaic word *Abba*: 'Father', or 'my Father', is deeply significant (Mk. 14: 36). This was a most intimate form of address used by Jewish children and older sons and daughters only when speaking to their fathers. The Jews never employed it when addressing God, because it would have been over-familiar. But it is apparent that Jesus used it, and on His lips it was the revelation of His unique relationship and communion with His Father. Men and women who receive Christ as Saviour and Lord are made children of God and are authorized to use the same mode of address (Mt. 11: 27; Jn. 1: 12; Rom. 8: 15; Gal. 4: 6).

d. THE LORD'S MODEL PRAYER

In Luke this prayer begins with the simple address, 'Father' (Lk. 11: 2 R.S.V.). The prayer is intended for use by the disciples of Christ (Mt. 5: 1). Only they can enter fully into its meaning. The model prayer is also noteworthy for the pattern which it provides for all prayer. The first half is devoted to God alone: His name, His kingdom, and His will. The second half is concerned with human needs, but only with the simple and basic ones: bread, the forgiveness of sins, guidance, and protection.

e. OTHER ASPECTS OF PRAYER IN THE NEW TESTAMENT

Prayer is to be offered 'in the name of Jesus Christ' (Jn. 14: 13, 15: 16, 16: 23 ff). To fulfil this requirement, it must be characterized by knowledge of Christ, faith in Him, and obedience to His will (1 Jn. 3: 22). One must recognize that he stands before God only in the righteousness of Jesus. Thus we pray 'in His name'.

It is not difficult to find teaching in the New Testament concerning all the main elements of Christian prayer, together with examples of them:

(1) *Adoration:* Romans 9: 5; Philippians 2: 10, 11; Revelation 1: 5, 6.

(2) *Thanksgiving:* 1 Corinthians 15: 57; 2 Corinthians 9: 15; Philippians 4: 6.

(3) *Confession:* 1 John 1: 9.

(4) *Intercession:* Philippians 1: 3, 4; 1 Timothy 2: 1-4.

(5) *Petition:* Matthew 6: 8, 7: 11.

f. DIVINE PARTICIPATION IN PRAYER

We are counselled to be diligent in prayer (Lk. 18: 1 ff; Eph. 6: 18) and to bring to it our undivided attention (Mt. 6: 6). But we are also assured that God Himself takes an active part in the prayer life of His people. In Romans chapter eight Paul draws back the veil to afford us a glimpse of Christ at God's right hand making intercession for His redeemed people (Rom. 8: 34; cf. Heb. 7: 25; 1 Jn. 2: 1). In the same chapter also the Apostle gives us an insight into the participation of the Holy Spirit in human prayers: 'We do not know how to pray as we ought, but the Spirit Himself intercedes for us with sighs too deep for words . . .' (vs. 26, 27, R.S.V.). Inevitably, there are many times when the Christian knows the will of God only in the most general way. He may be assured that the divine Spirit who prays within him translates his indefinite aspirations into specific requests which accord with the will of God.

6. THANKSGIVING

Dr John A. Mackay has written, 'The truth we need is a truth that sings' (*God's Order*, p. 40)—one which generates hope and joy. This need is abundantly met by the truth of the Bible. Among the words which occur most often in the pages of Scripture are those belonging to the vocabulary of gratitude: 'praise', 'thanks (giving)', 'blessing', 'gladness', 'joy', etc.

a. IN THE OLD TESTAMENT

'There is no word which is more central in the Old Testament than the word for joy.' (L. Koehler, *Theology of Old Testament*, p. 137.) Israel was repeatedly encouraged to make her religious acts and festivals occasions of joy (Lev. 23: 40; Num. 10: 10; Deut. 12: 7). And there is every reason to believe that she did so. The Psalter, which was the service-book of the Temple, abounds in praise and thanksgiving.

Among the reasons given in the Psalms for gratitude to God are: His personal deliverances, usually of an unspecified nature (Psa. 28: 6, 7, 34: 3, 4, 6); His creative activity and the gift of the harvest (Psa. 65, 95: 4, 5); His deliverance from Egypt (Psa. 136: 10–12, 16, 21); etc. Such thanksgiving is to be seen as a confession of the might and faithfulness of God, and of His people's utter dependence on Him (cf. H. Ringgren, *The Faith of the Psalmists*, p. 77). We may also note that in the passages which express Israel's eschatological hope —her faith in the final coming of God and the universal establishment of His kingdom—there is a mingling of both dread (Isa. 33: 14; Mal. 3: 2) and gladness (Isa. 9: 3, R.S.V., 35: 10, 65: 18, 19).

b. IN THE NEW TESTAMENT

The note of joy sounds again in the wonderful carols with which men and angels celebrate the advent of the Son of God (Lk. 1: 46–55, 68–79, 2: 14, 29–32). There is one significant reference to the thanksgiving of Jesus in the Synoptic Gospels (Lk. 10: 21). In the Gospel according to John, Jesus speaks of His joy and promises that His disciples will share in it (15: 11, 16: 20, 21, 22, 24, 17: 13).

The remainder of the New Testament witnesses to the fulfilment of this promise. Joy is part of the fruit of the Spirit (Gal. 5: 22). Immediately after the Pentecostal outpouring, joy and thanksgiving became part of the everyday lives of Christian disciples (Acts 2: 46, 47). This was one of their distinguishing marks in the first-century world; a world which contained little hope either for this age or the age to come. Thus it was an important ingredient in the witness which the Christians bore. There are many references to thanksgiving in the letters of Paul. Most of his letters open with expressions of gratitude to God for those to whom he is writing. He lays great stress on the duty of thanksgiving (Rom. 1: 21, 14: 6; 2 Cor. 1: 11; Phil. 4: 6).

c. THE COMMUNION SERVICE

In the accounts of the Last Supper we read that Jesus blessed the bread (Mt. 26: 26; Mk. 14: 22), i.e. gave thanks for it (Lk. 22: 19; 1 Cor. 11: 24), and that He gave thanks for the cup (Mt. 26: 27). It was the custom of Jewish piety to offer thanks to God for food and drink. We know that Jesus observed this custom (Mt. 15: 36; Lk. 9: 16). On this occasion, however, He gave thanks not only for the bread and wine, but also for the atoning sacrifice and the New Covenant which they represented. In the same way the worship of

Christians is meant to be, among other things, an occasion when they give thanks to God for the salvation which He accomplished in Jesus Christ. It should be a joyful experience. The Greek word for 'give thanks', which is used in the narratives of the Last Supper, is *eucharisteo*. In some sections of the Church the Communion Service is known as the Eucharist. This is not a New Testament usage, but it serves to emphasize the aspect of the service which is thanksgiving and joy.

7. SERVICE

In the section of this book headed 'Worship', it is pointed out that in the Greek word for worship there is a blending of the meanings 'worship' and 'service'. The same double meaning belongs to the two other nouns which are frequently used in the New Testament for service. *Leitourgia* means worship in Hebrews 9: 21 and service in 2 Corinthians 9: 12.

It appears, therefore, that a sharp distinction cannot be made between Christian worship, prayer, and service. Worship and prayer are man's response to God in whose image he is made and by whom he is redeemed. Service is his response to God who has given him dominion over the earth (Gen. 1: 26, 28). In the light of this we are entitled to draw the following conclusions:

First, the ideal for men and women is that all the activities of their lives shall be an offering of worship of God. This truth is expressed in Romans 12: 1.

Secondly, such a life is possible only where there is faith in Christ. Only then can human life glorify God and be acceptable to Him.

Finally, for the Christian to approach this ideal his personality must be cleansed and his will adjusted to the will of God by constant prayer and worship. Such worship will include the offering of life in all its aspects to God.

The New Testament sets before us parallel aspects of Christian service which must be held in creative tension.

Initially, Christians are frequently described—or describe themselves—as 'servants' of God or of Jesus Christ (Rom. 1: 1; Eph. 6: 6; Col. 4: 12). The word for servant in ordinary Greek meant 'slave'. The Christian is Christ's bond slave, 'bought with a price' (1 Cor. 6: 20). Yet he has been set free by Christ (Jn. 8: 36), and he is 'no more a servant, but a son' (Gal. 4: 7). He belongs to Christ 'whose service is perfect freedom'.

And the Christian is promised a reward for service and fidelity (Mt. 24: 45-47, 25: 21, 23; Rev. 2: 10). Yet there is no room for complacency in the Christian life. When we have done all that lies within our power we are to say, 'We are unprofitable servants; we have done that which was our duty to do' (Lk. 17: 10).

8. PERSEVERANCE AND ASSURANCE

a. PERSEVERANCE

'Final perseverance' has been defined as 'the doctrine that those who are elected to eternal life will never permanently lapse from grace or be finally lost.' This doctrine is one of the Five Points of Calvinism. The Arminians, on the other hand, regarded the final perseverance of all believers as very doubtful. There are still Christians who take up extreme positions on one side or the other.

The following are among the chief passages used to support the doctrine of final perseverance: John 10: 28, 29; Romans 8: 30, 35–39, 11: 29; Philippians 1: 6; 2 Timothy 1: 12; 1 Peter 1: 5, 8, 9. Passages which have been understood as pointing in the opposite direction are: Matthew 13: 5–7; John 15: 2, 6; 1 Corinthians 8: 11, 9: 27; Hebrews 6: 4–6, 10: 26, 27.

We have not space to examine these passages in detail. The student is referred to the commentaries. But it can be said that Scripture taken as a whole strongly supports the view that once a man is justified—put in a right relationship with God—he remains in this condition and that the new life he has received cannot die. 'It is remarkable that in the divinely-chosen biographies of Scripture no person appears who, at one time certainly a saint of God, at a later time was certainly a lost man.' (H. C. G. Moule, *Christian Doctrine*, p. 47.) This is because of the persistence of God's grace rather than of man's faith. As H. C. G. Moule remarks, it would be better to speak of the Perseverance of God.

The passages which point in the opposite direction are meant to serve as warnings. The bond which unites us with God is not physical, but moral and spiritual. We are *not* to presume upon it. We are bidden, rather, 'to make our calling and election sure' (2 Pet. 1: 10). The teaching of the New Testament concerning the persistence and climax of the life of faith is similar to that concerning its beginning. Salvation is something which men must seek (Acts 2: 40), yet it depends entirely on God's initiative (Jn. 6: 44). Such teaching is reconciled in experience, if not in logic; salvation is by grace through faith (Eph. 2: 8). In a parallel way, Paul instructs the Christians at Philippi to 'work out your own salvation . . . for God is at work in you, both to will and to work for His good pleasure' (Phil. 2: 12, 13). Faith is as important at the end of life as it is on the day of conversion (Heb. 3: 6).

b. ASSURANCE

The Bible reveals that, although the Christian may not be aware of the moment of his conversion, he certainly can know that it has taken place. There is the inner witness of the Holy Spirit (Rom.

8: 14–16). There is an experience of peace with God and of joy unknown before (Rom. 5: 1, 3). Life is controlled by new ideals, motives, and values (2 Cor. 5: 14; Phil. 4: 8). A new attitude of love for others is evidence that he has passed out of death into life (1 Jn. 3: 14). One of the purposes which John appears to have had in mind when writing his first epistle was that Christians might have assurance: 1 John 3: 19, 20, 5: 12, 13.

In spite of this, however, some Christians find that their emotional awareness of salvation is subject to fluctuation. There are even cases where all sense of the presence of Christ is lost, for a time at least. Those who experience spiritual desolation should remember that salvation is not dependent upon human feelings but upon God's grace. They should rest upon the promises of His Word and 'look unto Jesus' (Isa. 50: 10; Heb. 12: 2).

VI. THE FUTURE DESTINY OF MAN

1. THE FACT OF DEATH

Throughout the Bible there is a clear recognition of the transitory nature of human life. Whether or not it would have been so if man had continued in his original condition in which he was created is a matter of debate. We mentioned this issue earlier. Now it needs to be studied in a little more depth.

It is felt by some that the command to replenish the earth (Gen. 1: 28) carried with it the assurance that man's own life would by the same principle be renewed, but others have felt that this was never intended to be so. They point out that the fruit of the tree of life was as yet untasted (Gen. 3: 22) and man must therefore have been created mortal. To this argument, reply might be made that this tree of life is not represented as a prohibited one (Gen. 2: 16, 17), and it is only after the tree of the knowledge of good and evil has been sampled that the tree of life is removed from man's grasp. Certainly the first mention of death is in connection with sin (Gen. 2: 17). And this close relationship was maintained in the subsequent understanding of human experience (Rom. 5: 12).

In agreement with this relationship between sin and death it is to be noted that, as the consequences of sin multiply and become more apparent, man's lifespan is correspondingly shortened. The 969 years of Methuselah's life, which by our experience seem so astonishing, are gradually contracted until it becomes proverbially recognized that the normal length of a man's life is to be recognized as no more than three score and ten years (Psa. 90: 10). A few years more or less are as nothing compared with God's eternity (Psa. 90: 4), and no amount of thought or care can serve to lengthen it to any significant degree (Mt. 6: 27 footnote New English Bible).

2. DEATH ACCEPTED

The sentence of death appears to have been accepted by biblical personalities provided it was carried out in the fullness of time and not executed in a premature fashion (Gen. 15: 15; 2 Kings 20: 19). To come to the grave full of years was not felt to be an undue hardship—provided there were others to follow on. Consequently, blessing came to be expressed in terms of life which had run its full course so that a man was gathered to his fathers in old age while his offspring rose up to take his place (2 Sam. 19: 37).

In these circumstances, the importance of children could not be overestimated, and barrenness was regarded as so very much more than just a misfortune (1 Sam. 1: 10; 2 Sam. 14: 7). Here too the idea of tribal solidarity comes into prominence and is amply illustrated by the way in which the patriarchs gave their names to the tribes which sprang from them. So long as the tribe was perpetuated it could be felt with some justification that a man lived on.

All this will explain the relative paucity of the Old Testament references to the after-life. Even in some of the Old Testament examples, where in the light of Christian thinking we imagine we discern some glimmering of hope which looks beyond the grave, it has to be acknowledged that in fact the underlying thought is more limited.

3. OLD TESTAMENT CONCEPTS

a. SHEOL

The Old Testament ideas of life after death are typified in the Hebrew word *Sheol*. It is often translated merely 'the grave'. It is quite indefinite as far as descriptive language is concerned. More often than not, to be delivered from *Sheol* is not limited merely to being brought up out of the indefinite nether regions of death or the grave, but rather to be delivered from *first* going down thither. In other words, they take the form not of an affirmation concerning the after-life, but a confident assertion that God has power to deliver a man from his present distress and thus to prolong his life. *Sheol*, far from being a state into which a man might hope that he would eventually be brought, was a place to make men shudder; a place of darkness where only a shadowy existence might be known. Within *Sheol* the distinctions recognized upon earth have become blurred, and strong warriors have been brought to a state of utter weakness (Job 3: 17–19; Isa. 14: 9–11).

One can perhaps begin to discern the dawn of hope in that it began to be a growing recognition that *Sheol* itself falls within the universal sovereignty of God (Psa. 139: 8; Amos 9: 2). Israel began to realize that to go down into *Sheol* is *not* to be forever cut off. The power of God is there also, for it is ruled by the One who has already shown himself to be the Lord of heaven and earth. None of this, however, is clearly integrated into Old Testament man's thinking. The seeds of hope may be there, but they have not yet by any means germinated.

It is little wonder that such a conception was incapable of awakening an eager and intelligent spirit of anticipation. Even the extraordinary story concerning the witch of Endor (1 Sam. 28: 7–19) and the calling up of the spirit of Samuel is not described in detail. Thus, its interest in the after-life is not followed through.

There are a score of questions which one might wish to ask concerning the form and manner of Samuel's appearing, but none of them is adequately answered since the interest lies not with Samuel and the shadowy world from which he emerges, but with Saul and the more realistic historical setting within which his actions are portrayed. This is typical, for in fact throughout the whole of man's experience, first during the patriarchal period and then within the history of Israel, the scene is always set upon earth and in the sphere of human activity. The overwhelming consciousness is of a God who comes to visit and redeem His people here upon earth and to enter into personal relationships with those who trust Him.

b. THE PRINCIPLE OF FELLOWSHIP UNBROKEN

It is partly out of the sense of fellowship with God that there begins to grow the idea of a life beyond the present. At first it comes as no more than a fleeting glimpse. Gradually, however, it emerges as a developing aspiration and hope, making ready for the fuller realization which comes to light in the Christian revelation. Thus Enoch walked with God upon earth, and such was the bond of their fellowship that it became inconceivable that it should ever be destroyed. Enoch walked with God and he was not (Gen. 5: 24). Thus in enigmatic terms his passing is described. But behind the laconic expression there lies a wealth of incipient faith.

Similarly with the Psalmist; he is conscious of a walk with God which develops to the point where it has become unbreakable. The wicked may be cut off suddenly from the midst of their prosperity. But the man who trusts in God will be conscious of God's guiding hand upon him during his life and hopeful of this same Friend who will be waiting for him at life's end (Psa. 73: 23, 24).

c. THE CONCEPT OF RESURRECTION

There are two further passages which merit attention. The first in Isaiah 26 gives a clear and unmistakable hope of resurrection. Still, it is a hope which is limited to the righteous alone. Consequently, it can be said of Israel's enemies that they are dead, they shall not live. They are deceased they shall not rise, therefore hast Thou visited them and destroyed them and made all their memory to perish (Isa. 26: 14, 15). On the other hand, it is asserted with equal confidence that the righteous martyrs of Israel will live and their dead bodies shall arise (26: 19). It should be noted, incidentally, that the hope as it begins to emerge is one of *bodily* resurrection. This is fully in accord with the concern which had always been felt for the care of men's bones and their reverent burial (Gen. 50: 25; 2 Sam. 21: 12; 1 Kings. 13: 31).

The second passage in Daniel 12 goes further still, speaking of a resurrection of wicked and of righteous alike; some to everlasting life and some to shame and everlasting contempt (Dan. 12: 2). It is true that the *notoriously* wicked appear to be in mind, as well as the *outstandingly* righteous. So that the assertion is concerned with many, but not yet with *all*. Still, here again the principle is established and the realization of its universal application is only a matter of time.

Ezekiel's vision in the valley of dry bones, though not strictly related to personal resurrection, nevertheless deserves mention. Here too is material ready to be developed. It is cast in the form of a resurrection narrative (Ezek. 37: 1–14). It has to do with the revival of a nation which had been long dead, a fact signified by the very dryness of the bones (Ezek. 37: 2). Clearly, the hope of renewal and a return of vitality was a forlorn hope. The characteristic utterances of the book of Ezekiel are set in the form of a lament, for that was the mood of the exile period and the prophet reflects it with accuracy.

There is, however, other material interspersed which makes the prophecy distinctive. Now the unbelievable is asserted, and the prophet Ezekiel is sent to proclaim new life to a nation which was not merely dying, but one which had been given up as dead. True, the hope here is a national one rather than individual, but at least it was a step in the right direction. For if indeed the resurrection of a nation were possible through the inbreathing of the Divine Spirit, why should the resurrection of the individual be any more unthinkable?

d. THE PRINCIPLE OF SUFFERING

One other line of development is to be noted. It is related to a growing understanding of the experience of suffering—in particular, suffering which was pressed to its extreme limit of death. While life remained, there might be the possibility of a man's fortune being reversed. In many cases this did in fact take place. But when suffering reached its furthermost limit and culminated in death, then the fierceness of its challenge was felt most deeply. Thus the suffering Servant of Isaiah 53 is to be seen as the dying Servant.

To spend too much time trying to diagnose the nature of His suffering (e.g. leprosy, a judicial execution, etc.) is to miss the main point which lies in the fact that He was cut off out of the land of the living and nobody cared about His fate and that He had no descendants to preserve His line throughout the generations to follow (Isa. 53: 8). Similarly, in the vindication of the servant, the supreme consideration is not that God intervened on behalf of His Servant, for that had been true of other servants before Him. The significance is found in the fact that in this case, when suffering had been pressed to its extreme and had culminated in death, God was still able to raise up His Servant and quicken His life so that it could be said of Him that He would see His seed and would prolong His days (Isa. 53: 10).

e. THE UNCERTAINTY OF IT ALL IN THE OLD TESTAMENT

Not always, however, is this sublime faith matched when others considered the problem of suffering. Ecclesiastes 12 is typical of the pessimism of the whole book. It speaks of man's final destiny in terms of a gradual disintegration (Eccl. 12: 3–5), culminating in the dissolution of the body and the failure of the spirit. Now it should be noted that the return of the spirit to God is not to be understood in accordance with modern thought. It indicates here no more than the withdrawal of the life principle which first came by the inbreathing of God and the consequent reversion of an animated body to the lifeless dust of the earth.

Yet the writer cannot be content to leave it there. For paradoxically, he asserts the inevitability of a final judgment (Eccl. 12: 14). Thus he reaches out for the very thing which a moment before he had appeared to deny. Job too is subject to similar fluctuations of thought and faith. Thus at one moment he rises to the confident assertion of a future vindication (Job 19: 25), only to fall back into the despondency which allows the hope to be set aside or at least forgotten. Sometimes he raises the question of the after-life but seems unable to reach a decision concerning it (Job 14: 13–15).

When all the evidence of the Old Testament is taken together, we may sum up its teaching by saying that no doctrine of a future life is fully promulgated. There are earnest longings which arise amidst the frustrations of human experience. There are hopeful ventures of faith which spring from a sense of the righteousness of God who will not leave injustice unrectified. There are moments of revelation for those whose minds were open to receive them. But the note of certainty still waits to be sounded forth.

4. NEW TESTAMENT CONCEPTS

As a result of Old Testament doctrine on future life, we thus find carried over into the New Testament era conflicting ideas exemplified in the opposing views of the Pharisees who believed in a resurrection and the Sadducees who firmly denied it (Mk. 12: 18).

a. THE ARGUMENT FROM FELLOWSHIP

Jesus himself, however, had no hesitation whatever in supporting the Pharisees in this particular matter, rightly claiming that they had the support of the Scriptures for their view. The line of argument which He adopted is one to which reference has already been made, viz. the idea of fellowship. He cites the cases of Abraham and Isaac and Jacob and asserts that since these men of old had entered into fellowship with God during their lifetime, that relationship was a guarantee of their survival since God is not the god of dead people but of those who are alive (Mk. 12: 27).

b. THE ARGUMENT FROM INJUSTICE

Equally, Jesus appears to have accepted the need to put right the injustices of life. Thus with others of His time (Jn. 5: 29, 11: 24), He looked forward to a judgment which lies beyond this present world. He accepted the implication of a continuation of life by which such a judgment would be possible (Mt. 5: 22, 10: 15, 12: 36, 41, 42, 25: 31–46). It is true that Jesus often spoke of judgment as a present reality (Jn. 3: 18), but it was a judgment not yet apparent and the day of judgment would both confirm and make it clear.

c. THE FATE OF THE IMPENITENT

Jesus did not dwell to an unnecessary degree upon the fate of the impenitent. His purpose in coming into the world was not to condemn the world but to save it (Jn. 3: 17). However, He did say enough to give warning, speaking of eternal fire (Mt. 25: 41) and of the place where the worm dieth not and the fire is not quenched (Mk. 9: 48). True, this is figurative language and few today would understand it in a strict literal fashion. Still, behind these figures there lies the awful reality. Therefore, this part of the teaching of Jesus is certainly not to be set aside just because it is unpalatable in the thinking of this particular age. His words are true.

d. THE FATE OF THE BLESSED

On the other hand, Jesus spoke more freely of the eternal blessedness of those who trust Him, declaring that the pledge of these blessings was already given (Jn. 5: 24, 25, 6: 58), and that He Himself was the guarantor of a place in the Father's home (Jn. 14: 2). Above all, He linked the certainty of eternal life with the certainty of His own Resurrection (Jn. 14: 19).

i. The principle in Jesus' miracles

The miracles in which Jesus raised others from the dead teach nothing about man's state after death. Indeed, they are in themselves no more than a prolongation of life. The people concerned, such as Lazarus, presumably died again in due course. But as signs they are unmistakable in their message. They make it abundantly clear that in Jesus we are face to face with Him who holds the keys of both life and death (Rev. 1:18). They anticipate His own Resurrection. They testify of His claim to be the Resurrection and the Life (Jn. 11:25), and they are the pledge that others are to share in His rising from the dead.

ii. Hope based upon Jesus' resurrection

Paul was quick to see the close relationship between the Resurrection of Jesus and that of the believers (1 Cor. 15:16). For this reason he carefully marshalled the evidence to show that the Resurrection had actually taken place (1 Cor. 15:5–8). Being fully assured on this point, the resurrection of the believers became the confident hope which continually filled his heart.

iii. Awake or asleep?

Of course, there are aspects of the resurrection of the dead which are wrapped up in the mystery of God's counsel. Therefore, Paul was compelled to fall back upon the use of analogy in order to answer the curiosity and the hesitation of the Corinthians (1 Cor. 15:35–44). This is probably why he sometimes speaks of death as a sleep (1 Cor. 15:20, 51), as Jesus Himself had done (Mk. 5:39). But then at other times he suggests that the departed believer is consciously in the presence of Christ, and therefore this condition is to be preferred to the troubles of our earthly life (2 Cor. 5:8). However, such a seeming contradiction is more apparent than real. For example, it could well spring from our mortal conception of time and space. If such be the case, we should have no difficulty in holding the two thoughts together and finding comfort in these partial expressions of a mystery which is too deep for human comprehension. Moreover, it may well be that expression of Christian death as 'sleep' is to be understood purely figuratively. Most evangelical Bible students will opt for this latter view. Indeed, there is something of beauty in seeing the death of the Christian as 'sleep'. Death is conquered in the Resurrection of Christ. So a believer's body merely 'sleeps' until his resurrection. The idea of 'soul sleep' has little or no support in Scriptures.

iv. Linked with the Kingdom of God

Jesus' position was clear concerning the resurrection of the believers. It was not to be seen as an isolated phenomenon. Rather, it was to be part of the manifestation of the Kingdom of God. He linked it closely with the final day of judgment (Jn. 6:40) and His own return (Jn. 14:3). Thus Paul, writing in the same vein, holds back the destruction of the last enemy death until the kingdom has been delivered up to God at the second coming of Christ (1 Cor. 15:23, 24, 26).

v. Conclusion

So it can now be seen that by the time Jesus had arrived, the uncertainty of earlier thought has given place to the fuller revelation in Christ. The tentative suggestions of a future life have become the clear and categorical assurances of the New Testament, and these form the foundation of Christian hope today. It is true that death remains as a grim reality (2 Cor. 1: 9), but for the Christian it is transformed (1 Cor. 15: 54). When it does come in God's purpose and time, it is to be welcomed because through it there comes the revelation of the life of Jesus (2 Cor. 4: 10–11). Finally, it may be mentioned that this eternal life in Christ is not limited to an exceptional few. It is Christ's gift to as many as trust Him. At His second coming, multitudes from every nation are to share in His triumph and in the blessings of His eternal kingdom (Rev. 7: 9, 15–17). How wonderful heaven will be!

CONCLUSION TO BOOK TWO

It is marvellous beyond comprehension what God has done for man. Life, sustenance, love, care, redemption, salvation and an eternity in His actual presence are ours in Jesus Christ. Human terms can never exhaust the praise that is due Him because of His grace towards man. Perhaps the best way to glorify Him for His love is demonstrated in a life of praise and service. It is the theme of service to Christ through the Church that we now approach.

BOOK III

WHAT THE BIBLE SAYS ABOUT THE CHURCH AND ITS SERVICE

When we talk about 'the Church', and one's service through it, many different concepts arise in different people's mind. For example, consider the following everyday statements: 'As I went into the *church* I slipped and fell', or 'My brother went into a career in the Navy, but I went into the *Church*'. We hear it said 'I belong to the Baptist *church*,' or again, 'The *church* has been here since the time of Christ'. Often people say, 'The Sunday School is a part of our *church*'. There is obviously a fair degree of confusion as to the exact meaning of the word 'church'. We must differentiate between a building, a local fellowship, and ecclesiastical organization, a clerical order and a spiritual organism as set forth in the New Testament. Thus we raise the basic question:

I. WHAT IS THE CHURCH?

1. THE ESSENTIAL NATURE OF THE CHURCH

In the Bible the Church is not presented as a material building, a clerical order or a 'denomination'. It is not man-made, earthly, national or sectarian. Rather, it is eternal, spiritual and universal. It is the product of God's saving work in Christ.

a. THE COMPANY OF THE REDEEMED

Redemption is the great theme of the Bible. As we have previously seen, the word means liberation from bondage or oppression, either by acts of power or the payment of a price called a 'ransom' (Lev. 25: 25, 48; Jer, 31: 11, 32: 8; Hosea 3: 2, 13: 14). A great act of redemption was the liberation of Israel from Egypt, by which the people became known as 'The redeemed of the Lord'. The means used was the Passover lamb and the intervening power and presence of God. After this event, Redemption came to be applied to moral and spiritual deliverance from evil (Exod. 6: 6; Deut. 13: 5; Psa. 107: 2, 130: 8; Isa. 62: 12).

All this pointed to the Church, the spiritual Israel, which like the national Israel exists by the delivering work of God. Christ is the Redeemer, setting men free from the curse of the law, from all iniquity and from the power of evil by the price of His own blood. The 'redeemed' are purchased to God out of every nation, forgiven, translated into a new kingdom and sealed for final salvation. The Church is therefore that company of people for whom the atoning death of Christ has become effective with liberating power (Mk. 10: 45; Lk. 1: 68; Rom. 3: 24; Gal. 3: 13; Eph. 1: 7, 14, 4: 30; Col. 1: 13; Tit. 2: 14; 1 Pet. 1: 18; Rev. 5: 9).

b. THE COMPANY OF THE ENLIGHTENED

The first reference to the Church in the Gospels is in Matthew 16: 18. The circumstances are those of Peter's confession of Christ as Son of God, which comes as the result of revelation from God (Mt. 16: 17). It is on this rock, this kind of confession, Christ builds His Church. Every true believer comes through the same enlightenment and confession of Christ as Son of God. The Church is that company that has passed from darkness into marvellous light and continues to be enlightened by the Spirit (Acts 26: 18; 2 Cor. 4: 6; Eph. 1: 18; Col. 1: 12, 13).

c. THE COMPANY OF THE CALLED

The word 'church' in the New Testament is the Greek word *ekklesia*. It refers in Greek usage to a body of people called or brought together by means of a summons or proclamation. The Hebrew word is *kahal*, and is translated in the Old Testament 'assembly'. Again, it is derived from an ancient root meaning to 'summon a concourse of people together for a specific purpose' (Exod. 12: 6; Num. 10: 2, 3; Acts 19: 32, 39, 41).

One of the early uses in the New Testament is in Matthew 18: 17, referring to a gathering called to deal with an offending brother. Before this, however, we have Matthew 16: 18 (previously mentioned) where the word is used of the whole assembly of the New Israel in every place and age to be built on the rock of Christ's Messiahship and Deity. This 'call' comes through the word of God reaching, arresting and converting the individual. It is associated with 'the voice of the Son of God', and is shown in Scripture as the first element in the whole process of salvation; culminating in those who are called being 'glorified'. It is personal, inward and effective.

The imagery given in John 10 is pastoral. Christ the Good Shepherd calls His own sheep out of many folds into the one flock over which He is the one shepherd. Those who hear His voice and respond, receive eternal life. So arises the concept of the Church as the 'flock of God', over whom Christ is the great and chief Shepherd, under whose oversight local pastors are appointed to 'tend the flock of God'. The same pastoral image is seen in the Old Testament in which God is the 'Shepherd of Israel' (Psa. 23: 1,80: 1; Isa. 40: 11; Ezek. 34: 31; Lk. 12: 32; Jn. 10: 3–5, 11–16, 27–30; Acts 2: 39, 20: 28, 29; Rom. 8: 30; 2 Tim. 1: 9; Heb. 13: 20; 1 Pet. 1: 15, 2: 9, 25, 5: 2–4, 20).

The world *ekklesia* is used in two senses. *First, the universal*; all believers 'called' in every age and place (Eph. 5: 23–25). *Secondly, the local*; believers 'called' together into fellowship in one place (1 Cor. 1: 2). The local is an expression or 'outcropping' of the universal.

d. THE COMPANY OF THE REGENERATE

Entrance into the Church is by the new birth. It is called the 'church of the firstborn, whose names are written in heaven', the 'household of God', or 'family of God'. The Jew was born naturally into the family of Israel, sealed with the covenant of circumcision. The Christian is born spiritually into the family of the spiritual seed, by the second birth. This comes through faith in Christ and the regenerating action of the Holy Spirit in the heart. It creates a new relationship with God as Father and with other believers as brothers in the same family. Regeneration leads to the Church as the spiritual family of God, in which Christ is the 'Firstborn' (Jn. 1: 12, 13, 3: 5, 6, 7; Rom. 8: 29; Gal. 6: 10; Eph. 2: 19; Heb. 12: 23; Jas. 1: 18; 1 Pet. 1: 22, 23; 1 Jn. 3: 9, 14, 5: 1).

e. THE COMPANY OF THE INDWELT

The promise of our Lord was that the Holy Spirit would indwell believers. Strictly speaking, the Church came into being on the Day of Pentecost when the Spirit came to indwell the 120 assembled believers. At once there was created 'the fellowship', and the Lord then 'added to the church' those being saved (Jn. 14: 17; Acts 2: 4, 38–42, 47; Rom. 8: 9).

i. The indwelling creates the unity

The coming of the Spirit realized the presence of Christ in believers and their union with Him. This made them one, as the Father and the Son were one in the Godhead—by common essence or life. The Church was visualized on this basis in John 15 as the Vine and branches (Jn. 14: 16, 20, 15: 4, 5, 17: 21–23).

ii. The indwelling creates the Church as the Body of Christ

The unity thus created at Pentecost was a 'body' of which the risen Christ was the Head. This headship involved authority and lordship over the Body, communication of life and nourishment to the Body, impartation of fullness to the Body and expression of Being through the Body. Christ and Church are seen as one organism. As the body, so is the Christ (1 Cor. 12: 12). Believers are incorporated into the Body of Christ by 'baptism by the Spirit', i.e. the reception of the

Spirit as at Pentecost, thus bringing *into* the believer the life of Christ, and so also bringing the believer into the shared life of Christ—which is the life of the Body (Rom. 8: 9; 1 Cor. 12: 13, 27; Gal. 3: 27, 28; Eph. 1: 22, 23; Col. 1: 18, 2: 9, 10, 19).

iii. The indwelling creates the Church as the Temple of the Spirit

Every believer is a 'shrine of the Spirit (1 Cor. 6: 19). His body is referred to as a 'member of Christ'. He is made holy by the Spirit's indwelling. Hence he cannot be joined to that which is unclean (1 Cor. 6: 15–17). The whole fellowship of believers is created to be a 'temple of the Spirit' on earth. As the Spirit filled earthly temples in the Old Testament, so He fills the spiritual temple now. God dwells not in material buildings but in and among His people. This 'temple' is built on Christ, the foundation Rock. Christians are 'living stones', builded together in fellowship for the one purpose of being 'a holy temple for the Lord'. The emphasis here is upon the holiness and separateness of the Church from the world, upon the Church as the sphere of the Divine presence and of spiritual worship and ministry (Exod. 25: 8; 2 Chron. 5: 14, 6: 1–2; 2 Cor. 6: 14–18; Eph. 2: 20–22; Jas 4: 4, 5; 1 Pet. 2: 4, 5).

2. THE UNIVERSAL OR CATHOLIC ASPECT OF THE CHURCH

a. IN THE GOSPELS

Three main figures are used by our Lord. He speaks of 'my Church built on this Rock'. Peter is not the Rock, since he himself tells us that Christ is the chief corner-stone on which the Church is built. Paul also makes this plain. There is one Church built on one Rock (Mt. 16: 18; Eph. 2: 20; 1 Pet. 2: 4–7).

Then He speaks of 'my sheep' who are 'not of this fold' but are called by His voice and in response are brought into the one flock over which He is the one Shepherd. Again, Peter calls the Church the 'Flock of God' (Jn. 10: 16, 27–29; Acts 20: 28; 1 Pet. 5: 2).

Our Lord also speaks of Himself as the 'Vine' and His Church as the 'branches'. The image is of one organism through which there flows one life, producing one kind of fruit under the husbandry of the one Father. The Church here replaces Israel who is called in the Old Testament the vine of Jehovah (Jn. 15: 1, 5, 16).

Finally, Christ speaks of those who would believe and be made 'perfect in one'. The commission is given to 'make disciples of all nations, baptizing them in the Name of the Father, Son and Holy Spirit', and He would be with them 'to the end of the age'. Here is visualized a vast multitude in all ages and places who would be His disciples and bear the mark of baptism. For these He prayed and stated that their distinctive marks are:

(1) That they would believe through the Word.
(2) That they would belong to Christ and to God.
(3) That they would know Christ.
(4) That they would be kept from evil.
(5) That they would be *in* but not *of* the world.
(6) That they would be indwelt by Christ Himself.
(7) That they would be one as were the Father and the Son.
(8) That they would be marked by love.
(9) That they would be finally with Christ in glory.
(Mt. 28: 19, 20; Jn. 17: 2, 3, 6, 8, 10, 11, 14–16, 20–26.)

b. IN THE ACTS OF THE APOSTLES

The Church appears first in Jerusalem as a believing baptized company presided over by the apostles, continuing steadfastly in the apostles' teaching, fellowship, breaking of bread and prayers. All who believe are 'together' and the Church is added to daily by the Lord.

It then appears spreading out wherever the Gospel is preached according to the commission and plan of Acts 1: 8. The common elements are always faith in Christ, baptism in His Name and the reception of the Holy Spirit, while outward unity is shown by laying on of hands by the apostles.

Finally, the Church is seen everywhere throughout the Roman world—even in Rome itself—maintained in unity by the Holy Spirit and the ministry of apostles, evangelists and teachers. Members of churches are referred to as 'saints', 'believers', 'Christians', 'disciples', 'brethren' and 'the church of God purchased with His own blood' (Acts 1: 8, 2: 38, 39, 41–44, 47, 8: 12, 14–17, 10: 44–48, 11: 21–26, 14: 20–28, 15: 36, 41, 16: 5, 20: 28, 29).

c. IN THE EPISTLES
i. The Epistles themselves
These are written to Christians in many places, and for Christians of all ages they are in themselves evidence of the universality of the Church.

ii. The titles used for Christians
These titles themselves give evidence of oneness of life, experience and destiny. They are called: 'saints in Christ Jesus', 'the beloved of God', 'the called in Christ Jesus', 'the elect', 'those who in every place call on the Name of Christ', 'those who have received like precious faith', 'those who are sanctified and preserved in Jesus' (Rom. 1: 6, 7; 1 Cor. 1: 2; 1 Pet. 1: 2; 2 Pet. 1: 1; Jude 1).

iii. The fellowship expressed reveals catholicity
The spirit of love breathes through the epistles, shown in the mutual care of writers and readers one for another. There is joy in sharing the like common faith, stress on believing the same things and on

being of one mind and spirit, awareness of being in the same world
conflict and hope in the same apocalyptic destiny. So John writes:
'What we have seen and heard declare we to you that you may
have fellowship with us' (Rom. 1: 11, 12; 2 Cor. 1: 11; Phil.
1: 7–9, 30, 3: 20, 4: 21, 22; Col. 1: 4, 5; 1 Pet. 1: 1, 2; 2 Pet. 1: 1;
1 Jn. 1: 3).

iv. The pattern and doctrine of the Church

The pattern in the New Testament is that of separate local churches,
led by their own elders, yet all built on one foundation, called and
chosen by the one God, owning the one Lord Jesus Christ, indwelt
by the one Spirit, bought with the one price of the blood of Christ,
having the same regeneration and baptism in the Triune Name. It
partakes everywhere of the one loaf and cup in the communion and
is thus itself 'one loaf'. It pursues one mission, engages in one conflict
and anticipates one hope as it awaits God's Son from heaven.

The greatest passage emphasizing this is Ephesians 4: 3–6, which
sets forth the seven unities which underlie the 'unity of the Spirit
in the bond of peace'. This is the secret of the oneness of the Church.
The Church is thus seen as indivisible, universal and continuing
until the Advent of Christ. The doctrine of the Church universal is
shown under the following figures; 'the Flock of God', 'the Household of Faith', 'the Body of Christ', 'the Temple of the Holy Spirit',
'the One New Man', 'the Holy Nation', 'the Chosen Generation',
'the Royal Priesthood', 'the Purchased People', 'the Pillar and
Ground of Truth' (Acts 14: 23, 15: 41; 1 Cor. 1: 12, 13, 3: 11, 16,
10: 17, 12: 12, 13, 15: 51, 52; Eph. 1: 23, 2: 16, 19–22, 4: 3–6,
5: 23–27, 29, 30, 32; Col. 1: 18, 2: 19; 1 Thess. 4: 13–17; 1 Tim.
3: 15; Tit. 1: 5; 1 Pet. 2: 5–9, 5: 2, 3).

d. IN THE APOCALYPSE

The seven churches of Asia are depicted as a lampstand in which
is the one Lord, and are addressed by the one Spirit. The Church
universal is seen as an 'innumerable company redeemed from every
nation', and made a 'kingdom of priests'. Finally, she is seen as 'the
holy City', 'the new Jerusalem coming down from heaven' (Rev.
1: 6, 12, 13, 20, 2: 29, 5: 9, 7: 9, 21: 2, 10).

So through Gospels, Acts, Epistles and Revelation there appears
one Church, historically built on Christ and the apostles, and
appearing at the end of time as the Bride of the Lamb.

3. THE LOCAL ASPECT OF THE CHURCH

The New Testament speaks of both the 'Church' and the churches,
the local church being the expression or 'outcropping' of the universal Church in any given place. So we read of the church at
Jerusalem, at Antioch, the churches in Galatia, etc. Epistles given
for the universal Church were in fact written to local ones.

To belong to the universal Church involves belonging to the local church, since one is part of the other. In the local fellowship our membership in the whole Body of Christ is realized, developed, disciplined and expressed. The fullness of Christ imparted to the whole Church can and should be experienced in the local church. The rich teaching of the epistles was written to local churches (Rom. 1: 7; 1 Cor. 1: 2, 12: 27; 2 Cor. 1: 1; Gal. 1: 2; Col. 1: 9, 10).

It is in the local church that corporate Christian life and responsibility is realized and expressed in the following ways.

a. WORSHIP

This is the highest function of the human spirit. This the Father seeks, and this we owe to God above all else. The Church worships the Father through the Son and by the Holy Spirit.

i. The Divine presence

In the local church, God's presence is assured by the promise of Christ himself. This promise must be taken in full seriousness. It fulfils Old Testament types and situations in which the divine glory was manifested in Tabernacle and Temple, and is in keeping with the local church as the Temple of the Holy Spirit (Exod. 40: 34, 35; Ezek. 43: 7, 48: 35; Zeph. 3: 17; Rev. 1: 13–20).

ii. The nature of worship

True worship is spiritual and corporate. It is one through all the earth and with the heavenly hosts, yet expressed in local situations. It results from the encounter with the Living Christ and the realization of His presence in the midst (Mt. 28: 9, 17; Jn. 4: 20–24; 1 Cor. 14: 25; Phil. 3: 3).

iii. Such worship is priestly ministry

The Old Testament priests ministered before and to the Lord with sacrifices and incense. Levitical choirs sang and praised the Lord. The New Testament worship fulfils this and is referred to as 'serving' or 'ministering to the Lord' or 'offering up spiritual sacrifices' in the 'fruit of our lips' or the 'presenting of our bodies', which is our 'spiritual worship'. All this takes place personally or corporately in the local church (Deut. 10: 8; 1 Chron. 15: 16; Acts 13: 2, 27: 23; Rom. 12: 1; Eph. 5: 19; Heb. 13: 15; 1 Pet. 2: 5, 9; Rev. 1: 6).

b. THE LORDSHIP OF CHRIST

Christ is Lord of the Church and Head of the Body. Whilst this has universal reference, it has local application. It is within the local fellowship that this Lordship is to be realized and expressed by:

(1) The confession of the church that Jesus is Lord.
(2) The gathering of the local church in the Name or authority of Christ.

(3) The administration of the church by the Holy Spirit on behalf of Christ.

(4) The government of the local church by elders in Christ's Name.

(5) The administration of Christ's law and will in church meetings.

(6) The obedience of the church under the Scriptures.

(7) The proclamation of the church that Christ is Lord.

The local church is therefore a focal point of Christ's universal Lordship. And the presence of the Spirit in the church makes effective the Headship of Christ (Mt. 16: 16–19, 18: 18–20; Acts 13: 2–4, 15: 4, 6, 28; 1 Cor. 5: 4, 5, 12: 3–13, 27; 2 Cor. 4: 5; Eph. 1: 22, 23, 5: 23; Col. 1: 18, 3: 16, 17; Heb. 13: 17; 1 Pet. 5: 2, 3).

C. THE FELLOWSHIP OF BELIEVERS

The local church is the focus of fellowship. It was first called 'the fellowship' in Acts 2: 42. Fellowship means 'that which is shared' alike by all and is rooted in the word 'common', i.e. common land or common cause.

i. That which is common to all believers

It is the life they share in Christ that is the common share of all believers. It is Christ in and among them by the indwelling of the Spirit that creates the *koinonia*, or fellowship. Our Lord said, 'I in them that they may be perfect in one'. The fellowship is 'Christ among you, the hope of glory'. The basis of fellowship is the unity of the Godhead. The vital power of fellowship is the Holy Spirit, and the chief quality of fellowship is love (Jn. 13: 34, 35, 14: 6, 17, 23, 17: 11, 23; Acts 2: 44, 4: 32; Col. 1: 27).

ii. The environment in which fellowship is realized

Simply put, it is the 'Light' (1 Jn. 1: 5–7). Light is that which 'makes manifest' and involves honesty and openness in the clarity of truth.

iii. The pattern of fellowship is sevenfold

1) In the Gospel

There is a basic unity in Christian truth and ministry. Peter preached with the eleven. Paul worked in a team. The Church was one in the apostles' doctrine. There cannot be fellowship with those who do not abide in the doctrine of Christ (Acts 2: 14, 42; Phil. 1: 5, 7; 2 Jn. 9–11).

2) In the breaking of bread and worship

The communion is not only a symbol of Christ's death but of the Church's unity (1 Cor. 10: 16, 17).

3) In prayer

The early Church prayed together in fellowship (Acts 4: 24, 31, 32).

4) In church government

The New Testament had plurality of elders.

5) In activities and growth (Eph. 4: 12–16).

6) In association and caring

We read that all who believed were 'together', that they were of one heart and soul, and had all things in common. Love is the hallmark of fellowship, and mutual caring is the expression of love (Acts 2: 44, 4: 32; Gal. 6: 2; 1 Jn. 3: 16–18).

7) In witness and service

The disciples went out two by two. Peter and John went 'together' and said to the lame man 'look on us' (Mk. 6: 7; Lk. 10: 1; Acts 3: 1, 4).

d. MEMBERSHIP IN THE BODY OF CHRIST

Believers are said to be 'members of Christ', 'members of His Body' and 'members one of another'. This membership is not simply institutional but vital and organic and is realized by union with Christ through faith and baptism in the Spirit into the one Body. Membership in New Testament teaching involves:

i. Spiritual oneness with Christ and with other believers

And this means mutual dependence on and caring for one another, spiritual growth and participation in the fullness of Christ. All must be realized in the local church (Rom. 12: 5; 1 Cor. 6: 15, 12: 12, 13, 18–22, 25–27; Eph. 5: 30).

ii. Participation in the gifts of the Spirit

The Spirit manifests Himself in each member in some particular way. These gifts are sovereignly given and are to be used for the upbuilding of the church (Rom. 12: 4–8; 1 Cor. 12: 4–11, 27, 28).

iii. Responsibility in the local fellowship

Membership one of another involves *a right moral and spiritual relationship to one another*. There must be no lying, stealing, evil speaking, covetousness or sexual impurity among church members. Truth, kindness, purity and generosity must prevail. At the same time, membership in Christ eliminates fellowship with evil and impurity in the world (1 Cor. 6: 13–20; Gal. 6: 2; Eph. 4: 16, 25–32, 5: 1–7).

e. PRAYER

The Church is *a praying fellowship*. The early Church prayed continually. Its members were conscious of their need of strength, wisdom and guidance from God (Acts 1: 14, 24, 2: 42, 4: 24, 29–31, 6: 4, 6, 12: 5, 13: 2, 3). It was also *a praising community*. They were possessed with holy joy and a sense of the glory and greatness of God. The effect of the Holy Spirit is to produce praise and thanksgiving (Acts 2: 46, 47; Eph. 5: 19, 20). There are some definite reasons for this:

i. The church is a community of need
Only those with need really pray (Phil. 1: 19; 2 Thess. 3: 1).

ii. The church is a vessel of the Spirit
And since the Spirit prays, He will do so in and through the church (Rom. 8: 15, 26, 27). Hence we are told to 'pray in the Spirit' (Eph. 6: 18).

iii. The church is a priestly body
As such it has a ministry both of praise and intercession. Our great High Priest in heaven makes intercession for His church. We unite with Him in making intercession for one another and for the world (Eph. 6: 18, 19; Phil. 1: 19, 4: 6; Col. 4: 2, 3; 1 Thess. 5: 17, 25; 1 Tim. 2: 1–4, 8; Jas. 5: 13–16).

So the Church, as a praying body, stands in the succession of Israel as a praying priestly nation, of the great men and women of prayer of the Old Testament, of our Lord Jesus who lived a life of prayer, and of the apostles whose prayers and exhortations to prayer fill the epistles.

f. ORDINANCES (sometimes called 'sacraments' in some churches)
These are symbolic actions ordained for us by the Lord himself, and commanded for our observance. The churches of the Reformation regard baptism and the Lord's Supper as the two ordinances clearly given, although laying on of hands in confirmation, ordination and healing is widely practised and so for some takes on the character of a third ordinance.

i. Baptism
In the Gospels, baptism is given by the example and the command of Christ Himself. Baptized by John in Jordan, to 'fulfil all righteousness', Jesus made this rite the mark of discipleship for all believers (Mt. 28: 19; Mk. 16: 16).

In the Acts, baptism is seen as the immediate act of witness to repentance and faith in Christ and of initiation into the church. It was usually accompanied by the evident gift of the Holy Spirit. It appears as the normal practice throughout the early Church as the rite that stands at the heart of the conversion experience (Acts 2: 28, 41, 8: 12, 16, 36–38, 9: 18, 10: 47, 48, 16: 15, 33, 18: 8, 19: 5).

In the Epistles, there are several references to baptism as a symbolic act depicting the union of believers with Christ in His death, burial and resurrection. It is an initiatory act and relates to:

(1) Our repentance of past sin (putting off the old man).
(2) Our involvement in Christ's death, as being judged in Him.
(3) Our faith in Christ as Son of God, Saviour and Lord.
(4) Our new life in Christ, leading to righteousness and holiness.
(5) Our reception of the Spirit.
(6) Our incorporation into the body of Christ, the Church.
(7) The answer of a good conscience towards God.

(Rom. 6: 1–9; 1 Cor. 12: 13; Gal. 3: 27; Col. 2: 12, 13; Heb. 6: 2; 1 Pet. 3: 21.)

ii. The Lord's Supper

In the Synoptic Gospels (Matthew, Mark, Luke) this is given by the Lord's command to be an act of commemoration of His person and sacrifice. It more or less takes the place of the Jewish passover by which the people of God remembered their deliverance from Egypt. The wine is stated to represent the 'blood of the New Covenant' as distinct from the blood of animals shed at the inauguration of the Old Covenant at Mt. Sinai. The covenant of grace displaces that of law, the eternal sacrifice that of the temporal, the Divine Reality that of all types and shadows (Mt. 26: 26–29; Mk. 14: 22–25; Lk. 22: 14–20).

In the Gospel of John there is no account of the Supper. There is however, spiritual teaching inherent in the discourses of John 6 and 15. Christ is the 'bread of God which comes down from heaven and gives life to the world' whom we 'eat' by faith and by 'abiding in Him'. The bread is His 'flesh' which must be 'eaten' and His 'blood drunk'. A literal interpretation of this is impossible, being entirely out of keeping with all teaching of Scripture. The spiritual interpretation is shown by the emphasis on 'dwelling in me', 'living by me' and 'believing on me'. The same truth appears in John 15, where Christ is the True Vine in whom we 'abide' and from whom we draw our spiritual life (Jn. 6: 33–35, 47–58, 15: 1–5, 7–11).

In the Acts, the Lord's Supper is seen to be an integral and important part of early Church worship. Known simply as the 'breaking of bread', it was regularly observed in house meetings. The only reference to its regularity is the reference in Acts 20: 7, 'Upon the first day of the week when the disciples came together to break bread'. This does not indicate whether it means *every* Lord's day or *some particular* one when the supper was observed.

In the Epistles, reference is found only in the First Epistle to the Corinthians where it is described carefully in order to correct abuses which had arisen in Corinth. Here it is described as the 'Lord's

Table', the 'Lord's Supper' and the 'communion of the body and blood of Christ' and is shown to be:

(1) An act of memorial of Christ, by dominical command.
(2) A showing, or 'setting forth', of the Lord's death.
(3) A 'participation' in the body and blood of Christ.
(4) A symbol of the unity of the participants, in Christ.
(5) An act anticipatory of the Second Advent.
(6) A serious observance involving self-examination, self-judgment, and a manner worthy of the sacred mysteries symbolized in the Supper.
(7) A rite that involves separation from all that is unholy.

(1 Cor. 10: 14–21, 11: 20–34.)

In the Apocalypse. The 'marriage supper of the Lamb' in Revelation 19: 9 is generally regarded as the fulfilment of the Lord's words at the Last Supper, where He anticipates tasting the fruit of the vine, only in the Kingdom of His Father (Mt. 26: 29; Rev. 19: 9).

It is important to recognize that the ordinances are not mere symbols nor are they magical rites, they are actions by which believers show forth the truths of redemption and in which Christ is dynamically present by His Spirit to *make real* the meaning of His incarnation, death, resurrection and second coming and our union with Him by faith.

g. EDIFICATION

This means the building up of the Church not only in its numbers and organization but much more in the directing, strengthening and maturing of its spiritual life, in personal lives of members, local churches and the Church universally. The illustrations used are those of the Building and the Body.

i. A definition of edification

First, it means built. Christians are said to be *built upon* the foundation of Christ Jesus, the Gospel, the apostles and prophets, and their most holy faith (Rom. 15: 20; 1 Cor. 3: 10, 11; Eph. 2: 20; Jude 20). They are said to be *built up in* or *into* Christ, as an edifice or a body develops to fullness (Eph. 4: 15, 16; Col. 2: 7). They are said to be *built together,* one into another, as stones fitted into place from the one Corner Stone, or joined together as parts of a body from the one Head. This emphasizes the fellowship aspect of edification (Eph. 2: 22; Col. 2: 19; 1 Pet. 2: 4–6).

Secondly, it means stablished. Other words used are 'rooted', 'grounded', 'settled', 'established'. All these speak of strength of faith, depth of love, maturity of understanding and character which is all the effect of being built up in the truth. In consequence, believers are not easily moved away from Christ or unsettled in their

Christian faith. They do not act as unstable children but as grown men (Rom. 1: 11; Eph. 3: 17–19; Col. 2: 7; 1 Thess. 3: 12, 13).

Finally, it means nourished. The Church is nourished by Christ by means of the truth, and in the fellowship by means of the life communicated from the Head (Eph. 5: 29; Col. 2: 19; 1 Tim. 4: 6).

ii. Means for edification

i) The Holy Spirit
The Lord's teaching in John 14–16 shows the Spirit as being given for the complete upbuilding of the Church, by teaching all things, leading into all truth, guiding, showing the things of Christ and empowering the Church for all her ministry (Jn. 14: 16–18, 26, 15: 26, 16: 13, 14; Acts 1: 8; 1 Jn. 2: 27).

ii) The truth
The Word of God has been given especially for the instruction, equipping, spiritual upbuilding and perfecting of the saints. Paul commended the Ephesian elders to the 'Word of grace which is able to build you up and give you an inheritance'. Jesus said, 'If my words abide in you . . . you shall bring forth fruit'. Edification has a doctrinal aspect. It is being built up in sound truth (Acts 2: 42, 20: 32; Col. 1: 23, 2: 7; 1 Tim. 4: 13–16; 2 Tim. 3: 16, 17; 1 Pet. 2: 1, 2; 2 Pet. 1: 12).

iii) Spiritual gifts
These, as we have seen, have a significant place in the Church of the New Testament, being described and enumerated in Romans 12, 1 Corinthians 12 and Ephesians 4. They are the main practical means through which the edifying work of the Holy Spirit takes place. They may be classified as:

(1) Personal Gifts.
(2) Charismatic Gifts.
(3) General Gifts.

First, personal gifts are persons given to the Church by the ascended Lord with abilities of various kinds for the guidance, instruction and inspiration of the Church.

Apostles were given for foundational ministry, in establishing churches and giving basic truth. Paul calls himself a 'wise master builder' with authority to teach, guide and administer discipline for the edification—and not the destruction—of the Church. One of the qualifications of this office was to have seen the Lord. So this office is now gone, of course.

Prophets were given for the inspired uttering of the Word of God, either in preaching or in statements given for the specific instruction or guidance of the Church in a given situation.

Evangelists were given for the extension of the Church by bringing unbelievers to Christ.

Pastors and teachers had responsibility to care for and instruct the local churches in doctrine.

Certain men such as Paul combined all these gifts, but usually one man would excel in one particular ability (Acts 11: 27, 28, 13: 1, 21: 10, 11; Rom. 12: 6–8; 1 Cor. 3: 10, 14: 3; 2 Cor. 12: 19, 13: 10; Eph. 4: 11–16; 2 Tim. 1: 11, 4: 5).

Secondly, charismatic gifts. Nine of these are listed in 1 Corinthians 12. These are not persons as in Ephesians 4, but spiritual endowments given to members of the Church. They vary in value and use, but all are for the edifying of the Body of Christ. They are *not* natural abilities. Rather, they are spiritual gifts or 'operations of the Holy Spirit'. Such are utterances of wisdom, or knowledge, special faith (as distinct from saving faith), powers of healing, miraculous powers, prophetic utterances, discernment of spirits, speaking in tongues and interpretation (1 Cor. 12: 4–11, 28–31, 14: 1–40).

Thirdly, general gifts are mentioned in Romans 12 and 1 Corinthians 12: 28 and include ruling, showing mercy, exhortation, helps, governments. They refer to administration and such communication between church members as is for the general upbuilding of spiritual life and fellowship (Rom. 12: 6–8; 1 Cor. 12: 28).

It will be seen that while there are these distinctions in the types of 'gifts', i.e. gifts of people to the Church and functions in the Church, there is some overlapping in the lists. Moreover, they are most likely 'classes' of gifts. There may have been scores and scores of specific manifestations of them.

Finally, love. Paul devotes 1 Corinthians 13 to the emphasis on love as the chief factor in the edifying of the Church. In 1 Corinthians 8: 1, he shows that in doubtful matters, love must be the ruling principle. 'Knowledge puffs up, but love builds up'.

The importance of edification is that it should be the great objective in all mutual contacts between Christians and in all exercise of spiritual gifts and ministries. It must be for the equipping of the Church for its ministry to others. It is on the basis of the gifts of the Spirit that are evident in a local church that the local church should be structured for its ministry.

h. GOVERNMENT

By His resurrection and ascension, Christ has taken the place of authority. He is Head of the Church. He is Lord of all. The witness of this is the Holy Spirit. The apostolic message in Acts is that Christ is Lord in heaven, Lord on earth; and this Lordship is primarily realized in the Church. Christ as Head both enlivens His Body and governs it.

The means of Christ's government are:

i. The Holy Spirit

He is the divine executive on earth (Acts 2: 33, 1 Cor. 12: 3–6).

ii. The Word of God

Scripture is given for doctrine, reproof, correction. Truth originally given for the guidance of the Church is now set in Scripture that the Church may listen and obey (2 Tim. 3: 16–17).

iii. The local oversight

The apostles who first administered the Church were from Acts 11 onwards succeeded in local churches by elders, who are called 'overseers' or 'bishops'. They are men who 'pastor the flock of God'. They were also called rulers, leaders, guides and stewards of God, responsible under the Holy Spirit and the Word for maintaining spiritual purity of life and doctrine and for the spiritual health of the local church. As a governing body, they are to be respected and obeyed. Their authority is to be humbly exercised under Christ, and relates only to the local church in which they are appointed (Acts 11: 30, 14: 23, 15: 4, 6, 22, 23, 20: 17, 28; Rom. 12: 8; 1 Cor. 4: 1, 2; 1 Thess. 5: 12; 1 Tim. 3: 1, 4, 5, 4: 14, 5: 17; Tit. 1: 5, 7–9; Heb. 13: 7, 17; 1 Pet. 5: 1–3).

II. THE PLACE OF THE CHURCH IN THE PLAN OF GOD

1. THE ETERNAL POSITION AND FUNCTION OF THE CHURCH

Scripture shows the Church as not merely a human organization, i.e. people living on the natural earth plane in time and sense. The Church exists in the heavenly dimension and has an eternal destiny.

a. THE CHURCH ETERNALLY CHOSEN IN AND GIVEN TO CHRIST

It is constantly referred to as the 'elect' who are 'chosen' before the creation of the world and stands at the heart of 'the eternal purpose of God in Christ Jesus'. In John 17, our Lord continually referred to the Church as 'Those whom Thou hast given me out of the world' (Jn. 17: 2, 6, 9, 11, 12, 24; Rom. 8: 29, 30; Eph. 1: 4; 1 Thess. 1: 4; 2 Thess. 2: 13; 1 Pet. 1: 2; Rev. 13: 8 R.S.V.).

b. THE CHURCH A HEAVENLY AND ETERNAL TESTIMONY

The Church witnesses on earth, but far more she is a witness to 'principalities and powers in the heavenly realm'. She demonstrates the divine wisdom which in Christ has triumphed over all demonic intelligence and power. The Church, by redemption, is saved from cosmic ruin. She is also the eternal evidence of divine grace (1 Cor. 1: 24, 27, 28; Eph. 2: 6, 7, 3: 9–11).

c. THE CHURCH A HEAVENLY COMPANY WITH A HEAVENLY
   DESTINY

Our Lord spoke constantly in John 17 of the Church being 'not of the world'. The Church thus exists in two spheres at once: physically on the earthly plane and spiritually in the heavenly realm. She is 'in Colossae, in Christ'; 'in the body', yet 'in the Spirit'; living 'in the world', yet 'hidden with Christ in God'. Even while on earth, her membership and citizenship is in heaven. She is seated with Christ in the heavenlies, where she is blessed with all spiritual blessings and engages in spiritual conflict with spiritual weapons. She serves God on earth while awaiting her removal to be with Christ at His second coming. Her significance on earth is far exceeded by her significance in heaven (Lk. 10: 20; Jn. 14: 20, 17: 14, 16, 18, 24; 2 Cor. 10: 3–5; Eph. 1: 3, 20–23; Phil. 3: 20, 21, 4: 3; Col. 1: 2, 3: 1–4; 1 Thess. 1: 9, 10, 4: 15–17).

d. THE CHURCH THE BRIDE OF CHRIST

The concept appears first in St. Paul's reference to the Church being kept as a chaste virgin for Christ and, secondly, to marriage as being an illustration of Christ's relation to and purpose for the Church (2 Cor. 11: 2; Eph. 5: 25–27, 32). In the apocalyptic vision, the Church is seen as the Bride, the Lamb's wife, the New Jerusalem, coming down from heaven. She thus fulfils the Old Testament picture of Israel as the wife of Jehovah and Jerusalem as the city of the great King. The consummation of God's redemptive work in both the Old Testament and New Testament is seen in the following:

(1) The city is perfect and comes down from God. So the Divine thought and work is fulfilled.
(2) The gates are named with the twelve tribes of Israel. The Church of the Old Testament is seen as included.
(3) The foundations are named with the twelve apostles. The Church of the New Testament is here included. All who are written in the Lamb's book of life enter.
(4) Christ is the Lord and the Light of the city.
(5) The service and worship of God is the activity of the city.
(6) Sinlessness and purity is the quality of the city.
(7) Universal blessing is the effect of the city.
(Rev. 21: 2, 9, 27, 22: 1–5.)

The bridal aspect of the Church fulfils the New Testament teaching of the love of God in Christ for those He redeems and the response of the redeemed to that love (Jn. 15: 9, 17: 26; Rom. 8: 38, 39; 1 Jn. 4: 16–19).

2. THE EARTHLY, TEMPORAL POSITION AND MISSION OF THE CHURCH

a. THE MISSION OF GOD

The *missio Dei* is that divine outreach towards men in all ages in revealing Himself and His truth, so that men come to know God, to be saved and to be brought into His kingdom. This mission is motivated by holy love and by His eternal purpose to bring all things into fulfilment in Christ who is the First and the Last (Hab. 2: 14; Eph. 1: 8, 10; 2 Pet. 3: 9).

i. The divine mission in the Old Testament

This work involved the calling of Israel to be the witnesses of God in the earth. To them God sent His Spirit, His angels, His law and His prophets to reveal His truth and show His power. For them He overruled world events, since they had been redeemed to be the means of His world mission. Finally, to them He sent the Messiah —His Son (Psa. 111: 9; Isa. 43: 10; Jer. 7: 25; Acts 7: 53).

ii. The divine mission in the New Testament

This can be seen in the birth, life, death, resurrection and glory of the Son of God. He was sent by the Father to reveal Him, establish His kingdom and widen redemption to reach all mankind. The mission of God in Christ appears in:

(1) His witness to the truth.
(2) His works of power and mercy for both spiritual and physical needs of men.
(3) His announcement of the Gospel of saving power.
(4) His judgments both on persons and systems.
(Mk. 1: 15; Lk. 7: 22; Jn. 3: 17, 9: 4, 18: 37.)

b. THE CHURCH'S SHARE IN THE MISSION

The Church is seen as the instrument in the eternal and cosmic purpose of God to bring all things under the Lordship of Christ, to restore all things to God's original plan and to bring under one head all things in Christ. The very existence and witness of the Church is part of this process (Mt. 24: 14, 31; Acts 2: 19–21; Eph. 1: 9–11; 3: 9–11; Phil. 2: 9–15; Col. 1: 26–28; Jas. 1: 18; 2 Pet. 3: 9–14).

The Church's mission is concretely seen as:

i. The proclamation of the faith

By its preaching of the Gospel in obedience to the Great Commission the Church fulfils its mission. This mission is seen as reaching out to all nations through all ages until the second coming of

'Christ. The Church takes the place of Israel as God's instrument. So Jesus chose twelve and sent them out into the land and then into the world. In Acts and the Epistles we see this fulfilled according to Christ's command and strategy. The advent of the Spirit fulfils prophecy and supplies the power by which the Church is able to carry out its mission in the world by gospel preaching, the witness of believers, the establishing of churches in every place and the disseminating of the truth (Mt. 28: 18–20; Lk. 9: 1, 2, 10: 1, 2, 16: 16; Acts 1: 8, 2: 16–18, 5: 12–14, 8: 4, 13: 2–4, 27, 28: 28–31; Rom. 1: 5, 11: 11–15, 25, 32; 1 Thess. 1: 8).

ii. The evangelistic task

The prime responsibility of the Church is to preach the Gospel that men may be reconciled to God. It is a *lost* world whose primary need is to hear the Gospel that men may be saved. Paul is both example and teacher here. He is a pattern to those who believe. He calls on all to follow him as he follows Christ (Acts 26: 16–19; Rom. 1: 14–16; 1 Cor. 1: 17, 9: 16, 11: 1; 2 Cor. 4: 3, 4, 5: 18–20; Gal. 1: 15, 16; 1 Tim. 1: 16; 2 Tim. 4: 2). The *main thrust* of the Church's mission is thus *evangelistic*. When the Church forgets this, it does so at its own peril, not to speak of the tragedy it thus brings to the lost world.

C. THE NATURE OF THE GOSPEL

The New Testament defines the Gospel clearly. It is Good News for men in a bad situation. The situation is that 'all have sinned' and 'the wages of sin is death'. The world is 'guilty before God', all men are under judgment and all stand in need of redemption. Those who are not thus saved are still blind and dead in their sins and lost.

i. The Good News is that God loves this sinful world

To prove it, He sent Christ to be the Saviour. The *Kerygma*, i.e. message proclaimed is:

(1) Jesus Christ is the promised Messiah.
(2) The age has dawned: the Kingdom of God is with men.
(3) Jesus lived, taught, healed and ministered.
(4) Jesus died by crucifixion for the sins of all mankind.
(5) God raised Him on the third day.
(6) He is coming again.
(7) Forgiveness and the gift of the Holy Spirit comes to those who repent and believe.

This is the full message of the word 'Gospel'. This is what the Holy Spirit uses to bring men to God. When it is proclaimed, it should be proclaimed in *its fullness* (Jn. 3: 16; Rom. 1: 18, 3: 10, 19, 20, 23,

5: 6–10, 6: 23; 1 Cor. 1: 21; 2 Cor. 4: 3, 4, 5: 19–21; Eph. 2: 2, 3; Tit. 3: 4–7).

ii. The Gospel declares that salvation is by grace
Salvation comes only through faith and not by works of human effort or merit. It is by personal response to the Good News, which involves trust in Christ and His work of salvation. This faith also involves repentance, i.e. a complete change of attitude in that sin is renounced and Christ is received as Lord and King in one's life. Repentance is as vital as faith. Actually, one without the other is meaningless and an abstraction (Acts 2: 38, 16: 30, 31, 20: 21, 26: 20; Rom. 3: 24, 28; Eph. 1: 12, 13; 2: 8, 9; 1 Thess. 2: 13).

iii. The Gospel involves the new birth
By the operation of the Holy Spirit within those who believe, one becomes a child of God. This new life becomes the source of all spiritual blessing and is the root of holiness and of Christian fellowship (Jn. 1: 12, 13, 3: 3, 5, 7; 1 Pet. 1: 3, 23; 1 Jn. 3: 1, 9, 5: 1, 4).

iv. The Gospel is good news
It is a message of personal invitation, an announcing of facts rooted in God's love and revealed in history. It constitutes a call to faith and obedience. The New Testament emphasizes the importance of maintaining the purity of the Gospel for the salvation of men (1 Cor. 15: 1–4; Gal. 1: 8–12). As already emphasized, when one proclaims the Gospel by preaching or witness, he must be sure he presents the whole gospel, viz. the birth, life and character of Jesus, His death and glorious resurrection, the call to repentance and faith, the promise of forgiveness, the fact of His second coming and all as the fulfilment of prophecy that God long foretold. This is the 'Good News'.

d. THE FURTHERANCE OF THE KINGDOM
The Kingdom of God is His beneficent and righteous rule over men. And wholeness of life results from that rule. Christ preached and brought that Kingdom Himself, for He was and is the embodiment of it. This involved not only forgiveness of sins through the Gospel but the reorientation of one's whole life and the fulfilment of all needs, spiritual, moral and physical (Lk. 4: 18, 19, 21, 43, 7: 22, 9: 1, 2, 19: 10). The Church is called to continue the extension of the Kingdom of God. Hence her witness involves bringing to men soundness of mind, healing of body, rightness of relationships in all departments of life, freedom, social justice, equality of rights and opportunities and the application of God's laws in all areas of living—personal, domestic, industrial, social and inter-racial. The Sermon on the Mount is related to and issues from personal salvation. There is no biblical justification for separating a so-called

'social gospel' from a 'saving gospel'. God is interested in the *whole* man (Acts 3: 16, 4: 10–12, 5: 14–16, 9: 34, 35, 28: 31; Rom. 14: 17; Gal 6: 9, 10; Eph. 4: 25–28, 5: 25, 6: 1–9; 1 Thess. 4: 11, 12, 5: 11–15; 2 Tim. 1: 7; 1 Pet. 2: 17).

e. THE INVOLVEMENT OF ALL CHRISTIANS

While the New Testament shows the lead being taken by apostles, prophets, teachers and evangelists, it emphasizes that all believers are to be engaged in declaring the Gospel and furthering the Kingdom of God. All have a duty to 'go and tell'. If grace is active in one's life, there is an inevitable impulse so to do. Men healed by Christ went spontaneously to share with others the news of their healing. Those who received the Gospel in Acts went spreading it everywhere. The Holy Spirit empowers, and the love of Christ constrains, the members of the Body of Christ (Lk. 8: 38, 39; Acts 2: 44–47, 8: 4; Rom. 12: 5–11; 1 Cor. 1: 5–7; 2 Cor. 5: 14; Phil. 1 :27; 1 Thess. 1: 8; 2 Tim. 2: 2).

f. THE NEED FOR NEW FORMS

This must always be faced. Our Lord spoke of 'new wine in new bottles'. Thus the early Church broke free from the bonds and limits of Judaism, and moved out in new ways. The Holy Spirit is the Spirit of freedom, and the Church must ever watch the dangers of legalism and the deadening domination of structures.

The early Christian community at Jerusalem expressed the new life in fellowship (*koinonia*) which involved amongst other things the common sharing of goods. They met in houses for worship, breaking of bread, teaching and prayer. We must not close our minds to modern expressions of these two things.

The Church, while abandoning the false emphases of Judaism, took over some of her forms, such as the eldership, certain synagogue structures and baptism. Yet the Spirit developed new forms of ministry and worship (such as spiritual gifts) *and He continues to do so today*. The Church must always be alert to the moving of the Spirit. He leads continually into new spheres, ways and means of spreading the Gospel. To be wed to old forms just because they are traditional is tragic. Society changes, so must the Church's methods to reach society. To fail to do so is to miss God's purpose for the Church, viz. to communicate dynamically to its day.

Yet with all this there can be no changing of the Gospel or those basic principles at the core of Christian truth, which govern both the doctrine and the practice of the New Testament Church. Life ever seeks new forms. But it finds and shows them without doing violence to its basic principles (Mt. 9: 17; Acts 2: 44–46; Rom. 8: 2; Gal. 1: 7–9, 5: 1, 6, 13–18; Col. 2: 20–22).

III. THE SPIRITUAL WARFARE OF THE CHURCH

1. THE DEVIL

From Genesis chapter one to Revelation chapter twenty-one, the Bible describes a continuing conflict between the powers of evil headed by the Devil and the powers of good controlled by God.

a. WHO IS THE DEVIL?

He is the great enemy of God and man. He is the one who, assisted by his evil associates, promotes all that is evil and sinful in the world. He actively opposes all that is good and holy.

i. His names

The Devil is called by many names in the Bible. In the Gospels he is introduced to us as Satan (Mt. 16: 23; Lk. 22: 31), where he is called also the prince of the devils (Mt. 9: 34, 12: 24). While both Matthew and Luke refer to him as Beelzebub, it is John who introduces him as 'the prince of this world' (Jn. 14: 30). The apostles had their own favourite names for him. John refers to him mostly as the 'wicked one' (1 Jn. 2: 13), while Paul has a variety of terms; from the 'prince of the power of the air' in Ephesians 2: 2, to 'the God of this world' in 2 Corinthians 4: 4. When we turn to the book of Revelation the names become more dramatic and forceful. For instance, we find the Devil called both 'the dragon' and 'the old serpent' in chapter 12.

But probably the name most familiar to the reader is used both in the Gospels and the Epistles when the Devil is called the 'tempter' (Mt. 4: 3; 1 Thess. 3: 5).

ii. His origin

Long before the time of Adam it would appear that God's universe was divided into spheres of influence, each of which was under the supervision and control of an angel or heavenly prince, all of whom were responsible directly to God. In Colossians 1: 16 and Ephesians 1: 21, Paul tells of 'thrones, governments, princedoms and authorities' in both the visible and the invisible world. From the way the Bible refers to angels and archangels it appears that there was an established order among them, with some being more powerful than others.

The Bible seems to state quite clearly that the Devil was one of these powerful, heavenly princes who grossly abused his authority and was cast out of heaven (Lk. 10: 18). Ever since that time the Devil has been in opposition to God on the earth. With hosts of evil spirits at his command he has set himself up as a mighty prince of evil with his kingdom on earth (Mt. 12: 14).

b. THE DEVIL'S CHARACTERISTICS

i. His wickedness

The Devil is above all else 'wicked' (Jn. 17: 15) and very proud (1 Tim. 3: 6), because of his appearance of power (Eph. 2: 2, 6: 12). But despite his arrogance, he is cunning and subtle in his ways (2 Cor. 11: 3; Eph. 6: 11), even going to the extent of revealing himself in the guise of an angel of light (2 Cor. 11: 14) in order to trick unsuspecting men and women.

ii. His fierceness

The New Testament paints a vivid picture of his fierceness and cruelty (Lk. 8: 29, 9: 38, 42; 1 Pet. 5: 8) which no Christian should ever underestimate. As Paul warned the Ephesians, he is a constant danger to the believer (Eph. chap. 6). Even so, he is basically a coward for, as James says, if we resist him in the power of Christ he will flee from us (Jas. 4: 7).

iii. He is a liar

The Devil is able to be many sided in his character because he is a liar and the father of lies (Jn. 8: 44). Because he is wholly wicked, deceit is natural to him. The book of Job has much to say about the way the Devil seeks to spoil relationships between men and between man and God by making malicious accusations and false charges. One of the important practical themes of Paul's letters is that Christians should constantly be on their guard as the Devil attacks every aspect of life, spiritual, moral and physical.

iv. His cleverness

One of his most dangerous characteristics is that he is so clever. Beware, says Paul, of the wiles of the Devil. He is a creature of vastly superior intelligence to man, a mighty and gifted spirit of amazing resourcefulness. His reasoning is brilliant, his plans ingenious, his logic almost irrefutable. This is all part of his mighty craft and cunning (Eph. 6: 11).

c. THE DEVIL'S POWER

i. Over his 'children'

The Devil has power over all naturally born men and women. Since the Fall, we are all by nature children of the Devil (1 Jn. 3: 10). The result of his power over us before conversion is that we are held by him in spiritual darkness, for he has rendered us spiritually blind. How desperately one needs to be saved (2 Cor. 4: 4). The terrifying truth is that every person who is not born again through a personal faith in the Lord Jesus Christ is under the power and authority of the Devil and belongs to him (1 Cor. 5: 5; Eph. 6: 12; 1 Tim. 1: 20; 1 Jn. 5: 19). The ultimate penalty of the Devil's power over unregenerate men and women is that he controls their eternal destiny—hell itself. As Matthew 25: 41 teaches, they shall be punished together with him at the final judgment.

ii. He is a 'ruler'

Why does the Devil have such great power over the whole world at this time? Because, for the present, he is its ruler (Jn. 14: 30, 16: 11; 2 Cor. 4: 4; Eph. 2: 2, 6: 12).

This was the basis upon which the Devil came to Jesus and tempted Him when he showed to the Lord Jesus Christ all the kingdoms of the world in a moment of time (Mt. 4: 8; Lk. 4: 5).

iii. He is not to be underestimated

Jesus never underestimated the Devil's power. We read of Him praying for His disciples that God would protect them and keep them from falling into the power of the evil one (Jn. 17: 15). In Ephesians 6 Paul takes up this theme of Jesus and warns the Christians that they need to put on the whole armour of God in order to withstand the wiles of the Devil and to defeat his power and subtle attacks. Never a second of our waking or sleeping life are we without evil standing at our side looking for an opportunity of causing trouble to the Christian (Eph. 6: 11; 1 Tim. 3: 7; Jas. 4: 7; Rev. 12: 10).

As he tried to bring about the ruin of Jesus' life and ministry by tempting Him, so this is still his powerful weapon against the believer. By every means possible he tries one temptation after another—never giving up the struggle to regain full control of a redeemed human soul.

However, the Devil does not have unlimited power. For as his power was originally given to him by God, so it can be taken away from him. This is especially true now that he has been defeated openly by the Lord Jesus Christ on the Cross of Calvary. At the present time the Devil is allowed liberty, but this liberty has certain bounds upon it—especially in respect to his dealings with the relationship to believers. The Lord allows him to tempt and test Christians, as Job discovered (Job 1: 1–12, 2: 1–6). Jesus, speaking to Simon Peter, told him that Satan had desired to have him that he might sift him as wheat (Lk. 22: 31). But every Christian should realize that the Devil is *not* almighty in his power. He is very powerful and must never be underestimated as Paul often emphasizes, but the believer lives in the light of the triumphant resurrection of the Lord Jesus Christ. And he may live in the dynamic experience of it day by day.

d. THE DEVIL'S DEFEAT

From the moment of his head-on clash with the Devil on the mountain of temptation, Jesus was in open conflict with him. This conflict came to a head at the cross where Christ finally and publicly triumphed over him—the proof that He had done so being the resurrection of the Lord Jesus from the dead.

i. Jesus was unique
The only person to live on this earth over whom the Devil never had any power at all was Jesus (Jn. 14: 30). Now, because of His victory on the cross, Jesus has made it possible for the believer to defeat the Devil. As Paul assures us (Rom. 16: 20), the Lord's people enter into the Lord's victory over him. This is what Jesus promised when, in the Gospel of John, He said that the Father is able to keep from the 'evil one' those whom He has given to His Son out of the world (Jn. 17: 15).

ii. Victory comes 'in Christ'
The Devil's defeat is actual and experiential in the believer's life because of his relationship with Christ. In other words, it is made possible for us through our identification with the Lord. Being 'in Christ' we share in His victory, as was discussed earlier.

iii. The Devil's final destination and defeat
There is coming a time, at the last day, when the Devil's final defeat will take place, and his ultimate condemnation and punishment will be sealed for ever (Rev. 20: 10). Then he is to be totally crushed and at the final judgment will receive his reward together with his angels; and this reward is eternal fire.

2. DEMONS
When Satan fell, he took a host of fallen spirits with him. A demon is another description in the Bible for 'an evil spirit', i.e. those spirits who fell with the Devil. They are best described by seeing what they do. They assist the Devil in his programme of opposition to the word and the will of God. They do this by entering into men and controlling them in demon-possession (Mk. 5: 1–21). They are those who have power in the government of the Satanic world system, and inspire in men a desire to follow every human weakness, particularly that of idolatry and immorality (1 Cor. 10: 20).

Jesus spent much of His healing ministry casting out demons (Lk. 7: 21). There are those who seemingly desire to explain away these events. They attribute the idea of demon-possession to mental illness, inadequate understanding of early cultures, etc. Yet the Bible is so clear on this issue that it seems an error to attribute the phenomenon to anything other than that which the Scriptures themselves do. There are actual demons, fallen evil spirits, who desire to enter man, control affairs and war against God. Jesus Himself obviously held this view.

Paul said we were not to be ignorant of the Devil's ways (2 Cor.

2: 11). It is strange that segments of the Church have been silent
on this issue. There is currently a tremendous new thrust given to
spiritism and the occult. The Church must come alive to these
issues, for back of this new thrust lies 'the evil one'. The Church
and individual Christians are in a battle. We must not be ignorant
of our enemy and his strategy.

3. SIN

Not only does the Church war against Satan and his host of evil
spirits, we war against sin. Some things about this problem have
already been discussed. But now we must see sin as that which the
Church must overcome in its warfare.

Man's greatest problem is sin. It prevents him from realizing the
full potential for which he was created and condemns him to an
eternity without God. Sin is fundamentally the outcome of a man's
rebellion against God's creative authority over him and is the cause
of our separation from God since the Fall (Gen. 3: 1–24).*

a. WHAT IS SIN?

i. It is rebellion

Sin first reared its ugly head as a result of man ignoring God's word
(Gen. 3: 3–8), and is basically described in the Bible as being the
result of man turning aside from God's commandments and ordinances to do in preference his own desires (Dan. 9: 5). The essence
of sin is to be against God (Psa. 51: 4) and wanting things which
belong to God alone (Gen. 3: 4). This is nothing short of *rebellion*
(Deut. 9: 7; Jos. 1: 18). This rebellion produces lawlessness in the
human heart and in society (Hosea 4: 2; 1 Jn. 3: 4).

ii. It is falling short

As well as rebellion against the will of God, sin is also falling short
of God's glory (Rom. 3: 23). It is a falling short of the goal that
has been set and which before the Fall we were created capable of
realizing and enjoying. One of the reasons for which Jesus came into
the world was to show man what it is possible for him to achieve
here on earth. But when we fail to follow His example, we miss the
mark and fall short of the divine standard.

Sin is consequently the making of a positive choice to think and
act according to one's own wishes rather than according to God's
will. In other words, it is an attempt to live up to one's own standards rather than God's standards.

iii. It is corruption

Sin is the result of the corruption of the human heart. As Proverbs
says, 'As a man thinks in his heart so is he'. Sin consequently begins

* See pages 92ff and 98ff

in the heart (Mt. 5: 28, 15: 19), and God who searches the heart and tries the mind declares that the human heart is deceitful above all things and desperately wicked (Jer. 17: 9, 10).

b. WHAT IS THE RESULT OF SIN?

i. It separates us from God
Sin's first tragic effect is to separate us from God (Deut. 31: 17, 18; Psa. 78: 59–61; Isa. 59: 1, 2; Amos 3: 2, 3; Mic. 3: 4). God is holy and cannot permit any evil in His presence (Isa. 6: 3, 5), and so no sinner can know fellowship with God until something is done about his sin (1 Jn. 1: 6). As Psalms 51: 11 says, sin puts us at a distance from God—out of touch with God.

ii. It separates us from heaven
Having cut us off from fellowship with God in this life, it goes on to exclude us from heaven in the next (Gal. 5: 19–21; Eph. 5: 5; Rev. 21: 27).

iii. It draws God's wrath
These are perhaps what we might call the passive effects of sin. The active result of sin is that it draws forth God's wrath upon the sinner (Rom. 1: 18, 3: 5). Without Christ we live according to the passions of our flesh, and follow the desires of our body rather than the will of God, and are by nature the children of wrath, says Paul (Eph. 2: 3). We shall feel the full force of God's wrath on the day of judgment which is also described in the Bible as the day of His wrath (Rom. 2: 5–6). Those who stand before the Lord in their sin on that day and are not covered with the blood of Jesus Christ will then be punished for their rebellion by being cast into hell. One of the great clarion calls of the Bible is that all men need to be delivered from the wrath to come (Rom. 5: 9; 1 Thess. 1: 10).

iv. It is contagious
Sin is the basic disease of the human heart, and is very contagious. Sin is like leaven and spreads its corruption through the whole of a man's life and being, and right into the society in which he lives. Since Adam, with the exception of Jesus Christ, all men have sinned against God (Rom. 3: 23), and so we live in a world where sin has spoiled its original beauty and glory and left us with evil wherever we look. The misery and suffering that we see on every hand is a result of man's rebellion against God—his evil sinful nature. It is against all this the Church must wage war.

4. THE FLESH
Here too the Church is engaged in conflict. Paul is the main exponent of the biblical concept of the 'flesh' as the central and powerful principle of fallen humanity.

a. IT IS A PRINCIPLE OF SINFULNESS

The flesh is described as a powerful principle of sinfulness (Gal. 5: 17). The outward evidence of the evil nature of the 'flesh' is seen in the lust of man (1 Pet. 4: 2; 1 Jn. 2: 16, 5: 16) which dominates the mind (Eph. 2: 3) and enslaves the bodily members.

b. IT IS ROOTED IN DESIRE

The unregenerate man is dominated by 'sinful passions' or desire (Rom. 7: 5). Paul explains in Romans 8 that because of this he is unable to obey God's Law or to please God. Man's 'flesh' has been perverted by sin and because of this is both an instrument of sin and an avenue of its expression in the human life.

c. THERE IS VICTORY IN JESUS

It was to redeem man's body as well as his soul that Jesus came. One of the evidences of the completion of our redemption will be our receiving, as Christians, resurrection bodies at the personal return of the Lord Jesus Christ.

Until then, Paul warns the Christian that the flesh lusteth against the spirit and the spirit against the flesh (Gal. 5: 17).

The warfare of the Church is no minor or secondary issue. Every day is a battle for the people of God. But victory is assured through Christ (2 Cor. 2: 14). Moreover, the Church has great resources, these we discuss next.

IV. THE RESOURCES OF THE CHURCH

1. THE INSPIRED WORD OF GOD

a. ITS AUTHORITY

The word of God is the expression of the will of God. Inasmuch as His will is sovereign, His word is sovereign too. It is powerful and irresistible. When once His word is spoken, His will may be regarded as virtually accomplished. Hence, in the account of creation, God spoke at each successive stage and in a seemingly effortless manner the universe came into being (Gen. 1). Thus was creation understood and thus was it described in the language of the Psalms employed in the liturgy of Israel. God spake and it was done (Psa. 33: 9). It is the close correspondence between word and work which forms the basis of the prophetic consciousness. Rabshakeh, the Assyrian representative, can rightly discount the words of men, for they are no more than the movement of the lips (2 Kings 18: 20). But one cannot treat with similar disdain the prophetic word which comes from God Himself (2 Kings 19: 21). That word carries within itself the vitality of its own fulfilment and Sennacherib's doom is sealed.

Similarly, the word of judgment spoken by successive prophets against Israel came true. The miserable experience of defeat and exile were thought at first to be the sign that God had forsaken His people (Isa. 40: 27). Later it came to be seen that far from discrediting God's word, they fulfilled it (2 Kings 19: 25). Thus it became the pledge that in similar fashion, when God should turn from His anger and speak gracious words instead of words of judgment, these too would find their fulfilment. Therefore, it could be proclaimed to Israel in captivity that God's word of promise was as sure as the seasons which God has ordained. It would not return unfulfilled, but would run its course until God's gracious purpose was brought to pass (Isa. 55: 11).

b. its timeless character

Because God's words are so purposeful and because they cannot fail, they came to be treasured. The historical books of the Bible bore testimony to what God had done and what He had said (Exod. 32: 15, 16). The prophetical books recognized His hand at work in present history and confidently prophesied concerning the outworking of His plans in the future. Thus the word of God took on a timeless character. Equally, His words of command became not merely the criterion for present conduct but the norm by which the actions of future generations might be judged (Deut. 4: 9). The activity of God, and indeed His whole relationship to men, found expression in His word. To say, 'It stands written' was to invest the word with the authority and power which was inherent in its divine derivation. In this way it became possible to appeal to the written word, confident that it was incapable of being broken (Jn. 10: 35).

The Scriptures came to be the test of truth (Jn. 7: 52). Where there was correspondence between the word and the events which were taking place, it served both as a vindication of what had been spoken in an earlier generation and at the same time the authentication of what was taking place as being in very truth the activity of God (Lk. 4: 21). Jesus appealed to the Scriptures in this way, setting an example to His followers and showing them the manner in which they were to defend themselves against the assaults of the Devil. To each successive temptation, He quoted the words of Scripture (Mt. 4: 4, 7, 10). These were sufficient to send the tempter away.

How well Paul came to understand these tactics can be seen from the fact that he bade the Christian soldier to take the word of God as part of his armoury (Eph. 6: 17). He was confident that it would both give complete protection and prove powerful in battle.

c. ITS USES

Jesus took the Scriptures to be the guide of His conduct. When His actions were questioned (Mt. 12: 3), it was to the Scriptures that He appealed and by means of which He made His defence. In His teaching, He used them to give support. For example, in facing the question of divorce, He referred to the teaching of God's word concerning the relationship of marriage (Mt. 19: 4). Similarly, in regard to resurrection not only did He base His confidence on what God had spoken (Mt. 22: 31), but He pointed out to His opponents that if only they had had regard for the Scriptures they would not have fallen into such serious error (Mt. 22: 29). Further, reference to the Scriptures also provided illustration and pointed to the judgment which He so clearly foresaw (Mt. 24: 37).

d. THE WORD IS SURE

To Jesus, every word of Scripture was important. He asserted that not the slightest detail of it could go unfulfilled (Mt. 5: 18). No wonder that a later writer could speak confidently of the word of the Lord and declare that it endureth forever (1 Pet. 1: 25). It is not surprising, therefore, that the gospel writers made valid their claims concerning the person of Christ by appealing to what was written.

At times this appeal was of a character that it would at once grab the mind and make its telling contribution to Christian faith (Mt. 1: 23). At other times, the conviction that word and event must agree even to the point of utmost detail appears to have taken charge. Thus it was laboured to find such a correspondence (Mt. 2: 15).

e. ITS TESTIMONY TO CHRIST

The Scriptures were also of considerable importance when it came to the wider propagation of the Christian faith through preaching. Just as the synagogue provided the most appropriate setting for the preaching of the gospel (Acts 13: 14), so the Scriptures provided the most appropriate preparation. Often, especially at first, a broad sweep of the divine purpose through the lives of the patriarchs and of the chosen people was presented by the apostles and evangelists (Acts 7), making it clear that these events culminated in Christ. At other times, they used more specific scriptural references which were quoted in support of the Messianic claims of Christ (Acts 8: 32–35).

Paul appealed to the Scriptures to make good the claim that his was the authentic message of the Christian church (1 Cor. 15: 3 ff). It has been claimed that here Paul is referring not to the Old Testament Scriptures but to books of Christian testimony or to earlier gospels. This is argued on the ground that there is no specific text of the Old Testament where it is categorically stated that Christ will suffer death. To take this view, however, would require the same understanding of Matthew 26: 24 and Mark 9: 12. This is untenable. Moreover, Acts 3: 18 and Acts 26: 22, 23 (which speak of the prophets and Moses, not merely of the Scriptures) would be equally difficult. On the contrary, all these passages show that there was no such difficulty felt about an Old Testament presentation of the death of Christ. A clear identification was made between the Suffering Servant (Isa. 53) and other Old Testament passages of similar theme with the Suffering Saviour of New Testament theology. It is in line with this scriptural interpretation that Paul professes himself to be.

f. THE WORD IS HOLY AND INSPIRED

The special inspired nature of the Scriptures led to a recognition of a special relationship in which those men stood who first set them down. They were men holy in character and moved by the Spirit of God (2 Pet. 1: 20, 21). Indeed, so close was the liaison between the human instrument and the divine Spirit who was behind their utterance, that the two could be set down in the closest proximity to each other. Actually, what part was human and what part divine could no longer be determined (see Acts 4: 25 New English Bible).

Furthermore, if it were true that the inspiration of the Holy Spirit lay behind the Scriptures, making holy those who thus became fit to utter the word, it was equally true that those who received the word in sincerity of heart would themselves be partakers of the same holy qualities. So the Scriptures became part of the God-given resources of the Church. They became not only indispensable in the propagation of the faith but profitable in all manner of ways to those who made them the rule of their lives (2 Tim. 3: 15, 16). Thus they stand as the ruling guide and the pattern of conduct and spirit of the Church in all its ways (Heb. 4: 12).

g. THE WORD IS NOT TO BE ABUSED

One further word needs to be written concerning the inspired Scriptures. The authority given to the word spoken in God's name gave rise to those who wished to exercise influence for their own purposes and satisfaction. Consequently, it became necessary to regulate the word and to test its validity. In Israel there had been applied the test of fulfilment. If a prophetic word clearly came to pass, it had been inspired. If it failed, inevitably it came under question. But this kind of test could be applied only in respect of forthcoming events—and then only in retrospect. The word of God was much wider in its scope, and often it demanded action in the present.

How then could safeguards against abuse be provided? The safeguard was found in the consistency of God Himself. Clearly, He could not contradict Himself. Therefore, if any prophetic word ran contrary to the moral and spiritual standards already revealed, then—even if it were accompanied by telling signs—it was never-theless to be rejected (Deut. 13: 1–5).

The same kind of criterion was applied within the New Testa-ment Church. Not all revelation was clearly understood. This gave opportunity for it to be twisted to purposes alien to the spirit of the gospel (2 Pet. 3: 16). To counteract the danger, it had to be asserted that Scripture is not to be subject to purely private interpretation. It had been given within the fellowship of the people of God, and it was to be interpreted in the same manner. Thus the Church safe-guarded the divine Word.

So, we now have—in the providence of God—His own Word. It is the Church's resource of strength, wisdom, power and faith. It must be safeguarded, and it must be proclaimed.

2. THE HOLY SPIRIT

The Church was not only equipped with the Word to safeguard and proclaim, it was also given the gift of the Spirit to empower it for its task (Lk. 24: 49; Acts 1). We have already discussed much about the Holy Spirit. Here we shall see how He empowers the Church.

a. HIS WORK

This endowment of power was in accordance with the experience of those who in earlier ages had received a mission from the Lord. The gift of leadership had been Spirit inspired (Jdgs. 3: 10), physical strength had been similarly provided (Jdgs. 14: 6), and craftsman-ship too as occasion demanded (Exod. 31: 3). When the greatest need of the nation became the prophetic word, this too came through the Spirit (Num. 11: 29; Isa. 63: 10: 11).

It was not surprising then to find that Jesus too was equipped by the Spirit. Now, however, the temporary and partial character of the Spirit's endowment as seen in the Old Testament is replaced by His fullness and by His permanent presence. Jesus was born of the Spirit (Lk. 2: 25–27), baptized of the Spirit and empowered for His ministry (Lk. 4: 18 ff). In Him, the power of God and the enabling of the Spirit became synonymous (Lk. 11: 20, cf. Mt. 12: 28).

Furthermore, it was Jesus who promised the Spirit to His followers. He prayed to the Father in order that they might receive Him (Jn. 14: 16, 17), thus opening the door for the fulfilment of an ancient hope that all the Lord's people might be given the gift of prophecy (Num. 11: 29; Joel 2: 29). He taught His disciples that it was expedient for them that He should go away in order that the gift of the Spirit might be made (Jn. 16: 7). And when He came, Jesus said, He would provide all the resources which the Church would ever need.

The Spirit would quicken the Church's memory of the teaching of Jesus (Jn. 14: 26). More than that, He would provide His own testimony to Christ, supplementing and confirming the word of the apostles (Jn. 15: 26; Acts 5: 32). This was clearly of very great importance, for during His ministry there were many things which Jesus said and did which His disciples did not understand (Mk. 6: 52; Jn. 13: 7, 16: 3). Now they were not only to be reminded of them but an understanding of their meaning was to be given by means of the Spirit. For this reason, the teaching of the Church, as found within the Scriptures, goes further than the words of Jesus Himself. This is not to suggest that such teaching is the mere creation of the Church and therefore to be set aside as of inferior worth. By no means! It is evidence that the promise of Jesus was fulfilled, and that the Church far from creating the doctrine was taught it by the Holy Spirit of God.

Further, besides the Spirit's ministry to the Church, there was also a ministry of the Spirit within those to whom the Church's message was sent. Even the most eloquent preaching would not suffice unless the Spirit gave the conviction of sin and righteousness and judgment (Jn. 16: 7–11).

b. THE EXPERIENCE OF PENTECOST

It was for the fulfilment of the promise of Jesus that the disciples were instructed to wait in Jerusalem (Acts 1: 4). Then when the Spirit came, it was at once the signal for the great evangelistic effort to begin. True, on the day of Pentecost itself, this was facilitated by the presence in Jerusalem of a diverse gathering of peoples. But the opportunity was turned to good evangelistic advantage only because the Spirit enabled the disciples to speak the language of the people. This proved to be the first manifestation of the Spirit's dynamic presence (Acts 2: 4).

Another characteristic of the Spirit's presence was the way in which the fear of the apostles was utterly dispelled. Instead of cringing behind closed doors for fear of the Jews (Jn. 20: 19), they now came forth and spoke the word of God with boldness. Nor was their witness unconvincing, for Luke records that it was with great power that the apostles gave witness of the resurrection. Clearly, the reference is to the power of the Holy Spirit (Acts 4: 33).

This helps us to understand why Saul, when he was converted, needed above all else to be filled with the Holy Ghost so that he might be empowered for his missionary calling. Indeed, such an experience proved the reality of his conversion and became the norm not merely for outstanding Christian workers but for every true believer of any nationality (Acts 10: 44–48, 19: 5, 6).

c. THE SPIRIT IN PROCLAMATION

From the very first Paul realized that the Gospel which came from God could not be proclaimed in mere human strength. There was a vital difference between preaching the word and preaching it in the power of the Holy Spirit (1 Thess. 1: 5). So he rightly claimed, when writing to the Corinthian church, that he had not spoken with enticing words, but in a manner which enabled the power of the Spirit to be openly demonstrated. In this way, their faith was more firmly based than ever it could have been if Paul had spoken in his own strength (1 Cor. 2: 4, 13).

Once more it was shown in accordance with Jesus' own teaching that the Spirit not only enabled the speaker, a similar enabling was granted by the Spirit to the hearers. The Gospel, however clearly proclaimed, was still unintelligible unless the Spirit of God opened the eyes of those to whom the Gospel was preached so that they might receive the mysteries of the kingdom of God (1 Cor. 2: 9–12, 14).

d. THE WORK OF THE SPIRIT IN THE ADMINISTRATION OF THE
   CHURCH

In the administration of the local church, the gift of the Spirit was equally seen. When practical duties needed to be undertaken on behalf of the widows, it was to men full of the Holy Spirit to whom the task was entrusted (Acts 6: 3). The Spirit too was their constant guide, restraining (Acts 16: 6) and admonishing (Acts 16: 7) or urging them forward in their task (Acts 13: 2, 4), directing both the advance of the missionary purpose and the ordering of the Church which was thus created (Acts 15: 28).

Stephen in his lifetime was described as a man full of the Holy Ghost (Acts 6: 5), and in the moment when he faced martyrdom it was the Holy Spirit who opened his eyes and gave him the vision which enabled him to die in the spirit of triumphant faith (Acts 7: 55).

In the more general life of the Church, it was the Spirit who promoted the unity of the Church, binding together the diverse groups which made it up. Thus the divisions of sex and culture and race, which might otherwise have torn the Church asunder, were set aside.

Again, it was the Spirit who kept alive the vivid sense of fellowship with God in Christ, providing the means of access into the divine presence (Eph. 2: 18). This made meaningful and effective the prayers of the Church (Rom. 8: 26).

These examples have provided us with some idea of the manifestations of the Spirit in the life of the Church. They arise out of the varied experience which the developing experience brought. It was left to Paul to enumerate them more fully, and this he did in writing to the Corinthian church (1 Cor. 12).

e. ABUSES

Of all the Spirit's gifts, the most impressive to the Corinthians was that of tongues. This is something quite different from that to which reference is made in Acts 2. There the usefulness in the propagation of the Gospel is apparent. Here, it is a sign to the believers rather than to those outside. Indeed, Paul affirms that to the unbeliever coming unexpectedly into the community of the Christian Church, far from being an aid to faith, it might well constitute a stumbling block. So once again it is demonstrated that God's gifts are to be employed with discrimination, never for personal advancement but only for the building up of faith and of the Church (1 Cor. 12: 7).

We also see that the gift of the Spirit could be abused.* Simon (Acts 8: 19) wished to receive the gift of the Spirit in return for money so that he could use the gift for his own ends. Peter rebuked him and made it clear that this gift of the Spirit is to be exercised within the fellowship of the Church (Acts 8: 21). It is no more able to be privately exploited than could the Scriptures be subject to private interpretation (2 Pet. 3: 16).

Similarly, as already implied, it came later to be seen that the gifts of the Spirit can be simulated and the supreme test of their reality is the Spirit of love which inevitably accompanies the genuine thing (1 Cor. 12: 31). Above all, the spirits themselves are to be tested and any spirit which does not bear the characteristic testimony to Christ is to be rejected (1 Cor. 12: 3; 1 Jn. 4: 2, 3).

There is one final resource for the Church. To that subject we now proceed.

3. ANGELS

It may appear that the biblical teaching on angels should stand as a subject on its own. But the truth concerning this theme is usually in the setting of angels as ministering spirits, given to the Church to aid it in its warfare (Heb. 1: 14). So we approach the idea in this context. Several brief things can be said about them:

a. JESUS AND ANGELS

Angels were present when Jesus came to earth at His incarnation and also at the time of His resurrection and ascension. Moreover, we are assured they are to accompany Him at His return in glory (Mt. 24: 31). During Jesus' earthly life there are only two occasions when angels appear, and both of these occur at the beginning and the end of His earthly ministry (Mt. 4: 11; Lk. 22: 43). Jesus certainly believed in them and taught concerning them.

---

* See the discussion on the *'gift* of the Spirit' and the *'gifts* of the Spirit' on page 71 ff.

b. UNCERTAINTY AS TO DETAIL

Because angels belong to the sphere of heaven, it is very difficult for men to appreciate fully in earthly terms their nature and function, and the Bible gives us only a little knowledge about them.

c. THEIR BASIC REALM

Angels belong to the heavenly court and service of God, and their primary function is to be His ambassadors or messengers by doing and revealing His will in both heaven and on earth (Psa. 103: 20; Mt. 28: 2; Lk. 1: 26). In all of this they seek to express praise and worship to God (Rev. 5: 11).

d. THEY AID MEN

From time to time, angels have appeared to men (Gen. 32: 1) and assisted and strengthened men in their work for God (Jdgs. 2: 1; 1 Kings 19: 5, 7; Dan. 6: 22).

e. THE END OF TIME

At the end of time, when they come with Jesus at His personal return, they will be instructed by the Lord to be the executioners of His wrath to all unbelievers (Mt. 13: 24–30, 39–42).

Little, actually, is revealed in the Scriptures concerning angels and other heavenly beings (the cherubim, seraphim, the creatures of Revelation, etc.). We know they are creatures of God who serve and worship Him in His very presence. They make some excursions into the world, basically as messengers, e.g. Gabriel announcing the coming of Jesus (Lk. 1: 26–37). One thing is clear, we shall see them some day and worship with them for eternity.

f. THE 'ANGEL OF THE LORD'

This phrase occurs many times in the Old Testament. Here is a manifestation of God. The 'Angel of the Lord' is not an 'angel' in the created sense we have discussed here. He is actually God Himself.

4. THE ULTIMATE VICTORY OF THE CHURCH

No account of the Church's task and of its equipment for mission would be complete if the final outcome of it all were left in any doubt. The word of God is not only quick and powerful, it is destined to prevail and no distortion of its truth can prevent its free course (2 Thess. 3: 1). Similarly, the Spirit of God is not only the strong Comforter of the Church, He is the giver of victory.

Equipped then with the Word of God and with the Spirit of God, the ultimate victory of the Church is sure. Jesus Himself spoke of the impregnable rock upon which His Church was founded. At the same time, He foretold that its members would carry the battle against sin and Satan even to the very gates of hell which would themselves yield before the assault (Mt. 16: 18).

The results of sin might well be moving towards their climax. Trouble such as has never been heard of before might well befall the world (Mk. 13: 19), but the Lord will be mindful of His own (Mk. 13: 20). They are to be watchful in view of the uncertainty as to when their Lord will come. But whenever they discern the signs of the times, they are to look up and take heart knowing that the Lord will come to gather His own elect from the four winds and from the uttermost parts of the earth (Mk. 13: 27; 1 Thess 4: 13–17). Tribulation may be the lot of Christ's Church upon earth, but to those who are faithful unto death there is promised a crown of life (Rev. 2: 10).

So the Church can look for deliverance from the perils without and, with equal confidence, it can look for deliverance from its weaknesses and failings within. Peter was commended for his faith in Christ, for it was the faith which formed the foundation of the Church. Yet he could fall so quickly afterwards into such sin as made him bear the very name of Satan (Mk. 8: 33). Later on, he could even deny his Lord. But, nevertheless, Christ had hope concerning him and promised that in spite of everything he would still have a part in the service of the Church (Lk. 22: 32).

So was it true also of those who succeeded him in the generations which followed. Paul could write in 1 Corinthians of sins which were of such a nature that one would scarcely imagine that he was writing about the Christian Church at all (1 Cor. 5: 1). There were things which caused him anger and disgust. But the vigorous protest which springs from his heart is not the last word. Later he is able to say to the same Church that he has confidence in them in every respect (2 Cor. 7: 16). In the agony of his concern for the purity of the Church he may speak out in scathing terms of the fearful sins which threaten their very existence as a church, but when he has given full vent to what he feels, he proceeds to show that his hope is such that he is confident of better things concerning them.

This same hope is echoed in other epistles also (Heb. 6: 9). The Spirit might well have many things to rebuke within the Church (Rev. 2 and 3), but this was because He was jealous of the Church's welfare and mission and would not be satisfied until the Church was brought to perfection. In God's good time, the Church was to be presented as a Church without spot or blemish (Eph. 5: 26), fit to be the Bride of Christ (Rev. 21: 2).

Meanwhile, the Church would grow for the Lord and would be adding constantly to its number those who are being saved (Acts 2: 47). Sometimes its advance would be rapid (Acts 2: 41); sometimes its additions would be one by one (Acts 8: 27, 16: 14). But in the end it would reach enormous proportions, for the word of revelation affirmed that ultimately it would constitute a numberless multitude made up of every nation (Rev. 7: 9, 19: 6).

Thus would be fulfilled the prayer of Jesus that those who were His disciples might be one in Him (Jn. 17: 21), and that to their company there might be added those who hitherto had been of different folds (Jn. 10: 16).

All this might seem to the faint-hearted to be impossible, for the experience of the Church has not always seemed to point in this direction. There have been persecutions and setbacks. Sometimes even the elect have seemed to be in danger of being deceived (Mk. 13: 22). Perhaps above all, the Church has been disturbed by the passing of time and the delay in the fulfilment of the promise of Jesus' return (2 Pet. 3: 4). But this was no more than was predicted and marks not the slackness of God concerning His promises, but rather His long suffering which longs and waits for all men everywhere to be saved (2 Pet. 3: 9).

The fact that death has overtaken many of the believers will prove no difficulty. They will not be prevented from sharing in the fullness of redemption revealed at Christ's second coming. Those who have fallen asleep in Christ, God will bring with Him. And together with the Church on earth, which will have been caught up together with them in the clouds, they will be forever with the Lord (1 Thess. 4: 17). This is the hope that sustains the Church in the darkest of days and the truth with which we members of the Church comfort one another (1 Thess. 4: 18). A day of triumph for us all is *sure*. This is what the Bible says.

PSALMS

MATTHEW

MARK

JOHN—*cont.*

2 CORINTHIANS—contd.

90700